Transnational Dante

Critical Studies in Italian Migrations

Nancy C. Carnevale and Laura E. Ruberto, *series editors*

This series publishes scholarship on Italian migrations, mobilities, and other related transnational concerns. Authors include both emerging and established scholars with differing theoretical and methodological approaches, all rooted in humanities and social science disciplines. Books in the series seek to engage and extend questions of identity and community pertinent to the fields of ethnic studies, gender studies, and migration studies, among others.

Series Board

Transnational Dante

Inventing Argentine Cultural Identity

Heather Renee Sottong

FORDHAM UNIVERSITY PRESS

NEW YORK 2025

Fordham University Press also publishes its books in a variety of electronic formats. Some content that appears in print may not be available in electronic books.

Visit us online at www.fordhampress.com.

For EU safety / GPSR concerns: Mare Nostrum Group B.V., Mauritskade 21D, 1091 GC Amsterdam, The Netherlands, gpsr@mare-nostrum.co.uk

Library of Congress Cataloging-in-Publication Data available online at https://catalog.loc.gov.

Printed in the United States of America

27 26 25 5 4 3 2 1

First edition

CONTENTS

Transnational Dante

Introduction

> "I lost my way and tarried on paths until I forgot they were only paths, and I but a traveler, and you the end of my voyage."
>
> —LEOPOLDO MARECHAL, *Adán Buenosayres*[1]

"Dante in Argentina? What could Dante possibly have to do with Argentine identity?" This was the question, accompanied by the familiar furrowed brow and look of bewilderment, that I was confronted with whenever I told someone my research interests. The question was inevitably followed by other questions like "What got you interested in this topic?" Being neither Italian nor Argentine, I have to admit that I did not *choose* this topic because of my own identity. Rather, the meandering path of my research led me here.

I am, first and foremost, a lover of the *Divine Comedy*, because it is one of the greatest, most complex, and most encompassing works of literature ever written. It exemplifies just how powerful and enduring literature can be. One could study it an entire lifetime and never exhaust its depths. After seven centuries (2021 marked the seven hundredth anniversary of Dante's death), there is still more to be said, and scholars have generously expended great quantities of ink, arguing over the meaning of one single line. However, as a scholar I am less interested in micro issues and more interested in the text's expansiveness and Dante's transnational legacy. For example, what are the textual and thematic characteristics of Dante's *Divine Comedy* that make it an ideal vehicle for literary appropriation, and what are the historical and cultural factors that account for Dante's enduring popularity both in Italy and beyond? I am particularly interested in the literary appropriation of Dante in the Americas, which has only recently become a hot topic, as is evidenced by the fact that in May 2021, the Dante Society of America and Harvard University organized an international symposium on the reception and influence of Dante in the Americas aptly titled "*Tra liti sì lontani.*" But this was not the case just ten years ago. Although Dante's presence in the United States has received a great deal of critical attention ever since Henry Wadsworth Longfellow's seminal translation of the *Divine Comedy* in 1867, the important role he played in Hispanic American literature is still a new frontier in Dante scholarship.

For this reason, in 2011 I co-organized, with Prof. Massimo Ciavolella, Prof. Efraín Kristal, and the UCLA Center for Medieval and Renaissance Studies, the symposium "Dante in the Americas." As was evident from the conference, Dante's literary presence is pervasive throughout Central and South America: in Mexico (in the poetry of Octavio Paz and the novels of Juan Rulfo and Ignacio Padilla); in Brazil (in the novels of Machado de Assis); in Peru (in the poetry of Jorge Wiesse and the novels of Mario Vargas Llosa); in Argentina (in the works of Leopoldo Lugones, Jorge Luis Borges, Leopoldo Marechal, and many more). The more I researched, the more I understood that focusing on Argentina was inevitable. Not only did Argentina offer considerably more material, but the instances of Dante reappropriation were not isolated cases nor simply due to a single author's admiration for Dante. Rather, rewriting Dante was a means for Argentine authors to enter into dialogue regarding the state of their national literature.

The presence of Dante in Argentine literature begins with the Generation of '37, a group of writers who rejected the Spanish cultural heritage of the country and strongly opposed the dictator Juan Manuel de Rosas. In the 1890s the *Divine Comedy* was translated into Spanish by none other than Bartolomé Mitre, president of Argentina from 1862 to 1868. Subsequently, Dante was appropriated by the most prominent authors of the Argentine literary canon, such as Leopoldo Lugones, Jorge Luis Borges, and Leopoldo Marechal. Although there are a number of articles and a few books on the influence of Dante on Borges, there exists no comprehensive study of the impact of Dante's work in Argentine letters. What I found, remarkably, was that rewriting Dante was a way for Argentine authors to voice their views on the direction that should be taken to develop Argentine letters, in the same way that the courtly love poetry of Dante's era was often a dialogue between poets concerning the phenomenology of love and the stylistic conventions of lyric love poetry. Understanding it fully requires understanding the relationships/rivalries between authors, their stylistic views and poetic agendas, and in this case, the pressure Argentine authors felt to produce a great work of literature that would fulfill the role of the *Divine Comedy* within Argentina. More than that, rewriting Dante became a means to parody one another's divergent viewpoints.

To understand this interliterary Dantean dialogue, one must first understand the importance of the *Divine Comedy* within Italy for creating cultural cohesion during the Risorgimento period, and then look at the comparative lack of cultural cohesion in Argentina during the same period, given that their nation-building phases coincided. In nineteenth-century Italy, Dante was envisioned by intellectuals such as Giuseppe Mazzini as a prophet of national unity. This is because politically speaking, Dante advocated for empire as the only means to achieve peace on the Italian peninsula, which during the fourteenth century was comprised of warring city states. Five centuries later, during the struggle for national unification, Risorgimento thinkers equated Dante's ideas on empire with their ideas on nationhood. They drew parallels between the political strife during the medieval period and the situation mid-nineteenth century, when the Italian peninsula was split into several parts. In the north, Austria had Lombardy and Venetia. To the west was the rival Kingdom of Sardinia-Piedmont, consisting of the mainland territories of Piedmont, Nice, and Savoy, plus the island of Sardinia. South of Lombardy were the duchies of Parma, Modena, and Tuscany. In the middle of Italy, along both coasts, were the Papal States ruled by the pope. South of the Papal States was the Kingdom of the Two Sicilies, consisting of Sicily and the mainland section forming the bottom half of the peninsula. How does a diverse conglomeration of separate regions become one nation? There must be an ideological framework to unify the population and give individuals a sense of nation, peoplehood, collective identity, and national purpose. The groundwork was laid by Risorgimento thinkers, and the movement was both political and literary.

On the literary front, Risorgimento ideologues such as Giuseppe Mazzini actively promoted an idea of Dante as a prophet of their eventual unification. He had, after all, already created cultural cohesion linguistically, by being the first to write a major work of literature in the vernacular, at a time when Latin was the predominant literary language. Furthermore, in *De vulgari eloquentia* (*On Eloquence in the Vernacular*) Dante makes linguistically based arguments regarding cultural identity. Since borders are always changing, one could, as he suggests, think about identity and unity not through geography but through language. Thus Dante subdivides Romance languages into those that use "sì," "oui," and "oc": the language of Sì (Spanish, Italian, and Portuguese), the language of Oïl (now contemporary French), and the language of Oc (Occitan). In other words, he divides the populations of areas of present-day southern Europe according to language. He further subdivides the Italian peninsula into fourteen spoken dialects. Interestingly, he understands the division of Italian dialects morally, seeing it as part of the larger problem of the division of tongues which he views as punishment for human presumption in the building of the tower of Babel. Mankind, having lost the language of Eden (a stable, unchanging language), replaced it with diverse vernaculars. What he seeks to promote in this work is a single unified Italian language, a linguistic cultural unification.

In the sixteenth century the rediscovery of Dante's *De vulgari eloquentia* and a renewed interest in linguistics played a key role in the *questione della lingua* (the problem of language), the debate regarding the criteria that should determine the establishment of a modern Italian literary and spoken language. But a much greater revival of Dante and a more pronounced reappropriation of his work for political purposes was not to occur until the nineteenth century. Dante had, for the most part, fallen out of fashion from the fifteenth to the late eighteenth century, when Petrarch's poetry was the predominant literary model. But toward the end of the eighteenth century, Dante was increasingly embraced by intellectuals involved with the political emancipation of Italy.

When Romantics sing the praises of Dante, the aspects that come to the forefront most frequently are his moral integrity, his defiance of political injustice, and his defense of political unity. Andrea Ciccarelli argues in his article "Dante and Italian Culture from the Risorgimento to World War I" that the recovery of Dante by nineteenth-century Italian culture was based "mostly on political and ethical reasons, and that these patriotic reasons converted Dante into an emblem of national unity."[2]

Giuseppe Mazzini was extremely influential in inspiring many patriotic readings of Dante. His first essay, *Dell'amor patrio di Dante* (1826–27), concerns Dante's love for Florence. In *Sopra alcune tendenze della letteratura italiana del XIX secolo* (1829), he links Dante's moral righteousness with contemporary Italian writers. In *Ai poeti del secolo XIX* (1832), he promotes the use of poetry as the voice of the people. As Andrea Ciccarelli explains, these essays helped establish a parallel based on ethical convictions between Dante and late eighteenth- and early nineteenth-century writers: "Mazzini sees Dante as an example, actually, *the* example of Italian integrity for his refusal of moral compromises with the political power of his times, and he draws an analogy with the writings of some late eighteenth- and early nineteenth-century writers, especially with those of Vittorio Alfieri and Ugo Foscolo."[3] Establishing analogies between Dante and the historical protagonists of the Risorgimento was to become a trend.

Mazzini, who read Dante primarily in a political vein, was very adept at using his name as a rallying point. His essay "Dante," written for Operai Italiani in London in the *Apostolato Popolare* for September 15, 1844, is essentially a call to action. Mazzini begins by asking the question, "Who was the man whose name belongs to the Italian people?"[4] First, he establishes that Dante's aims of unity were the same as those of the present day. Second, he thanks Dante for the formation of a common language "that will one day represent National Unity among us."[5] Not only was Dante a great poet and great thinker, but he was also a great politician, who "understanding better than any other the mission of the Italian man, brought together the theoretical and the practical, Power and virtue—Thought and Action)."[6] The notion of thought followed by action was at the center of Mazzini's political creed.

Mazzini also helped promote the idea of Dante as *pater patriae*. "Patria" was, according to Mazzini, the dominant thought of Dante's life, and the dream for which he suffered and sacrificed. In his brief biographical sketch, Mazzini emphasizes the elements of Dante's life story that make him an ideal patriot. For example, he emphasizes that Dante was involved in the civil affairs of his city, and that he fought valorously at the battle of Campaldino.[7] Since his aim is to depict Dante as a moral hero and ideal patriot, he devotes a significant section of this short essay to explaining that Dante was neither Guelph nor Ghibelline, but rather, as he says in his own poem, "s'era fatto parte per sè stesso."[8] In other words, his ideas were above the petty party rivalries because it was the idea of future nationhood that predominated in his soul.[9]

Furthermore, Mazzini provides examples of Dante's moral righteousness and his refusal to compromise himself. He describes Dante, the errant exile, who in 1315 was invited to return to Florence only if he paid fines and declared himself pardoned, and thus guilty. Mazzini, outraged that Dante be asked to pay his oppressors, includes the letter of the offended Dante, refusing the offer.[10] The episode is meant to be indicative of Dante's dignity and his sound ethics.

Although Dante was unable to return to his beloved Florence, Mazzini claims that he died comforted, knowing that Italy would one day become "Nation, and for the third time, director of European civilization."[11] Patria, he says, was for Dante a religion, and he believed his land to be "destined by God to the great mission of giving moral unity to Europe and through Europe to Humanity."[12]

At the end of his laudatory essay Mazzini asks how Italians can honor this great man who gave them their language and foundational book. His answer is a call to unity in the name of Dante:

> Do you, Italians, really want to honor the memory of your Greats and give peace to the soul of Dante Alighieri? Make true the concept that fatigued him during his life on earth. Make ONE and powerful and free your land. Extinguish among yourselves all those petty divisions against which Dante preached so much, to the point that he, the man who most of all felt and loved your future, was condemned to misfortune and exile, while you remain doomed to a centuries-old impotence. Free the tombs of your Greats, the men who have placed a crown of glory on your country, from the shame of being trampled upon by the foot of a foreign soldier. And when you are made worthy of Dante

> in love and hate—when Dante's soul can look upon you painlessly and glad of all its Italian pride—we will raise the statue of the Poet to the highest elevation in Rome and write on the base: TO THE PROPHET OF THE ITALIAN NATION FROM THE ITALIANS WORTHY OF HIM.[13]

His essay is essentially a plea to "do it for Dante." Mazzini makes Dante a national idol, a point of convergence for all Italians.

Dante's great revival during the Risorgimento period is a strong example of how literature can play a key role in the creation of cultural cohesion. Later we will further investigate the Romantic idea of epic in particular as the presumed reflection of national essence. In this regard, Italy is well represented by both Virgil's *Aeneid* and Dante's *Divine Comedy*. Not every country, however, has a text that successfully functions as what Nicolas Shumway terms a "guiding fiction," that is, a narrative that gives individuals a sense of nation, peoplehood, collective identity, and national purpose.[14]

Before we turn to the case of Argentina, let me just clarify that I am considering national identity as something that is carefully constructed and refined over time, more or less successfully. The narratives that contribute to the underlying guiding fiction are both literary and overtly political. As Edmund S. Morgan explains in the opening of his book *Inventing the People*, successful government requires the acceptance of fictions.

> Government requires make-believe. Make believe that the king is divine, make believe that he can do no wrong or make believe that the voice of the people is the voice of God. Make believe that the people *have* a voice or make believe that the representatives of the people *are* the people. Make believe that governors are the servants of the people. Make believe that all men are equal or make believe that they are not.[15]

In particular, Morgan analyzes the notion of popular sovereignty. He points out that the federal system of the United States with its three branches of government is not in any complete sense "government of the people, by the people and for the people." Rather, actually analyzing the system and its parts, it becomes clear that the US government is at best "a government by competing special interests (including the government itself and its several agencies) who represent no one but themselves."[16] Yet he argues that the fiction of representative government is both necessary and positive. It is necessary because the belief that the government represents our interests impels US citizens to consent to state rule. It is positive because through attempts to make reality resemble the fiction of representation, reform is most frequently undertaken. In other words, "by the people, for the people" is a myth; the myth is necessary for cooperation; and to ensure that the myth remains believable, positive reforms are often undertaken.

Similar to this line of thinking and useful for our present analysis are the theories of Eric Hobsbawm, Benedict Anderson, and Nicolas Shumway, who coined the concepts of "invented traditions," "imagined communities," and "guiding fictions," respectively. The "invention of tradition" is a notion developed by Eric Hobsbawm and Terence Ranger, who explore the creation of new traditions which appear or claim to be old in origin. Although every epoch, they explain, most likely gave rise to invented tradition, it occurs more frequently when a rapid transformation of society weakens or destroys previous social patterns. This phenomenon is especially apparent in the development of nationalism, and often involves the dismantling and restructuring of images of the past. It is not to be confused with genuine traditions: "Where the old ways are alive, traditions need be neither revived nor invented."[17] Hobsbawm identifies late nineteenth- and early twentieth-century Europe as a place and time in which invented traditions flourished. Benedict Anderson goes a step further, identifying nations in general as social constructs, existing only in the minds of those in the community and constructed by the political and cultural elites. In his book *Imagined Communities: Reflections on the Origin and Spread of Nationalism*, rather than focusing on nineteenth-century Europe, he traces the emergence of community in South America.[18]

The concepts of "imagined traditions" and "imagined communities" can be applied to the case of Argentina, which after the War of Independence from Spain (1810–18) had to develop its own national cultural identity. At the end of the colonial period Argentina was a largely unpopulated land, with an estimated population of around 500,000.[19] Unlike Mexico and Peru with highly developed Indian civilization, Argentina had mostly nomadic tribes, which were annihilated over time and excluded from the construction of a national identity undertaken by Argentina's forefathers. Nicolas Shumway explains in his book *The Invention of Argentina* that during the last half of the 1700s Argentina was "a land of isolated settlements, autonomist townsmen, nomad gauchos, relatively docile employees of estancieros, unconquered Indians, minimal economic and political development—and no sense of national destiny."[20] European immigration was encouraged and supported to populate the expanses and modernize the economy. The great European immigration wave to Argentina took place in the late nineteenth and early twentieth centuries and resulted in a heterogeneous population of predominantly Spanish and Italian origin. Symbolical or ideological identification among the population had to be established and "argentinidad" invented.

According to Shumway, the attempt of Argentina's forefathers to invent a collective identity was a failure. He argues that the nineteenth-century intellectuals who first framed the idea of Argentina were unsuccessful in creating an ideological framework for union.[21] Rather than creating a mythology of inclusion, nineteenth-century Argentina gave rise to opposing "guiding fictions," which resulted in a mythology of exclusion. He argues that from independence onward, two divergent streams of thought dominated the country's guiding fictions: one elitist, liberal, pro-European, and *porteño*,[22] and the other populist, nationalist, nativist, and federalist. Developed in the nineteenth century during the period of national consolidation, these guiding fictions, according to Shumway, continue to exert their influence on Argentina's present.[23]

If we take for example one of Argentina's literary classics, José Hernández's *Martín Fierro*, we can see that the work comes down clearly on the pro-federalist side of the divide. *Martín Fierro* is the story of an impoverished gaucho who, with no possibility of social integration, is forced to remain an outlaw. The work is highly critical of Argentine institutions such as the military and government for their exploitation of Argentina's gaucho minority and rural inhabitants. Critical of an elitist, liberal, pro-European, and *porteño* government, the book clearly cannot be said to foster any sort of national consolidation. It would be more likely to foster unrest and rebellion. For this reason, the opinions of Argentine authors regarding the status of this work as Argentina's epic are polarized and will be discussed thoroughly in each chapter.

I will be seeking to answer the following questions: How does literature play a role in the formation of national identity? Can texts like *Martín*

Fierro that offer a mythology of exclusion successfully function as guiding fictions? How can cultural cohesion be achieved among a population predominantly composed of immigrants? How was the Italian diaspora in Argentina either incorporated or excluded from this formulation at various stages? What sort of anxieties and identity negotiations took place between the Argentine creole culture and the Italian diasporic culture?

It is important to note that Italian immigrants in Argentina were not, as was the case in the United States, a relatively small minority compared to other migrant populations.[24] Italians began immigrating to Argentina in large numbers during the latter half of the nineteenth century. Between 1857 and 1900, 2,000,000 European immigrants were admitted, 1,116,000 of whom remained in the country. Among those who remained, 660,392 were Italian. In other words, approximately 60 percent of all European immigrants at the time were Italian, making them an significant part of the demographic.[25] Furthermore, as seen in table 1, from the 1860s to the 1880s more Italians immigrated to Argentina than to the United States.

Furthermore, the Italians in Argentina enjoyed, on average, a higher relative status than did Italians in the United States. This is for several reasons. First, Italians arriving in Argentina were favored over natives as tenant farmers and urban workers. In the nineteenth century (although decidedly less so in the twentieth, as we shall see later on), they were met with positive

Table 1. Italian immigration to Argentina and the United States

PERIOD	ARGENTINA	UNITED STATES
1861–70	113,554	11,728
1871–80	152,061	55,759
1881–90	493,885	307,309
1891–1900	425,693	651,899
1901–10	796,190	2,104,209
1911–20	347,388	1,165,246
Total immigrants, 1860–1914	2,270,525	4,083,000
Total immigrants, 1900–1914	1,137,475	3,156,000

Source: Samuel L. Baily.[26]

rather than negative prejudice on arrival. Indeed, the founding fathers of the nation viewed them as intermediaries whose presence would have a "civilizing" effect on the rest of the population. The Argentine elite perceived European immigrants to be superior to the native population, symbolized by the *gaucho* and the *caudillo*. Economically speaking, Italian immigrants were welcomed wholeheartedly to "populate the desert." It was not until the early twentieth century that the local elite felt threatened by their growing numbers and perceptions shifted. In contrast, in the United States Italians were from the start largely perceived as an inferior race in comparison to Northern Europeans, and the negative stereotyping they endured no doubt made for a more complicated integration process.

Another relative advantage enjoyed by Italians immigrating to Argentina is that many of them had the opportunity to become landowners rather than mere tenant farmers, as Herbert S. Klein and Roberto Cortes Conde have shown.[27] Although locals did dominate the land market, and it was certainly not easy nor common for the recently immigrated to be able to obtain land, as table 2 shows, in Argentina a significant number of Italians did manage to become rural property owners or even ranch owners.[28]

Table 2. Property ownership by nationality (as a percentage) in Argentina, 1914

NATIONALITY	NON-RANCH RURAL PROPERTY OWNERS	RANCH OWNERS	RELATIVE IMPORTANCE AMONG PROPERTY OWNERS	ADULTS OWNING PROPERTY
Argentines	59.4	77.8	62.2	32.4
Italians	21.0	6.4	18.9	25.1
Spaniards	6.4	4.7	9.7	15.9
Russians	3.0	0.6	0.9	13.9
Uruguayans	0.8	0.9	1.2	20.6
All others	9.4	9.6	6.3	171.9
Total population in category	72,429	66,561	1,074,964	4,016,739

Source: Herbert S. Klein.[29]

Other Italians who were not involved in farming rural areas prospered in river navigation and trade. Still others became leading and respected members of the mercentile community.[30] A closer look at the census of Buenos Aires in 1887 reveals that as early as the late 1880s Italians accounted for 32 percent of the total population, 53 percent of the workers in industry, 57.5 percent of the owners of industrial establishments, 39 percent of the workers in commerce, and 16 percent of the owners of commercial establishments.[31] In New York, on the other hand, only a small percentage of the population was Italian, and therefore they were not able to dominate any sector of the economy to the same degree.[32]

In general, in Argentina there were greater opportunities in skilled, career-oriented jobs, while in the United States, there was higher demand for unskilled, temporary, urban workers. This may partially account for the slightly lesser return immigration from Argentina back to Italy compared to that from the United States back to Italy.[33] On the whole, the Italians arriving in Argentina were better educated that those arriving in the United States. As Jorge Balán has pointed out, this may be because more northern Italians migrated to Argentina while more southern Italians migrated to the United States, and northern Italy had higher literacy rates.[34] Italian immigrants to Argentina also played a more significant role in local workers' and employees' organizations than the Italians in New York, likely due to their sheer numbers.[35] Overall, the evidence on property ownership, economic activity, occupational mobility, and community organizations all seems to indicate that the Italians in Buenos Aires adjusted more quickly and easily than did those in the United States.[36]

One last thing should be noted when considering the relatively favorable conditions for Italian immigration to Argentina—the large Italian community already in place on their arrival. Very early on, even before reunification, there was already an important Italian community in Buenos Aires to welcome newcomers. Already in 1869 Italians made up 23 percent of the population of Buenos Aires.[37] In contrast, Italians in the United States arrived relatively late; even as late as 1910 Italians accounted for under 10 percent of the foreign-born population.[38] Although incomplete data make it difficult to precisely measure social mobility, land ownership, and assimilation, Herbert Klein concludes that the indices we have all point in the same direction, to the "extraordinary success for a people who had only just entered the national economy and were still overwhelmingly of the first generation."[39]

As a natural consequence of the large and relatively well-integrated Italian community present since the mid-nineteenth century, Argentine culture has been undeniably influenced by Italian culture in terms of language, customs, and traditions. When it comes to literature, Dante is perhaps the author who has proven most influential to Argentine letters. In this investigation, I seek to answer the following questions: Did the strong presence of Italians in Argentina influence cultural production in the nascent nation? Why did Argentine authors consistently call upon Dante in their attempts to develop a uniquely Argentine literature? And how are the rewritings of Dante in the Argentine canon in dialogue with one another?

The book begins with a chapter on Bartolomé Mitre, president of Argentina (1862–68), and the first Argentine translator of Dante. He translated the *Divine Comedy*, which was decidedly a nation-building, foundational text within Italy, with the intention of adopting it as a nation-building text in Argentina. In chapter 1 I discuss how Mitre's reading of Dante was influenced by Risorgimento Italians such as Giuseppe Mazzini who associated Dante with political unity, morality, and high culture. Mitre's translation coincides with his larger project to create a national mythology and national heroes via his *Historia de Belgrano* (1858–59) and *Historia de San Martín* (1887–88).

My discussion of Mitre's motives for translating the *Comedy* is framed within the context of Argentine debates on immigration. Mitre welcomed Italian immigration in particular, and his translation of the *Divine Comedy* appropriates the Italian classic for incoming and extant Argentine citizens. Liberal leaders such as Mitre construed immigration as a means to bring people from supposedly more "civilized" countries into a sparsely populated land, in hopes of creating a modern society with a dynamic economy. From 1862 to 1868 (the years of his presidency), of the 289,409 recent immigrants, 205,442 were from Italy (that is, approximately 70 percent).[40]

In chapter 2 I turn to textual analysis and argue that Mitre's translation of the *Divine Comedy* can be considered a counteroperation to the aesthetic and thematic tendencies and social message promoted by José Hernández, Mitre's political adversary and author of what is today considered Argentina's greatest epic—*Martín Fierro* (1872). In his letters on the state of Argentine literature, Mitre disregarded the importance of Hernández's greatest work, which can be read as a protest against the government's oppression and exploitation of minority social groups. Hernández was strongly opposed to Mitre's Buenos Aires–centric political policies and Eurocentric cultural production, which disregarded the needs and the identity of the indigenous population, the gauchos, and the poor inhabitants of rural Argentina. Mitre's decision to fill what he perceived as a "cultural void" with translations of classics from Old World Europe was a means of negating the importance of the local literary production that ran counter to his vision of a post-Independence, progressive Argentina, an Argentina that embraced Italian immigration.

Shifts in the perception of Italian immigrants in postcolonial Argentina are central to my research. At the time of Mitre's translation in the late nineteenth century, Italian immigrants were depicted as the bringers of progress and culture, who would "civilize" the largely uninhabited pampas. Just three decades later, however, the same immigrants came to be seen as materialistic, uncivilized, and uncouth. The Creole[41] elite who had previously championed them began to resent their ever-growing presence, which they perceived as a threat to their social hegemony. The growing xenophobia is reflected in the literature of the time. Despite the ever-changing demographics and political situation, the popularity of Dante and the Argentine preoccupation with questions of identity remained constants. In response to the volatile demographic flux of the first decades of the 1900s in Buenos Aires, intellectuals felt it a pragmatic necessity to define what exactly it meant to be "Argentine." The following chapters explore divergent responses to this question, all of which incorporate Dante, who became something of a literary guide as Argentine intellectuals navigated the complex labyrinth of their national identity.

Chapter 3 is dedicated to Leopoldo Lugones (1874–1938). Lugones was heavily influenced by the *Divine Comedy*. In the first poem of his collection *Lunario sentimental* (1909) he claims to have learned his verse from Dante, "Abuelo arduo y conciso,/Por cuyo Paraíso/Jamás pasó un pedante" (Arduous and concise ancestor/Through whose Paradise/No pedant ever passed).[42] His short story "Francesca" (1909) is a creative reinvention of the fifth canto of *Inferno*. Subsequently, however, Lugones abandoned his Eurocentric style of writing in order to embrace gaucho literature, and in particular the epic poem *Martín Fierro*, as the literature which best expresses "the heroic life of our race."[43] Jorge Luis Borges (1899–1986), who was well aware of Lugones's story "Francesca"[44] and its lack of correspondence to the literary nationalism he advocated in *El payador*,[45] set out to write a Francesca of the pampas. His short story "The Intruder" simultaneously subverts Dante's fifth canto and Lugones's adaptation (chapter 4). In chapter 5 I examine Borges's famous story "The Aleph," which, I argue, is not only a parody of the *Divine Comedy*, but also a subtle critique of Lugones in the figure of Carlos Argentino Daneri, a pedant whose poetics the protagonist (Borges) despises.

Although studies have focused on Dante in the works of Leopoldo Lugones and Jorge Luis Borges individually, scholars have failed to address the relationship between Borges's adaptations of the *Comedy* and those of his distinguished antecedent and rival. In chapters 4 and 5 I show how Borges's rewritings of Dante are in direct dialogue with those of Lugones. Borges uses Dante primarily to parody Lugones's pedanticism and also his nativist nationalistic views expressed in *El payador*.

Chapter 6 looks at Leopoldo Marechal's views on immigration and Argentine identity, and chapters 7–8 at his use of Dante in *Adán Buenosayres* (1948). In this novel of epic proportions, Marechal, a pro-Perón Catholic nationalist, rewrites Dante to parody the snobbism and lack of consensus among the intellectual elite, the primary producers of culture. Through the voice of the main character, Adán, Marechal articulates the need for a return to tradition and a spiritually directed literature. As the title suggests, Adán Buenosayres is the first man (Adam), as well as the primary representative of Buenos Aires. Just as the protagonist of the *Divine Comedy* is also its author, so too Adán is the literary incarnation of Marechal. In book 7, Adán, guided by the astrologer Schultze (Virgil), descends through limbo (a slum) and then through nine circles of hell, which are divided into neighborhoods of Buenos Aires. Not only does the book closely follow Dante's *Inferno* in structure, but just like the *Comedy*, it is the story of a penitential journey in hopes of spiritual realization. A second, and equally important, motif of the novel is also Dantean in nature: the *Mujer Celeste* or *Madonna Intelligenza*.

Book 6, "The Blue-Bound Notebook," is a philosophical reflection that closely parallels Dante's *Vita nuova* and is heavily influenced by the doctrine of the Fedeli d'Amore.[46]

The novel is set in the 1920s, and the protagonists correspond to important members of Argentina's literary elite: Borges (Luis Pereda), Xul Solar (the astrologer Schultze), Francisco Luis Bernárdez (Franky Amundsen), and Jacobo Fijman (Samuel Tesler). Each character represents one of the contradicting trends of Argentine literati in their endeavors to produce a uniquely Argentine literature. Marechal parodies Dante in order to underscore the country's failure to produce its own *Divine Comedy*, that is, a guiding text that is representative of Argentina's national identity.

This study was written with many readerships in mind: Danteists; Italianists interested in Italian migration and transnationalism; scholars of Argentine literature; Latin Americanists; and anyone interested in migration and transnational issues. For the benefit of the Italianists I have provided basic historical contextualization as a necessary framework for each chapter. I have also translated the Spanish quotations into English. Both the original Spanish text and the parallel English translations are provided in the case of poetry or a particularly worded prose passage. Unless otherwise noted in the footnotes, all translations are mine. As regards Argentine readers, as a foreigner I can hardly teach them anything about their own national history. Instead, my goal was to enrich their reading of Argentine classics through newfound knowledge of Dante, and to enable a better understanding of the role of literature in the formation of a sense of Argentine national identity.

One need not be Italian nor Argentine (as I myself am not) to be fascinated by Dante's afterlife in Argentina. The consistent rewriting of the *Divine Comedy* in the Argentine context testifies to the fact that great works of literature can be revived during different eras and even reappropriated by different peoples to foster mythologies of inclusion or exclusion related to national identity.

ONE

Bartolomé Mitre on Immigration and Argentine Identity

> Italy is the fertile mother of modern civilization. She gave to human language the most harmonious of her notes; to literature the most original of the Renaissance poets; to science the revealer of the laws of the Universe; to Geography the discoverer of the New World; to the visual arts the works that gave form, color, and body to the ideal; to music the melodious inspirations that stir souls; to human rights the abolition of the death penalty and to the political world a Free and United Italy . . . !
>
> —BARTOLOMÉ MITRE, *1902*[1]

Bartolomé Mitre, president of Argentina from 1862 to 1868, was an important advocate of Italian culture within the country.[2] An influential military leader, diplomat, legislator, journalist, and historian, he was also the first Argentine to translate the *Divine Comedy*. Mitre's first full translation of *Inferno* was published in 1889 under the title *El infierno de la Divina Comedia*. This was followed by the 1891 publication of *La divina comedia: Juicios críticos sobre el ensayo de traducción del Infierno del Dante por Bartolomé Mitre*, a compilation of corrections and criticisms of his translation. Shortly thereafter in the same year, the French publisher Félix Lajouane printed a luxury edition of *Inferno* that was the first to include Mitre's theory of translation. But his work on the translation was far from finished. He would continue to meticulously correct errors, publishing two further editions with emendations.[3] In 1893 a new edition of *Infierno* with over 1,400 corrections was published in Buenos Aires, and in 1894, *La divina comedia* in its entirety was published by Peuser. Finally, in 1897 a definitive edition updated with corrections was made available.

As is clear from the sheer number of editions with all their copious corrections, the translation of the *Divine Comedy* was not something that Mitre took lightly. He dedicated a decade of his life to this gargantuan task: legend has it that during the war with Paraguay he spent all his downtime translating. As a famous anecdote goes, one day when combat was halted, an official entered his tent to find him immersed in his work, surrounded by dictionaries and scattered sheets of paper. The curious official inquired:

—¿Qué anda haciendo, mi general?
—Aquí me ve, traduciendo al Dante.
—Hace bien, a esos gringos hay que darles con todo.[4]

(—What are you doing, General?
—Just as you see me, translating Dante.
—It is good: you must go hard on those gringos, General.)

The term "gringos"—used at the time to refer to all foreigners—here refers to Italians. The official's comment thus suggests that Mitre's translation was butchering the original text so badly as to injure "the gringos" themselves. Although probably fabricated in subsequent years, the anecdote circulated widely. While the location of the exchange (either in a tent near the battlefield or in Mitre's office) and the identity of the interlocutor can vary in the telling, the ending is always the same and demonstrates the mystery surrounding Mitre's literary labor.[5] In some versions the interlocutor is told to wait outside for some time, emphasizing the importance of the translation above and beyond that of the visitor. According to Ángel Battistessa, who followed in Mitre's footsteps as a translator of Dante, Mitre considered the translation of the *Comedy* to be more an act of government than a literary endeavor.[6] Why did Mitre assign such importance to the translation? And what could the translation of an Italian epic poem have to do with Argentine politics? As I hope to show in this chapter, translating Dante was part of Mitre's project to fill a "cultural void" that he perceived in Argentina, addressing this lack with the classics of Old World Europe in the hopes of creating a linguistic model to serve as a foundation for a nascent cultural identity. This involved adopting a literary work that Mitre found ideal for creating cultural cohesion among the existing population and incoming Italian immigrants.

If we consider Mitre's position in terms of the ideological divide Nicolas Shumway outlines in *The Invention of Argentina*, Mitre epitomizes the elitist, liberal, pro-European, and *porteño*[7] stream of thought (as opposed to the populist, nationalist, nativist, and federalist).[8] This is true not only of Mitre's governance, but also of his literary endeavors. As we shall see, he minimizes (or ignores) the significance of local literary production treating of nativist topics, instead translating and promoting works of European high culture such as Dante's *Divine Comedy*.

Mitre's pessimistic views on local literary production can best be seen in a 1887 letter to Señor don Miguel M. Ruíz addressing the possibility of creating a course on South American literature, which as of yet was not taught in universities. Ruíz had written to Mitre asking his opinion and advice on the matter, having heard from Prof. Alió at the Colegio del Uruguay that Mitre believed such an endeavor to be impossible. Alío had seconded Mitre's opinion, informing Ruíz: "there isn't any material to form a text with which to teach a course on Argentine and American literature."[9]

Mitre's response to the proposal, which he refers to as "a matter in which I didn't want any part, neither direct nor indirect," is less than enthusiastic. Not only, he claims, is there no extant didactic material for such a course, but none could be created even if they wanted to: "the work is not only difficult, but even materially impossible."[10] Why impossible? Because in Mitre's eyes, anything that could be labeled under the umbrella "South American Literature" was yet to be written:

> In order to teach a literature course, the first thing one needs is literature. In our case, we are lacking not only the complete materials to teach such a course, but also the very material that constitutes the subject itself.[11]

Even after spelling out this opinion in black and white, Mitre then refers to a character from folklore to drive home what he considers an obvious truth:

> There is a well-known cooking recipe among the many truths of Pero Grullo: in order to make a chicken stew, the first thing one needs is a chicken.[12]

Pero Grullo is a folkloric character known for his habit of stating truisms, always with comical effect. Believed to have been a real person who lived in the 1200s in Palencia, he entered into the popular imagination through anecdotes and eventually became a literary character.[13] Francisco de Quevedo included him in his 1622 book *Los sueños*, wherein Pero Grullo gives ten prophesies which Quevedo terms "perogrulladas."[14] Mitre's mention of Pero Grullo in this context is particularly significant because it draws attention to the distinction Mitre sees between folklore and literature. As the letter progresses, Mitre's preference for high literature and the classics becomes apparent. At the same time, he openly concedes that elements of popular culture can indeed develop into material for high culture over time.

In Mitre's opinion, although some South American "literary" materials did exist, they were fragmentary, and could not be studied as a fully formed "literature":

> If by the word literature one understands quite simply a certain number of books written by the natives of a specific region about a few of the subjects that make up the treasure of art or human thought, South America could be said to have its own literature; a literature which is *fragmentary, just budding one could say*, and which up till now has contributed more material to the bibliography than to the wealth of ideas or criticism. If, however, by literature one understands what the word actually means, that is, *a collection of works which embrace the vast field of human thought, which includes, in addition to all extant genres, original creations that mark progress in literature or writers who, without having gained universal renown, nourish with its essence the genius of a nation*, then no: South America does not have a literature. And that which it has does not even include simple examples of the diverse forms or genres.[15]

His criteria for literature are that (1) it encompass the vastness of human thought, (2) it include works of all genres, (3) it include original creations which demonstrate progress, or (4) it is produced by writers who are able to nourish the genius of a nation.

The idea that literature must "nourish with its essence the genius of a nation" is a Romantic one, as is Mitre's idea of the history of literature, which he defines as "a document which records customs and the spirit of a people, the way men think and feel at a given time, reflecting collectivity."[16] In the current era of globalization, we tend to think of "national literatures" as a "well-founded fiction," to quote Pierre Bourdieu.[17] For Mitre's generation (apart from forward thinkers such as Goethe, harbinger of *Weltliteratur*), literature was very much associated with the particularity of nations and considered a key factor in the construction of national identities. A history of literature is thus something Mitre perceives as always related to national, cultural, and linguistic boundaries, rather than geographical ones:

> For this reason, no one has ever thought to write a history of European literature simply for geographical reasons, even though the materials to do so are abundant and superfluous, for doing so would entail writing artificially without logical order and under a very limited point of view, the history of humanity with all the confusion of the Tower of Babel.[18]

Interestingly, this recalls what Dante says in *De vulgari eloquentia* regarding language as a better means than geography to divide peoples, as well as his discussion of the Tower of Babel as the reason for linguistic confusion. In book 1, chapter 6 he writes that if not for the fault of man's presumption and God's subsequent punishment, all men would still be speaking in Hebrew like Adam: "in this form of language spoke all his [Adam's] descendants until the building of the Tower of Babel (which is interpreted as 'tower of confusion.')"[19]

An important criterion for Mitre's history of literature is that it have a guiding thread: "Literature courses must have a unifying criterion, whether it be linguistic, genre-related, or philosophical."[20] He uses the example of Schlegel's course on dramatic literature, "which examines over the course of time the formation of a language and the genius of a nation, or the development of an art form in its multiple and analogous manifestations."[21]

In summary, according to Mitre, the language and genius of a nation are reflected in its literature, developing gradually over time, and so the study of this development is the history of literature. Mitre believed the literature of South America and Argentina to be in an embryonic state, requiring an incubation period of several centuries for great genius to develop. He applies this reasoning not only to literature, but also to other art forms such as painting, sculpture, and music. Interestingly, he sees the duration of this artistic incubation period as something that can be calculated by modern science:

> Modern science has mathematically determined how many millions of men and how many centuries are necessary to produce a great musician, a great sculptor, and a great painter. It is a question of time, a combination of elective affinities, an evolution that occurs gradually and which has as its principal factor hereditary ability and *intellectual accumulation*, which like capital is accumulated over time. Can South America claim for itself a musical, pictorial, or sculptural art when it has only produced a few musicians—only one of whom created an opera—or a dozen good painters and a few sculptors?[22]

Mitre believed such developments to be impossible in a sparsely populated country such as Argentina, which only a short time before had been a colony of Spain. In all of South America, he points out, "there are many voids to be filled, both territorial and intellectual. The vast majority of the land is uncultivated, and even unoccupied, and the literary colonies lack representatives and personifications to populate her terrain, which is profound but yet untilled."[23]

The main question Mitre asks is "How to fill the great voids?"[24] Not only must the desert be populated, but the cultural voids must be filled, and the former colony must break away from the cultural influence of Spain. Mitre's plan was to fill the void with non-Spanish European high culture, in particular that of Italy, which he considered the cradle of civilization (as he would express fifteen years later). In contrast to uncultivated Argentina, Italy stood as the "fertile mother of modern civilization."[25] Until homegrown seeds of genius could develop and intellectual capital accumulate, it was necessary to adopt foreign texts. And of the great Italian authors, Dante was an obvious choice: the "father of the Italian language," known for having provided the moral sustenance to nourish the genius of his nation. The Risorgimento thinkers considered him the harbinger of Italian unity, and he was widely popular among the Romantic-period poets that Mitre admired and translated, such as Byron and Hugo.

Mitre's translations of foreign texts became part of a strong literary tradition of translation in Argentina. As Sergio Waisman demonstrates in his article "Foundational Scenes of Translation," translation played an important role in the formation of the Argentine nation from its very inception, when it was first used by the *criollos* who sought to break away from the Spanish empire and forge a new literary language.[26] More generally, translation is often key to the development of national identity in peripheral traditions:

> The nation, intimately related to but ultimately different from the State, is a cultural and linguistic concept. The nation is formed, and at times dismantled and then reformed, in and through culture and language. Translation in peripheral traditions participates actively in the complex processes of the formation of nations and their subjectivities. . . . The act of translation reveals nodes of potential that bring to the forefront issues of identity and representation.[27]

According to Itamar Even-Zohar, there are three main conditions that set the stage for translation to play a major role within a literary polysystem:

> (a) when a polysystem has not yet been crystallized, that is to say, when a literature is "young," in the process of being established; (b) when a literature is either "peripheral," (within a large group of correlated literatures) or "weak," or both; and (c) when there are turning points, crises, or literary vacuums in a literature.[28]

All three of these conditions applied to Argentina at the time of Mitre's translations. The independence movement having only just started in 1810, Argentine literature was yet in its infancy. Not only was its literary canon a mere shadow of those of European countries, its people continued to see themselves as existing on the periphery of Western civilization. Indeed, a key characteristic of the Argentine literature that would follow was its lasting preoccupation with defining its place among other Western traditions. Finally, during Mitre's life Argentina was at a major turning point in its history. The territory had been united, the caudillos largely suppressed, and the modernization of the economy was under way, largely thanks to Mitre's own presidency. Mitre continually sought to usher in progress and to "civilize" and populate what had very recently been a largely uninhabited pampa. His translation of the Divine Comedy was a means to bring high culture to the country and to enrich Argentinean Spanish by broadening its expressive possibilities. Before further discussing why Mitre turned to Dante in particular, we must briefly investigate why he saw Italian immigration specifically as key to the country's development.

Populating the Desert: Italian Immigration in Argentina

Following independence, Argentina's governing elites sought to populate and modernize the vast expanses. The population of the entire Argentine territory at the time of independence from Spain is estimated to have been a mere 400,000.[29] Intellectuals such as Juan Bautista Alberdi, the major political thinker behind Argentina's 1853 constitution, emphasized the importance of adding to this meager population. Like Mitre, Alberdi was a member of the "Generation of '37" intellectual movement, named after the date of the literary salon that marked its inception. Members of the group sought to distance themselves from Spanish tradition and were strongly opposed to the federal governor Juan Manuel de Rosas.[30] Following the battle of Caseros in 1852, when Rosas was defeated, Alberdi wrote his book *Bases y puntos de partida para la organización política de la República Argentina*.[31] The book seeks to outline simple and rational bases for organizing the nascent country. He points out that the foremost enemy of pure unity in the Argentine Republic is not Don Juan Manuel de Rosas, but "the space of 200,000 square leagues in which the handful of our scarce population of one million is diluted, like a drop of red paint in the Paraná River."[32] Ten chapters of the *Bases* are devoted to exploring the problem of deficient population and to proposing possible solutions.

Alberdi's primary solution was to populate the desert. He coined the phrase "gobernar es poblar" ("to govern is to populate") and argued that the only civilization on Argentine soil was European: "We do not have a single important city that was not founded by Europeans. . . . Even now, after independence, indigenous people are neither important nor numerous in our political civil society."[33] Europe had brought to the Argentine territory the notion of order, the knowledge of liberty, the art of wealth, and the principles of Christian civilization.[34] Everything that Argentina had, he argued, was thanks to Europeans: "If it had not been for Europe, America today would be worshiping the sun, the trees, the beasts, burning men in sacrifice, and would not know marriage."[35] He felt that the native population was incapable of self-rule and that without a rebirth of culture the country was doomed to stagnation and barbarism. He encouraged Argentines to recognize their need for progress and "call again for help from Europe for our *incomplete culture*."[36] The only way to fill the void and bring civilization to the otherwise "empty and gloomy territory" was by encouraging mass immigration from Europe.[37] The ideas articulated by Alberdi heavily influenced the Argentine constitution of 1853, the Preamble of which invites "all good-willed citizens" of the world to immigrate to Argentina.

But deeper into the document, Article 25 specifies that the federal government will encourage "European immigration."[38] Julia Albarracin demonstrates in her dissertation, "Selecting Immigration in Modern Argentina," that notions of ethnic and/or cultural "eligibility" of certain immigrant groups have influenced Argentine immigration policy and shaped the "imagined community" that this policy tried to construct. She argues that although economic factors are important in explaining the number of immigrants a country is willing to accept, identity politics tend to dictate who is admitted.[39] As she shows throughout her study, the conceptions of the ideal citizen were redefined over time, but Argentine immigration policies reveal a recurrent preference for European immigration.[40]

While the Founding Fathers of Argentina were all in favor of immigration, they each had slightly different ideas of what constituted the "ideal" immigrant. Let us compare Alberdi, the so-called Father of the Constitution; Mitre (president from 1862 to 1868); and Sarmiento, Mitre's successor and author of one of the cornerstones of Argentine literature, *Facundo* (1845). As we have seen, in Alberdi's view, immigration was the only means "for this American desert to swiftly become a world of opulence."[41] For Alberdi, the ideal immigrants were European (preferably Anglo-Saxon), and they would civilize the extant population by serving as a model with their modern work and consumption habits. In chapter 15 of *Bases* he writes: "How and in what form will the life-giving spirit of European civilization come to our soil in the future? As it has come in every epoch: Europe will bring her new spirit, her habits of industry, her practices of civilization in the immigration she sends to us."[42] Alberdi felt that the best way to impart the desired European "civilization" was through the example set by Europeans themselves, rather than through the educational system. He continues: "Every European who comes to our shores brings us more civilization in his habits, which he then passes on to our inhabitants, than in so many philosophy books. . . . A hard-working man is the most effective catechism."[43] Because education was insufficient, the *gauchos* and the indigenous population were to acquire culture through firsthand contact. Alberdi argues that even if the *roto*, the *gaucho*, and the *cholo* were to have the best education system, "in one hundred years you will not make him an English laborer who works, consumes, lives decently and comfortably."[44] Although all of the articles of Alberdi's constitutional project advocate immigration from Europe in general, the fact that he here specifies "English" rather than "European" indicates that the English are indeed the ideal.[45] Throughout his *Bases*, he mentions the English as an economic example and a model of "liberty," with the French as the epitome of culture, and the United States, particularly California, as the ideal constitutional model. The Italians go unmentioned.

Sarmiento's writings reveal a similar bias. In his search for models for Argentine institutional development, he explores the systems in place in Northern European countries. Sarmiento also wrote extensively about the United States, having traveled there to analyze political and educational institutions.[46] In his primary literary work, *Facundo*, he contrasts the lovely and orderly houses of the German and Scottish settlements south of Buenos Aires with the "barbarous aspect" of the housing in the city center.[47] Like Alberdi, he believed immigration from "civilized" nations to be the cure for Argentina's "barbaric" state, which was largely the cause of the *gauchos* and, even worse, the *caudillos* such as Juan Manuel de Rosas. At the end of the book Sarmiento contrasts France and Argentina, representing civilization and barbarism respectively. Sarmiento predicts that a transformation from barbarous to civil society could be achieved through education, foreign capital investment, and immigration.

Although Alberdi's and Sarmiento's envisioned transformation of Argentina from a predominantly Indigenous-Mestizo population to one of primarily white European immigrants *did* occur over the next half a century, the majority of these immigrants came not from Anglo-Saxon nations, nor from France. Between 1857 and 1900, 2,000,000 European immigrants were admitted, 1,116,000 of whom remained in the country. Among those who remained were 250,135 Spaniards, 106,334 Frenchmen, 18,240 Austro-Hungarians, 18,095 Britons, 15,521 Swiss, 14,862 Russian Jews, 14,737 Belgians, and 17,989 Germans.[48] The number of Italians was 660,392: 60 percent of all European immigrants who arrived during this period. In the following section I intend to show that Mitre not only recognized Italian immigration as Argentina's reality, but also saw it as the country's future.[49]

Mitre on Immigration

Throughout his political career, Mitre advocated Italian immigration for a variety of economic, social, and cultural reasons. He saw Italians as responsible in large part for the country's economic prosperity, and as the bringers of moral progress. Politicians at the time were divided as to whether the government should have a "laissez-faire" immigration policy or if official arrangements should be made with other nations and subsidies offered. On September 23 and 24, 1870 (two years after the end of his presidential term), Mitre delivered four discourses defending the "spontaneous immigration" policies he had advocated during his presidency.[50] Having studied immigration in the United States and Australia, and because of his experience as leader of the nation, he was strongly opposed to what he called "artificial immigration" (i.e., subsidized or incentivized). Not only was it costly for the nation, he argued, but it also ran the risk of creating a country full of unintegrated minority groups who did not adapt to the host country.

He begins his discourses by stating that he would defend the system of spontaneous immigration that had been in operation throughout his presidency, which began with 6,000 yearly immigrants and ended with 30,000.[51] The existing system of immigration, he explains, was not born of chance; rather, it was the logical consequence of a clearly conceived idea and a dedication to its development during the course of his administration.[52] And this idea did not cost the country anything more than "sixty cents a head." Furthermore, he argues, the man who comes of his own free will and with his own capital is more likely to find success upon arrival:

> The energetic man who immigrates of his own free will, who deliberately chooses his new patria, who comes with open arms and his own capital, can exercise his liberty of action more vastly and with better means and results than he who obeys a foreign impulse, who is tied to a contract, with no more resources than those which the government generously grants him or loans him.[53]

Whom, then, does Mitre see as this "energetic man" who will bring progress to Argentina? The immigrants in question are the Italians, whose presence in Argentina bolsters Mitre's defense of spontaneous immigration. Italians, the best on land and at sea, have modernized a formerly backward Argentina. Mitre praises them as cultivators of the land:

> Who are the people who have made the ten leagues of arable land encircling Buenos Aires fertile? To whom do we owe the green belts surrounding all our towns along the coast of our great rivers, and even those oases of wheat, maize, potatoes, and woodland *that break up the monotony of the uncultivated Pampas*? To the Italian planters from Lombardy and Piedmont, or even from Naples, who are the *most able and hard-working farmers in Europe*.[54]

Mitre's mention of the "uncultivated monotony" of the pampas speaks to what Sarmiento wrote at the beginning of *Facundo*. Sarmiento's book begins with a lengthy geographical description of Argentina and an explanation of how the bleak and featureless geography of the pampas was a major barrier to civilization. Mitre's solution to the problem of the underpopulated pampas is the Italian.

Mitre then points to the benefit the Italian presence has brought to the Argentine shipping industry. To these "fellow countrymen of the discoverer of the New World" Mitre attributes the development of Argentina's coastal shipping fleet, the ease and cheapness of river transport, and the crews of her warships. He notes that despite these contributions, the Italians are "expressly excluded by this scheme from the benefit offered to other races, who, whatever their qualities, have not necessarily contributed to our workforce the way the Genoese have done and still do."[55] Evidently frustrated by the tendency of his fellow politicians to associate progress only with immigrants from Northern Europe, Mitre speaks out to bring the Italians their due recognition.

Finally, Mitre argues, Italians are good for the banking industry. Twenty percent of the money deposited in the Bank of Buenos Aires belongs to Italian immigrants, "who set the example of capital accumulated through savings."[56] Here the Italians set a civilized example for the local population by means of their good habits, the very process by which Alberdi insisted the barbarism of Argentina must be purged.

Mitre devotes much more of his discourse to lauding the Italians than he does to any other migrant group. Of the nationalities mentioned, only the Irish and the Italians receive more than a page of commentary. To the next largest population group after the Italians, the Spanish, he dedicates only two sentences. To the French, a brief paragraph.[57] Although the envisioned ideal immigrant of Alberdi and Sarmiento was the English and the French, the reality was the Italian. Not only were Italian immigrants the major migrant group during Mitre's presidency (1862–68), as well as at the time of his four discourses supporting spontaneous immigration (1870), they would also continue to be the dominant migrant group in the following decades. Of the 289,409 recent immigrants to Argentina from 1882 to 1886, 205,442 came from Italy.[58] By the time Mitre published the first installments of various cantos of *Inferno* in 1889,[59] Italians had long been a permanent part of the fabric of Argentina.

Why the Divine Comedy*?*

Having filled the territorial void with Italians, Mitre intended to fill the cultural void with Italian literature. As we saw in his letter to Miguel M. Ruíz, Mitre believed literature could "nourish with its essence the genius of a nation." Since he did not believe this sort of literature existed yet in Argentina, or for that matter anywhere else in South America, his hope was to import it via translation of the literary work best known for having provided the moral sustenance to fuel the genius of a nation. Let us return briefly to Mitre's letter on South American literature to get a better understanding of his insistence that a work of literature be a transcendent "guiding text" of supranational influence.

In his letter Mitre states that South America contained only a handful of great lyric poets. As far as prose authors, "they are limited to a few historians, not even two of whom could call themselves classical."[60] Furthermore, he says, South America does not have epic literature, nor dramatic literature, nor even philosophical or imaginative writings, apart from its spontaneous bursts of lyric poetry.[61] Nor can the continent claim any significant philosophers or authors with transcendent ideas that gain renown abroad:

> Let's not even talk about philosophers, nor of great thinkers in the domain of transcendental ideas, who in their pages reflect in literary forms the ample flights of human thought. It doesn't even have to be as original as Emerson. We do not have any work of literature with wings sufficiently powerful to fly over national borders, and certainly not into the future. Their work couldn't even walk within these borders.[62]

For Mitre, a true work of literature (whether poetry or prose) must be a guiding text which transcends borders. The South American authors who do get a mention in his letter to Ruíz are those whose names had achieved a certain degree of influence in European literary circles.[63] In his opinion, one could hardly expect a nascent literature that had only recently emerged from chaos to produce many original works that provide moral and spiritual guidance:

> The genesis of American literature has emerged from chaos: it has defined its forms and is in the process of acquiring original characteristics; but the stars that will illuminate its horizons have not yet appeared in its firmament. Given such conditions, to aspire to teach a course of American literature, and in addition Argentine literature, without fundamental causes, connections, and genres, is like wanting to illuminate the world in the middle of the day with a candelabra with four of its candles extinguished.[64]

Although it is clear that all Mitre says of South American literature is true of Argentina, he stresses the point:

> And what I say in regards to what is called South American literature—which has no drama, poem, novel, nor philosophical treatise of any import—pertains as well to that which we call Argentine literature, which has only recently begun to take shape and which still does not consist of a collection of works which merits such a name, and cannot even be classified according to genres.[65]

In truth, however, Argentina was not without important and original works of literature. Significantly, Mitre makes no mention of what would become, in the twentieth century and beyond, Argentina's most renowned literary classic, *Martín Fierro* (first published in 1872). Many Argentine intellectuals, most notably Leopoldo Lugones, would later tout the work as the greatest reflection of Argentine national identity.[66] In his 1913 lectures, Lugones declared the work to be the epic of Argentina, comparable to Italy's *Divine Comedy* or Spain's *Don Quixote*. Mitre, who acknowledged the nation's need of an epic, chose not to embrace *Martín Fierro*, but instead to translate the *Divine Comedy*, to him the epitome of national unity, justice, and high culture.

What Did Dante Mean for Mitre?

In order to understand what Dante represented for Mitre, we must return to his youth, long before his presidency, long before the influx of Italian immigration and the publication of his translation. According to Mitre himself in the "Translator's Theory," the *Divine Comedy* had been his "bedside book" for more than forty years, and although he had long believed himself to be "impregnated with its spirit," it wasn't until the 1880s that he had the courage to translate it.[67]

Mitre's fascination with Dante dates back to his days in Montevideo, when Argentina was divided by constant internal struggles between the *Unitarios* and the *Federales*. While the *Unitarios* (Unitarians) advocated a Unitary state—a centralized government with Buenos Aires as the capital—the *Federales* (Federalists) supported a federation of independent provinces. The provincial *caudillo* leaders constantly vied with one another for power, creating an unstable political situation which Mitre saw as a recipe for continuous internal strife.

For most of Mitre's adolescence (he was born in 1821) and young adulthood, the *caudillo* Juan Manuel de Rosas held control of the Argentine provinces as governor of Buenos Aires Province from 1829 to 1832 and again from 1835 to 1852. Rosas was born to a wealthy family of landowners and grew up in the countryside, where he learned the ways of the *gauchos*. His knowledge of rural Argentina would later make him adept at governing its otherwise unruly population. In the areas he controlled, his rule was absolute, and his opponents considered him a tyrant. Not only did he restrict the press, but he also resorted to brutal tactics, using spies and the *mazorca* to discourage revolt among those who opposed his rule.[68] His supporters considered him a strong leader who would safeguard the interests of the landowners, the *gauchos*, and the rural population.

For Mitre and the other *unitarios*, Rosas's way of governing was backward and despotic. Rosas sought to maintain his influence with an iron fist and resisted pressure to create a national constitution, insisting that Argentina was not ready for such an institution. Mitre made it his mission during his earlier career to oust Rosas and pave the way for progress, modernization, and his own political legacy. Mitre spent his youth in Buenos Aires when Rosas was in power, going into exile with his family in Montevideo in 1837. They were not alone there: many other exiled intellectuals lived in Montevideo, a hub of anti-Rosas activity. Newspapers, literary works, and political commentaries became the means for them to stir up further anti-Rosas sentiment both at home and abroad, in the hopes that this would eventually lead to armed uprisings, foreign support, and Rosas's downfall.

The picture that such young Argentine exiles had of Rosas is best summed up by Sarmiento's *Facundo*, which contrasts the barbarism of the *caudillo* dictatorship with the progress and civilization of enlightened Europe. For Sarmiento, Mitre, and other exiled intellectuals, Rosas represented an archaic providential mindset, a stagnant world order reinforced by tyrannical rule. It wasn't until the battle of Caseros in 1852 that Rosas was finally defeated, Justo José de Urquiza leading an army of 24,000 soldiers (mostly Argentine, but also coming from Brazil and Uruguay) into the provinces of Santa Fe and Buenos Aires. A thirty-year-old Mitre commanded a division during this, the battle that put an end to Rosas's twenty-year rule over Argentina.

The backdrop of this uprising against *caudillismo* in Argentina shows why the poets and thinkers of "Young Italy" and Risorgimento Italy appealed to the romantic generation of exiled Argentines, Mitre among them. While Argentina had been dominated by *caudillismo*, Italy had been dominated by foreign powers. The revolutionary ideas of Young Italy served as a blueprint for Young Argentina and inspired a similar program of liberation. As we shall see later, Mitre was inspired not only by their political vision, but also their patriotic reading of Dante as an emblem of national unity.

Young Italy, Young Argentina

Young Italy (La Giovine Italia) was a political movement founded in 1831 by Giuseppe Mazzini. Mazzini's goal was to create a popular uprising against the Austrian Empire in order to bring about a unified Italy, which did not become the Kingdom of Italy until 1861 (just one year before Mitre began his presidency). Having witnessed the failed revolts attempted by the secret society of the Carbonari (literally "charcoal makers"), Mazzini's intent was to attract Italians to his independence cause through a broad moral and spiritual revival. Education and then insurrection were the means by which his patriotic movement sought to liberate Italy.

Mazzini's ideas quickly spread beyond the Italian peninsula, resulting in the formation of Young Germany, Young Switzerland, Young Poland, and in 1834, Young Europe. But his influence was not to be confined to one continent. In Argentina, the model established by Young Italy inspired the River Plate intellectuals to organize themselves politically into the Asociación de la Joven Argentina (Young Argentina).[69] On the night of June 23, 1837, a group of approximately thirty-five young men founded this new association: Esteban Echeverría, the group's leader, read a credo he had written entitled "Symbolic Words," receiving an enthusiastic response. On July 8 the group gathered once again to give their oath, which was, according to Echeverría, based on that of Young Italy:[70]

> 1. They swear to combine their intelligence, property, and manual labor in service of the realization of the principles formulated in the *symbolic words* that form the basis of the pact of alliance; 2. They swear to not give up in the endeavor, no matter what the dangers that may threaten each of the social members; 3. They swear to sustain these principles in every difficult situation and to use all the means at their disposal to defend and disseminate them; and 4. They swear reciprocal fraternity, close union, and perpetual silence regarding anything that could compromise the existence of the Association.[71]

The group was the Argentine version of a secret society, defining notions of liberty and patriotism and opposing the perceived tyranny of Rosas. They produced a great deal of anti-Rosas propaganda, gaining support from fellow Argentines and Europeans alike. Their dogma, articulated by Echeverría, was first published in 1838 as *Declaraciones de principios que constituyen la creencia social de la República Argentina*, and republished in 1846 as *El dogma socialista*.[72] This idealistic and effusively patriotic document bears similarities to the 1832 *Istruzioni generali per gli affratellati della Giovine Italia* (General instructions for the members of Young Italy) and Young Europe's *Pact of*

Fraternity, signed in Berne, Switzerland, in 1834. In their dogma the members of the association declare themselves to be "builders of the sacred mission of defining their nations."[73]

Mazzinian ideas were further diffused among Argentine exiles in Uruguay, via the journal *El Iniciador*, founded on January 1, 1839, by Andrés Lamas and Miguel Cané (the elder). The Italian journalist Giovanni Battista Cuneo, who was instrumental in spreading the ideas of Mazzini in South America, collaborated with the editors. The Mazzinian slogan "Bisogna riporsi in via" (We must set out on our journey) was printed on the front of every edition in Italian, along with the Spanish translation "Es necesario ponernos en camino." Mitre, who contributed to the journal's pages along with other exiled Argentine intellectuals, was by then steeped in the ideology of Young Italy.[74]

Standing as a testament to Mitre's enthusiasm for the Young Italy movement is a poem published in *El Nacional* on November 30, 1838. Although published anonymously, Mitre signed his name "B. Mitre" underneath the poem in his personal copy of the issue, kept in his library (see figure 1):

¡Italia! ¡Italia! De mil héroes patria,
Alza tu frente entre la nada hundida,
Un siglo de existencia carcomida
Se borra con un día de igualdad.
¡Juventud Italiana! La esperanza
No reneguéis en vuestros corazones,
Hermanos son los santos pabellones
Que llaman a la Gloria y Libertad.
¡Joven Italia! El mundo te saluda
Y te saluda el pueblo Américano.
¡Desterrados! os damos nuestra mano. . . .
Ahora los himnos de la unión, cantad.
¡Joven Italia! El estandarte santo,
Alze a tu vez la juventud potente,
Caiga el tirano, el trono y esplendente
Se sublime la Santa Libertad.[75]

(Italy, Italy, land of a thousand heroes,
Raise from the ruins your downcast head,

A century of existence in decay
Is erased in one day of equality.
Young Italy! Do not reject
The hope in your hearts,
Brothers are the sacred peoples
Who strive for Glory and Liberty.
Young Italy! The world salutes you
And the American people salute you.
Exiled, we give you our hand . . .
Now sing the hymns of union!
Young Italy! May the holy banner
Elevate the powerful youth,
Let the tyrant fall, the throne, and resplendent,
Be transformed into Holy Freedom . . .)

Proclaiming all Americans, and all the world, to be the friends and brothers of the Italians, he calls for solidarity and liberation through battle. While the poem speaks ostensibly in support of the Risorgimento, it also implicitly

EL NACIONAL.

Y te saluda el Pueblo Américano,
Desterrados! os damos nuestra mano. . . .
Ahora los Himnos de la union cantad.
Jovén Italia! el estandarte santo,
Alze otra vez la juventud potente,
Caiga el tirano, el trono y esplendente
Su sublime la Santa Libertad.
B. Mitre.

FIGURE 1. Detail of a page of Mitre's personal copy of the November 30, 1838, edition of the newspaper *El Nacional*, archived in the Museo Mitre. Underneath the last lines of the poem "A la Joven Italia," one can see his signature (B. Mitre) written in ink.

opposes the hegemony of Rosas, cast again as a tyrant preventing the unity and progress of Argentina. In their fight to bring about Rosas's downfall, the members of Young Argentina looked to Young Italy as a model, but beyond Mazzini's political ideals, his views on the power of poetry to inspire patriotism and action were well known to the young Mitre.[76]

Mitre's Risorgimento Reading of Dante

Influenced by the thinking of the Italian exiles they encountered in Montevideo, Mitre and his fellow Argentine exiles associated Dante with liberty and political union. Mitre illustrates this association in a letter to Miguel Cané (the younger), written in justification of his *Divine Comedy* translation. Cané was skeptical regarding the benefits that Mitre's translation could have for the country. He seems dumbfounded that a man like Mitre, so engaged in the formation of a modern nation, would have the "colossal force" to translate Dante's poem.[77] And for what purpose? He doubts even the relative importance of the translation, believing that most Argentines will not actually read the work:

> How many men in Argentina do you figure have read the *Divine Comedy* unhurriedly and in its entirety? I'm not talking about the Italians, of course, who live in our land. For them reading Dante is an obligation from the time they learn to read, something like the final stamp on a document of citizenship.[78]

His concern, in fact, is that the *Divine Comedy* is a work only accessible to men of letters, and not of much import to the greater population. He refers to the work as "obscure" and "difficult," suggesting that Mitre's time would have been better spent writing another history.[79] Cané calls the translation a "titanic caprice" and jokingly warns Mitre against deciding next to learn Sanskrit and translate the *Ramayana*.[80]

For Cané, just one generation younger than Mitre, the latter's undertaking a translation of the *Divine Comedy* was almost incomprehensible. Perhaps in Cané's liberal (and un-Romantic) view, the consolidated state of 1894 did *not* need an epic to galvanize the nation. He recognizes, however, that the importance of Dante for Mitre has everything to do with the influence of the Italian exiles (such as Cuneo) during Mitre's days in Montevideo. At that time, Argentine and Italian exiles alike read Dante and dreamed of unity for their sister countries:

> The *sensation* of Italian that the exiles awoke in you, back in your youth, I have also maintained as a household tradition. Cuneo, just before his death, spoke to me about you and my father, about the whole group of Argentines that made Montevideo shine in the night of Silver. Cuneo wanted me to recite cantos of Dante and sonnets of Petrarch from memory, like my father did, back in the cult of that Italy that you all saw at the time as sad and enchained like our own country, and that today we see, with a secret suffering, in triple alliances that prove sickening for her sort, her history, and her destiny.[81]

When Mitre responded to Cané, he confirmed that this period in Montevideo indeed held the key to the significance of Dante for his generation. Mitre recalls the deep friendship he formed with Cané's father (Miguel Cané the elder), the two of them united in the fight against Rosas.[82] Mitre thanks the younger Cané for reminding him of "the distant epoch in which the *Divine Comedy* was observed in great detail . . . , chosen by the exiles who dreamed of the united Italy presented by the Poet, at the same time as the Argentine immigrants hoped for the liberty of their country."[83]

Italian and Argentine National Debates

Mitre's Risorgimento fanaticism is evidence of the widespread influence of the Italian unification movement noted by Albert Russell Ascoli and Krystyna von Henneberg in their introduction to the book *Making and Remaking Italy*: "Risorgimento heroes and myths flourished in places as far away as Argentina and Australia, consoling symbols of what the nation might have been, and creators of transnational patriotism."[84] Although Argentine nation-builders such as Mitre may have idealized the unification process in Italy, with its comparatively stronger cultural basis, Italy's national project had its own fractures and weaknesses, and the Italian national debate was no less fraught and contested. There were debates between radicals and moderates, unitarians and federalists, republicans and monarchists. Other areas of friction included the Papacy's claims to sovereignty over the Papal States and the Northern and Southern divide, with the Southern areas of Italy adversely affected by inadequate economic infrastructures, poor crop yields, and high unemployment.

A central difficulty in constructing a national past in Italy lay in the existence of many separate regional or municipal histories. But struggles against a foreign invader held a common place, as did the idea that centuries of foreign domination had produced servile citizens. In the first half of the nineteenth century, when the revolutionary attempts repeatedly failed, Mazzini used Dante to raise morale among revolutionaries, arguing that Dante had prophesied the rebirth of Italian civilization.

A major challenge that Italian nation-builders had to grapple with was the difficulty of translating a cultural ideal into a political fact. As Ascoli and von Henneberg point out, "it is the contrast between the fragility of the political nation on the one hand, and the cultural conviction of 'Italianness' on the other, that makes Italian history useful to scholars re-evaluating the impact and reception of other nation-building projects."[85] Politically speaking, Italy had not had any unifying institutions since the Roman Empire. As Madame de Staël aptly noted, for Italy culture and literary language were particularly important given the lack of political success: "Other nations can look to glory in war or politics; the Italians must acquire prestige from culture and the arts."[86]

Not just Madame de Staël but many foreigners who embarked on the Grand Tour wrote travel narratives or works of literature which portrayed Italy as a place that was culturally rich but politically and morally degenerate. Foreign observers continuously described Italy as a destination that was both exotic and luxurious; burdened by its classical past; boasting of illustrious ancestors; but languishing in a degenerate present.[87] Perhaps too comfortable resting on its laurels, the peninsula appeared to some travelers to have fallen asleep.[88] As Silvana Patriarca demonstrates in her article "Indolence and Regeneration: Tropes and Tensions of Risorgimento Patriotism," the patriotic discourse of the Risorgimento had to refute the negative representations and stereotyping of foreigners who envisioned Italy as a country of ruins and former glory but of current decline.[89] Cesare de Seta even argues that Italians acquired a consciousness of themselves on account of the "mirror" that was held up to them in Grand Tour narratives.[90] In response, there was much bold articulation of cultural superiority among Italian intellectuals. As literary historian Giulio Bollati famously wrote, nineteenth-century Italian history was marked by "the simultaneity of primacy and decadence, of objective inferiority overcompensated by an invincible sense of superiority."[91] We can see this, for example, in the rhetoric of Vincenzo Gioberti, author of *Del primato morale e civile degli italiani* (*The Moral and Political Primacy of the Italians*), who proclaims Italy to be the "mother nation of mankind."[92] Mitre uses similar rhetoric in the quotation that opens this chapter, wherein he calls Italy "the fertile mother of modern civilization."[93]

In terms of character, within Europe and in comparison to Northern Europeans, Italians were negatively stereotyped as lazy, superstitious, and morally lax.[94] Cesare Balbo, author of *Delle speranze d'Italia* (On the hopes of Italy, 1844) encouraged Italians to travel to distant lands to follow the example of "more civilized" countries.[95] This is in notable contrast to the way that Argentine nation-builders envisioned Italians as the bringers of civilization. Furthermore, the negative stereotyping is notably absent from Mitre's discourses on immigration, in which he envisions the Italians as industrious and energetic.

In conclusion, as Ascoli and von Henneberg explain, "from the start, the Risorgimento, with its emphasis on ensuring historical continuity, embodied the paradoxes of building anew what was supposed to exist inherently."[96] Argentina, on the other hand, was building anew what did not yet not exist. Both Italians and Argentines were concerned with the image of their nation abroad. Italian patriots agreed that Italians had fallen into a state of degradation on account of centuries of foreign oppression and that they were heading toward resurgence. But while Italy needed newness and regeneration, Argentina wanted a past founded in European tradition. Italian patriots endeavored to regenerate Italy to the levels of her illustrious past, and Argentine patriots aimed at forgetting Argentina's colonial past and instead emphasizing her sisterhood and solidarity with Italy. For Mitre, just as for Mazzini, Dante had prefigured Italian unity and was the poet associated par excellence with "patria," "liberty," and "justice." Mitre chose to translate the *Divine Comedy* because he saw it as literature that exemplified the transcendence of borders, a work which embodied the same ideas and values that he wished to propagate in the new Argentina.

TWO

Bartolomé Mitre's Translation of the *Divine Comedy*: An Anti–*Martín Fierro*

> Just as Italy has its *Divine Comedy*, Spain its *Don Quixote*, and Germany its *Faust*, Argentina has its *Martín Fierro*.
>
> —PABLO SUBIETA, online

José Hernández's *Martín Fierro* has long been considered Argentina's most prized literary classic.[1] Originally published in two parts, *El gaucho Martín Fierro* (1872) and *La vuelta de Martín Fierro* (1879), it enjoyed immediate and popular success. Within two years of its publication, *El gaucho Martín Fierro* had been printed nine times.[2] It was sold in rural *pulperías* (small grocery stores) and read aloud at public gatherings in the countryside. Many Argentine intellectuals, most notably Leopoldo Lugones (1874–1938), would later uphold *Martín Fierro* as the greatest reflection of Argentine national identity. In his 1913 lectures, Lugones declared the work to be the epic of Argentina, comparable to Italy's *Divine Comedy* or Spain's *Don Quixote*.[3]

It is interesting to note, then, that Bartolomé Mitre, a contemporary of Hernández who was fully aware of the book's popular success, chose not to mention it when asked about the state of Argentine literature. In chapter 1 I examined Mitre's 1887 letter to Señor don Miguel M. Ruíz, in which he argues that a university course on South American literature cannot be offered, given that said literature is yet to exist.[4] In Mitre's opinion:

> There are many voids to be filled, both territorial and intellectual. The vast majority of the land is uncultivated, and even unoccupied, and the literary colonies lack representatives and personifications to populate her terrain which is profound but yet untilled.[5]

By envisioning nineteenth-century South America as culturally barren, Mitre is negating the existence and importance of the indigenous cultures, as well as the local literary/cultural production that had occurred in situ since colonization.

In light of his stark views regarding the state of South American literature discussed in chapter 1, it becomes easier to understand why he dedicated a great deal of time and energy to the translation of European classics, such as Horace, Byron, Hugo, and, most importantly, Dante. He labored on his translation of the *Divine Comedy* for nearly a decade, beginning translations of various cantos of the *Inferno* in 1889, and publishing a definitive edition of all three *cantiche* in 1897. The amount of time Mitre devoted to the translation becomes all the more impressive when we consider that during the 1890s, approximately three decades after his presidency, he was still extremely active politically. For example, in 1890, he founded the Civic Union party along with Leandro Alem, and instigated the Revolution of the Park to oust then president Juárez Celman. In 1892 he was, along with Bernardo de Irigoyen, on the Civic Union's presidential ticket, although he later renounced the candidacy. Throughout the decade he exerted his political influence by way of the newspaper *La Nación*, which he had founded in 1870. The questions that beg asking, then, are, first: Why did Mitre see the hugely laborious task of translating Dante as a priority amid so much political activism? And further, what did the translation of an Italian epic poem have to do with Argentine politics? To shed light on these questions, I will consider this translation in conjunction with Mitre's negation of local literary production, namely Hernández's *Martín Fierro*, before turning to Mitre's translation of Dante.

Martín Fierro: *Argentina's Epic*

El gaucho Martín Fierro, which I will hereafter refer to as *La ida* (1872), is a poem about an impoverished gaucho of the Argentine pampas who sings of his many misfortunes, most of which are directly related to his persecution by Argentine institutions such as the military and government. Drafted into the army, Fierro leaves his family, only to be exploited and mistreated by the military men who were misusing the conscripts as free labor. After realizing the futility of remaining on the front, he deserts and returns home to find his house destroyed and his family gone. In a country that offers him no alternative, he is forced to live as an outlaw. By the end of the book, Fierro and his friend Cruz have withdrawn from civilization.

The book's author, José Hernández (1834–1886), was raised on his father's ranch near Buenos Aires, where he became deeply familiar with the rural life of the gauchos, as well as their speech, mannerisms, and rugged lifestyle. He was not a gaucho himself, but rather a member of the ruling elite. He was economically liberal but, unlike Mitre, felt that the economy should be based on cattle ranching rather than on agriculture and industrialization, which were more labor-intensive and required immigration. Gauchos, rather than immigrants, were a key component of a cattle-ranching economy. Hernández was a federalist, and his life and works were dedicated to safeguarding the interests of the landowning population of the provinces. He shared with other rural landowners the growing sentiment that rampant "progress," excessive immigration, and the arbitrary power of the city of Buenos Aires over the provinces could lead to a loss of tradition and values.

Hernández made his voice heard as a journalist, politician, and author of fiction. In 1851 he began working as the Paraná-Entre Ríos correspondent to *La Reforma Pacífica*. From 1852 to 1872 he defended the provinces against what he considered to be the excessive centralization of the government in Buenos Aires. He also took part in the gaucho uprising led by Ricardo López Jordán, which ended in 1871 with the defeat of the gauchos and Hernández's exile to Montevideo. He was openly against Mitre's extreme liberalism and military contradictions during the War of Paraguay.[6] He also spoke out against Domingo Faustino Sarmiento, who was elected president in 1868.

From 1869 to 1870, Hernández was the editor of the newspaper *El Río de la Plata*, which published articles against the persecution and exploitation of the gauchos, among other political issues, and whose goals were explicitly stated in the first issue:

> Situated in a line of thinking independent from Sarmiento and Mitre, as well as from Urquiza, the newspaper will support a few essential tenets: defense of the men of the countryside, total and systematic opposition of the War of Paraguay and the attack on Brazilian interests, indefatigable postulation of the municipal regimen and the judgment of the jury, concord and national unity, liberty for all, equality in front of the law, political and economic federalism, industrial protectionism, and economic nationalism.[7]

One of the controversial topics opposed by Hernández was the military draft of the gauchos, who he believed were needed in the countryside to raise the cattle which he saw as the economic future of the country, rather than on the warfront fighting Indians or other American countries, as they did in the Paraguayan War. In his opinion, universal conscription was bound to end in disaster: "It's not necessary to possess the secrets of the future in order to predict what will happen. It's enough to know the countryside, the nature of our gauchos, their customs, and the terror and panic that military service provokes in them."[8]

These sociopolitical arguments are at the heart of *El gaucho Martín Fierro (La ida)*. Hernández began writing the poem following the suppression of his newspaper and his exile. In 1872, he received amnesty and was able to return to Buenos Aires, where he would publish it. With *La ida* Hernández addresses social and political inequities, and the bitterness of his recent political bruising emerges in pages that are extremely critical of the central government. The book concludes with no hope of integration of the rebel gaucho into society. Conversely, the second part, *La vuelta de Martín Fierro* (1879), is much more conciliatory, no doubt because it was written when Hernández's political situation was far more favorable on account of the presidency of Nicolás Avellaneda (1874–80).[9]

In March 1879 Hernández himself sent Mitre, his longtime political adversary, a copy of *La vuelta* in which he inscribed the following words:

> For 25 years I have been among the ranks of your political adversaries—few Argentines can say the same; just as few have dared as I have to rise above this

> distinction, to ask the illustrious Author that he concede a small space in his Library for this modest book. I ask you to please accept it as a gesture of respect from your fellow countryman.[10]

Although Mitre did not yet own a copy, he was most certainly aware of the book's popularity, which he acknowledges at the beginning of his response letter: "*Martín Fierro* is a work and a figure who has earned citizenship in Argentine literature and society." Ostensibly putting politics aside, in the same letter Mitre accepts Hernández's literary offering, saying that he appreciates the benevolent words that accompany the book. But his disapproval of the work's sociopolitical message becomes evident in the criticisms that follow.

Still in the same letter, Mitre begins by describing the book as "a truly spontaneous poem, a slice of real life." Although seemingly a flattering remark, it is most likely a slight that insinuates that the poem was written with little heed to formal perfection. He goes on, however, to praise the work, which seems to meet the criteria for literature as he himself laid out in the aforementioned letter to Miguel M. Ruíz, wherein he insisted that a nation's literature possess new genres or "original creations that mark literary progress."[11] Of *Martín Fierro*, he writes:

> It has intention, philosophy, poetic flights, and beautiful descriptions which signify the third or fourth form that this genre of literature has taken on among us. Hidalgo will always be its Homer because he was the first, and like you he was inspired by a poetics that you have summed up in the following verses:
>
> > Porque yo canto opinando
> > Que es mi modo de cantar
>
> Ascasubi, who followed in Hidalgo's footsteps, putting the gaucho in the presence of civilization and exalting his patriotism; and Estanislao del Campo, who made the gaucho judge works of art and the society according to his own criteria, mark the intermediary forms of the genre.[12]

Mitre recognizes the gauchesque as a literary genre unique to Argentina that has developed over time, culminating in *Martín Fierro*.[13] His perception of the development of a whole genre is probably his greatest achievement as a literary critic. Yet, despite his identification of *Martín Fierro* as the apex of this original literary genre, he is very critical of its lexicon, style, and content, as he writes in the letter just quoted above:

> I find that you have been overly realistic and have exaggerated the local color in verses without meter which you intentionally sowed into your pages, as well as certain barbarisms which were not necessary to make your book accessible to the world.[14]

Mitre does not seem to appreciate the extent to which *Martín Fierro* is formally sophisticated. While Hernández maintains the eight-syllable line of the *payadas*, the rural ballads, he implements a rhyming six-line stanza with the second, third, and sixth lines rhyming, and the fourth and fifth lines rhyming independently. The first line is kept unrhymed. Furthermore, Mitre does not seem to understand Hernández's mythologization of the gaucho. He most likely could not get past the work's subject matter to recognize its literary potential, fearing that its pessimistic portrayal of the political situation gave a negative impression of the new nation and of both his own and Sarmiento's presidencies.

Mitre's Translation of the Divine Comedy*: An Anti–*Martín Fierro

Mitre's translation of the *Divine Comedy* can be considered an anti–*Martín Fierro*. It is a way to mitigate the linguistic and aesthetic tendencies of Hernández's work, and most importantly, to promote the opposite social message—cultural cohesion modeled upon Risorgimento Italy, with which the *Divine Comedy* was associated. To explain, Risorgimento thinkers saw Dante as a prophet of national unity, given his opposition to foreign domination. Giuseppe Mazzini, in particular, was influential in promoting the idea of Dante as *pater patriae*.

Mitre was familiar with the culture of the Italian Risorgimento. He was introduced to Mazzinian ideas and the ideology of Young Italy while he and his family were exiles in Montevideo, Uruguay, when Juan Manuel de Rosas was in power in Buenos Aires. It was in exile that a young Mitre came to know Giuseppe Garibaldi and other Italians, themselves exiles, who were involved in spreading the ideas of Mazzini in South America.[15] Mitre's association of Dante with political unity is confirmed in a letter to Miguel Cané (the younger), in which he recalls the time when "the *Divine Comedy* was observed in great detail . . . , chosen by the exiles who dreamed of the united Italy presented by the Poet, at the same time as the Argentine immigrants hoped for the liberty of their country."[16]

A second reason that a translation of Dante made sense for Mitre within the context of nineteenth-century Argentina was due to the considerable presence of Italian migrants in the region. Following independence, as the Argentine territory remained largely unpopulated, the governing elites, such as Juan Bautista Alberdi, who coined the phrase *gobernar es poblar* (to govern is to populate), promoted immigration as the means to "civilize" and modernize the nation. As we have seen in chapter 1, in the second half of the nineteenth century, roughly 60 percent of the European immigrants who settled in the country were Italian;[17] and Mitre himself was pro–Italian immigration during his presidency.[18] A version of the *Divine Comedy* translated into Spanish was both a gesture of welcome for Italian immigrants and, as becomes apparent from the prologue to the translation and the publication announcements, a way of associating Argentina with Old World high culture.

Associating Argentina with High Culture

A closer look at Mitre's translation reveals that men of letters and urban intellectuals were the intended audience. This stands in stark contrast with Hernández's *Martín Fierro*, which was addressed to and appreciated by the rural population. Thus, *Martín Fierro* and Mitre's translation of the *Divine Comedy* diverge on both an aesthetic and a thematic level.

In *Martín Fierro* Hernández incorporates expressions characteristic of the popular Argentine Spanish of the pampas, considered unworthy of high literature, in much the same way as the Italian vernacular was considered inferior to Latin at the time of Dante. When he lived among the gauchos, Hernández absorbed their way of speech and employed its expressive power for the storytelling "duels" of his poets of the pampa. Dialect pronunciations are frequently imitated via orthographic changes. For example, Hernández replaces "f" with "j" ("juerte" for "fuerte" and "juera" for "fuera"); "b" with "g" ("gueno" for "bueno"); and "v" with "g" ("guelta" for "vuelta"). Similarly, the "d" is more often than not omitted from the suffix "-ado," which is written as it was pronounced by rural Argentines as "-ao." The simple change of leaving off the final "d" of the suffix "-dad," thereby lengthening the "a," gives his gaucho poetry a unique phonetic quality:

que nunca peleo ni mato
sino por necesidá
y que a tanta alversidá
sólo me arrojó el mal trato.

(lines 105–8; Hernández, *Martín Fierro*, 10)

In addition to the omission of the final "d"s, the first "d" in "adversidad" is changed to an "l." While such pronunciations were typical of the gauchos, they were not the norm among urban intellectuals like Mitre. Hernández's goal was to be a poet for the rural population, and therefore his protagonist proclaims at the onset, "yo no soy cantor letrao,"[19] to convey a sense of humility, although such verses could only be written by a man of letters.

Perhaps even more interesting are the humorous plays on words that bring together the pronunciation and imagery of the pampas, such as when the drunk Martín Fierro insults a woman he fancies when out dancing:

Al ver llegar la morena	Upon seeing the woman enter
que no hacía caso de naides	paying no attention to anyone,
le dije con la mamúa:	I said to her drunkenly:
"Va . . . ca . . . yendo gente al baile."	"*Va . . . ca . . . yendo gente al baile.*"

(lines 1151–54, 69)

Fierro, slurring on account of "la mamúa" (Argentine slang indicating drunkenness), points out that people are starting to show up to dance ("va cayendo"). However, because his speech is slurred and drawn out, "va . . . ca . . ." is interpreted by the woman as an insult, "vaca" meaning "cow." The woman retaliates, "más *vaca* será su madre" (your mother is more of a cow). This only escalates the animalesque vulgarity of Fierro's advances, as he continues to offend her in the low language of the rural dance halls:

"Negra linda" . . . dije yo,
"me gusta . . . pa la carona";
y me puse a talariar
esta coplita fregona:

"A los blancos hizo Dios,
a los mulatos San Pedro,
a los negros hizo el diablo
para tizón del infierno."

"Beautiful negress" . . . I said to her
"*Me gusta . . . pa la carona,*"
and I started to sing
this little verse:

"White men were made by God,
mulatos by San Pedro
and blacks were made by the devil
to stain the fires of hell."

(lines 1163–70, 69)

Fierro tells her he would like to mount her, since "carona" could be understood as "saddle," thereby likening her to a horse. Shortly thereafter he gets into a brawl and ends up killing a Black man. He says to him at the beginning of the fight: "Por . . . rudo . . . que un hombre sea/nunca se enoja por esto" ("*Por . . . rudo* . . . as a man may be/he should never get mad over this."[20] Similar to the tenzone of Dante's time, Hernández packs as many insults into one line as possible, *porrudo* meaning hairy in addition to rude (*rudo*). Elsewhere, the text even pokes fun at the speech of Italian immigrants, who were not as refined as the country's forefathers had initially envisioned.[21]

The style, of course, is low, comic, and characterized by rural colloquialisms that Mitre considered undesirable and referred to as "barbarisms," which in philology designates words or expressions that are badly formed according to traditional philological rules; for example, a word formed from elements of different languages. More importantly, "barbarism" means an absence of culture and civilization; it was a politically charged word ever since Sarmiento's *Facundo* depicted the opposition between "civilización" and "barbarie" as the central conflict in Argentine culture. For the urban intellectual elite, the gauchos and the *caudillos* represented the barbarism believed to derive from the nature of the Argentine countryside. Their way of life stood in opposition to the civilization that was to be cultivated via modernization and the importation of European cultural ideals. By contrast, Sarmiento and Mitre most likely perceived the speech patterns of the pampas as a degradation of language.

In Mitre's opinion, rather than using low language in a work of literature to make it accessible, one should elevate "the vulgar intelligence to the level of language used to express ideas and feelings common among men."[22]

This is an important point with regard to his translation of Dante, which eliminates much of the low language so characteristic of the original text. Linguistically, his translation of the *Divine Comedy* is a counteroperation to that performed by Hernández. Mitre seeks to reverse the tendency to bring creole colloquialisms into the language, employing instead an antiquated Spanish enriched by Italianisms and Latinisms.

In his prologue to the translation, entitled "Teoría del Traductor," Mitre declares that the best translation of the *Divine Comedy* into Spanish would approximate the style of the Castilian poets of the fifteenth century, such as Juan de Mena, Manrique, or the Marquis of Santillana. At this time, Mitre writes, Spanish came into being as a romance language, free of its original ties to Latin and marking the transition between the anticlassical and classical periods of Spanish literature. According to Mitre, a translation in this style would be most capable of mirroring Dante's original text, since adopting the style of these Castilian poets would reproduce the sounds and metrical combinations of syllables of Latin derivation.

Mitre further declares that he will introduce antiquated terms and idioms when they happen to "harmonize" with the tone of the original composition, but not when they would "disfigure" the poem. In this way he hopes to give the translation "a light archaic touch, without taking its language back to anti-classical Spanish, which would result in a pedantic and spurious affectation."[23] Moreover, since he says that the *Divine Comedy* was written "in a Tuscan dialect that sprang like a murky spring from the crystalline torrent of Latin," Mitre offers an implicit judgment that favors the linguistic purity of Latin over the developing vernacular.[24] Not surprisingly, Mitre's version retains numerous Latinisms and Italianisms, where the latter seem to be used in Spanish to create a parallel archaic feel in the translation that aligns with his theoretical approach. As an example, in *Purgatorio* 11.103–5 Mitre replaces the colloquial language employed by Dante with a more formal register:

Che voce avrai tu più, se vecchia scindi,
da te la carne, che se fossi morto
anzi che tu lasciassi il "pappo" e 'l "dindi"

(*Purg.* 11.103–5)

Pappo and *dindi* are baby talk words for bread (*pappo = pane*) and money (*dindi = denaro*). Mitre translates the lines as "¿Qué más fama tendrás desde el momento/que te separes de tu carne vieja,/o papa digas con *pueril acento*?" Instead of employing infantile speech, Mitre includes the Latinism "pueril acento." Whereas José Hernández's *Martín Fierro* (1872/79) incorporated colloquialisms into a new poetics, Mitre reverses the trend. Rather than replacing Dante's many colloquialisms with Argentine equivalents that would be familiar to the general population, he frequently leaves the terms in Italian, or replaces them with Latinisms or archaisms.

As Claudia Fernández Speier has argued, Mitre's many archaisms, Italianisms, and neologisms may have impeded comprehension for many nineteenth-century readers. To determine the degree of difficulty his translation would have presented to readers at the time, Speier consulted the 1869 to 1884 *Diccionario de la lengua Castellana por la Academia Española*. She argues that Mitre's frequent selection of antiquated terms and Italianisms made the text fairly inaccessible to readers not versed in Golden Age Spanish poetry as well as in Italian. Speier concludes that if a Dantean term existed in the "italianized Spanish" of the sixteenth and seventeenth century, then Mitre retained it.[25] Perhaps realizing the difficulty some of these terms may have presented to readers, Mitre accompanies many archaisms with brief notes explaining that the term is antiquated and providing the modern equivalent.[26]

Regardless of his goal, the result of his word choice is at times a loss of colloquiality and a change in tone. This pattern emerges early in the first canto when Dante meets Virgil, his beloved mentor and soon-to-be infernal guide:

"Or se' tu quel Virgilio e quella fonte che spandi di parlar sì largo fiume?" rispuos'io lui con vergognosa fronte.	Tú eres Virgilio, la perenne fuente que expande el gran raudal de su oratoria! le interrumpí con ruberosa frente,
"O de li altri poeti onore e lume, vagliami 'l lungo studio e 'l grande amore che m'ha fatto cercar lo tuo volume.	¡Oh! de poetas, luminar y gloria, ¡válgame el largo estudio y grande afecto que consagré a tu libro, y tu memoria!

Tu se' lo mio maestro e 'l mio autore, tu se' solo colui da cu' io tolsi lo bello stilo che m'ha fatto onore.	¡Oh mi autor y maestro predilecto! de ti aprendí tan sólo el bello estilo, que tanto honor ha dado a mi intelecto.

(*Inf.* 1.79–87)

In the original, Dante the pilgrim seems humble, and his meeting with Virgil has the intimate feel of a young pupil encountering his greatest master. In Mitre's version, Dante the pilgrim comes across as pedantic on account of grandiloquent phrasing. In his translation of the line, "Or se' tu quel Virgilio e quella fonte," Mitre eliminates the more colloquial "quel" (ese) and replaces the demonstrative adjective "quella" with the descriptive adjective "perenne" (perennial), from Latin *perennis.* The next line, "el gran raudal de su oratoria!" is magniloquent in comparison to the original, as is the adjective "ruberosa," from Latin *rubor, -ōris*, which could have been translated with the more common "vergonzosa," also more analogous to the Italian "vergognosa." In the original, the image of Dante searching for Virgil's book is tender ("che m'ha fatto cercar lo tuo volume"), while Mitre's rendition ("que consagré a tu libro, y tu memoria!") is more austere and abstract, with the verb "consagrar" (instead of "buscar") and the noun "memoria" (memory), which is not in the original.

The incongruously lofty register of certain parts of the first canto led me to wonder how Mitre had handled *Inferno* 18–23, which exemplify Dante's plurilingualism. Most notably in *Inferno* 18, one finds low, comic language and explicit sexual language mixed in with elevated language. As Zygmunt G. Barański has argued, canto 18 of *Inferno* features "un vocabolario spinto ai limiti del linguisticamente accettabile. In tal modo, Dante mette a nudo l'avvilente realtà, celata solitamente dalle 'parole ornate' (v. 91) dei peccatori, di colpe dalla forte carica sessuale":[27]

Appresso ciò lo duca "Fa che pinghe",
mi disse, "il viso un poco più avante,
sì che la faccia ben con l'occhio attinghe
    di quella sozza e scapigliata fante
che là si graffia con l'unghie merdose,
e or s'accoscia e ora è in piedi stante.
    Taïde è, la puttana che rispuose
al drudo suo quando disse "Ho io grazie

grandi apo te?": 'Anzi maravigliose!'
 E quinci sian le nostre viste sazie."

(*Inf.* 18.127–36)

As Barański explains, Dante's language is phonetically "aspro" (harsh), and features, on one hand, low words such as "sozza e scapigliata fante" (v. 130), "graffia" (v. 131), "merdose" (v. 131), "puttana" (v. 133), and the rhyme in—*inghe* (vv. 127 and 129); and, at the same time, words such as "drudo" (v. 134), which are clearly courtly, with feudal-chevaleresque connotations. Even the exchange between Thaïs and her lover is in high style and includes a blatant Latinism: "apo" (v. 135), from *apud.*[28] In short, the canto is indicative of Dante's plurilingualism, in the heterogeneous uses of language and style.

The question is whether Mitre's translation succeeds in conserving the phonetic roughness of the original or its different stylistic registers.

Già eravam là 've lo stretto calle con l'argine secondo s'incrocicchia, e fa di quello ad un altro' arco spalle.	Llegamos a un extremo, donde alcanza el arco con sus bordes a juntarse, y es pilar de otro puente que se avanza;
Quindi sentimmo gente che si nicchia ne l'altra bolgia e che col muso scuffa, e sé medesma con le palme picchia.	siento de allí una grita levantarse, con bufidos de gente condenada, y unos a otros coléricos golpearse.
Le ripe eran grommate d'una muffa, per l'alito di giù che vi s'appasta, che con li occhi e col naso facea zuffa.	La pendiente está toda embadurnada de sucio órin, que la nariz ofende, y que náuseas provoca a la mirada.
Lo fondo è cupo sì, che non ci basta loco a veder sanza montare al dosso de l'arco, ove lo scoglio più sovrasta.	En vano el ojo penetrar pretende, aquella hondura, sólo percibida de la alta roca a cuyo pie desciende.
Quivi venimmo; e quindi giù nel fosso vidi gente attuffata in uno sterco che da li uman privadi parea mosso.	Vimos allí una turba zabullida, que chapoteaba en una cloaca inmunda, a estercolar humano parecida;
E mentre ch'io là giù con l'occhio cerco, vidi un col capo sì di merda lordo, che non parëa s'era laico o cherco.	y en medio a la asquerosa baraunda, uno de ellos, que clérigo barrunto, con excremento su cabeza inunda.
Quei mi sgridò: "Perché se' tu sì gordo di riguardar più me che li altri brutti?" E io a lui: "Perché, se ben ricordo,	¿Por qué miras" preguntó el del unto, "y no a esos brutos?" Con el ojo fijo, le respondí: "Porque eres un trasunto,

già t'ho veduto coi capelli asciutti, e se' Alessio Interminei da Lucca: però t'adocchio più che li altri tutti."	de uno limpio de pelo, y bien colijo, eres Alessio Interminei, de Luca: por eso en verte aquí me regocijo."
Ed elli allor, battendosi la zucca: "Qua giù m'hanno sommerso le lusinghe ond'io non ebbi mai la lingua stucca."	Y él, entonces, golpeándose la nuca, dijo: "Aquí purgo la lisonja aviesa, que con la lengua al prójimo embaüca."

(*Inf.* 18.100–136)

Dante's description of the *bolgia* contains explicit visual and olfactory terms and crude vocabulary such as *sterco*, *privadi*, *merda*, *unghie merdose*. Phonetically speaking, there is an abundance of harsh-sounding words, such as *s'incrocicchia*, *nicchia*, *scuffa*, *grommate*, *appasta*, and *stucca*. Mitre's translation often does not conserve the rough alliteration, as in the line "e sé medesma con le palme picchia" ("y unos a otros coléricos golpearse"), where he inserts the word "coléricos," which was not in the original and expresses a more formal register. Though he preserves the animalesque nature of the sinners somewhat with "bufidos," this approximation is not as graphic as "col muso scuffa." Furthermore, the lines "La pendiante esta toda embadurnanda / de sucio orín que la nariz ofende, / y que náuseas provoca a la mirada" uses a much more formal register and conveys nothing of the colloquial or phonetically "aspro" quality of the original, "Le ripe eran grommate d'una muffa, / per l'alito di giù che vi s'appasta, / che con li occhi e col naso facea zuffa." As Teodolinda Barolini points out in her commentary on the canto, "The inventive rhyme-words, taken from everyday life and resolutely non-literary—for instance 'scuffa'/'muffa'/'zuffa' (*Inf.* 18.104–08)—are used to give a plebeian tone to the degraded surroundings of the final two sinners of *Inferno* 18."[29] Rather than employing everyday vocabulary to reproduce a "plebeian tone," Mitre chooses to incorporate words of Latin origin wherever possible. For example, "pendiente" (instead of "inclinado") from Lat. *pendens*; "orín" from Lat. vulg. *aurīgo*; "offender" from Lat. *offendĕre*; "náuseas" from Lat. *nauseāre*; "provocar" (instead of "producir" or "causar") from Lat. *provocāre*.

The same can be said of the following lines:

Lo fondo è cupo sì, che non ci basta loco a veder sanza montare al dosso de l'arco, ove lo scoglio più sovrasta.	En vano el ojo penetrar pretende, aquella hondura, sólo percibida de la alta roca a cuyo pie desciende.

(*Inf.* 18.109–11)

Mitre's choice of vocabulary, "en vano," "penetrar," "hondura," "percibida," and the use of the pronoun "cuyo," give his version a loftier feel. When it comes to references to excrement, instead of using the common term "mierda," Mitre opts for "estercolar" from Latin *stercorare*; "cloaca" also from the Latin; or he adopts an Italianism, writing "uñas de merdosa" for Dante's "l'unghie merdose."

While this particular canto is predominately low in style, with Thaïs's speech Dante suddenly switches to a courtly register, which Mitre maintains by translating "drudo" with "cortejo," and Thaïs's speech as "Estoy en gracia?" and "¡Y muy maravillosa!" But he adds the adjective "licenciosa" (licentious) to describe her, where there is no such qualifying term in the original; and in the last line he adds the cumbersome word "podredumbre" (rottenness/corruption), which, although well suited to the subject matter of the canto, is not in Dante's version.

In summary, while Mitre's antiquated Spanish may be better suited for some of the loftier sections of the poem, it fails to convey the harsh quality of the comic sections of the original. It is ironic that Mitre would use Dante as a means to counteract the literary tendencies exemplified by works such as Hernández's *Martín Fierro*, because it reveals a misunderstanding of Dante's plurilingualism, and his ability to write in a style that is at times rough and vulgar, at times gentle and plain, and at times lofty and refined. It seems that Mitre associated the *Divine Comedy* strictly with high, as opposed to popular, culture.

Hernández, on the other hand, incorporates low language into a sophisticated poetics. Like Dante, Hernández envisioned his work being read in all corners of the countryside, and not just in the circles of the educated. In the prologue to the 1879 edition he calls the work

> a book destined to awaken the intelligence and the love of reading in an almost primitive population, and which will serve as a beneficial recreation after tiring labor for thousands of people who have never read. As such it must be adapted to the uses and customs of these same readers; it must render their ideas and interpret their feelings in the same language, and in their most common phrasing, even if this be incorrect.[30]

His notion too of a work of literature is Romantic, in that it should reflect the social customs of a population. The difference between Hernández and

Mitre is that Hernández writes for both a popular readership and men of letters, while Mitre's work is intended for the intellectual urban elite, or the ideal future citizen who has been "elevated" via education. Such intent is further reflected in the marketing of the translation, which was meant for the most "civilized" of readerships. For example, the publication announcement of September 1890 for the first version of *Infierno* declares that "for the first time" an Argentine work will have the honor of being a luxury commodity.[31] More than once the advertisement emphasizes that this is no ordinary edition, but a distinguished publication to be appreciated by the erudite: "The *Inferno of Dante*, which is destined exclusively for men of letters and Argentine bibliophiles, just went to press in one of the most important Parisian publishing houses."[32] The book is referred to as "a refined luxury," and, as such, the number of copies must be limited to make it an exclusive possession: "Because it is an exclusive, luxury edition, we limited ourselves to only 600 copies which are all individually numbered by the publisher."[33]

The edition included original illustrations by artists in imitation of the "most elegant works" published by Parisian editors.[34] Six illustrations by the painter Cornillier, winner of the *Prix de Rome*, grace its pages. The pictures were reproduced in watercolor by señor Abot, known for his popular illustrations of fashionable books printed in Paris. The book also featured portraits of both Dante and his translator. Even the paper was a luxury, having been ordered expressly for this edition, every page with a watermark. The printing was entrusted to none other than the presses of Chamerot, the preferred printer of the Parisian editors. Mitre himself went to Paris to personally discuss his corrections with the editor. The result was advertised as "a worthy edition which will be of interest to those who admire the laboriousness and erudition of the historiographer of San Martín and Belgrano."[35]

While Hernández endeavored to cultivate his image as a spokesman for the humble rural population, Mitre, as translator of the *Divine Comedy*, sought to cultivate his image as a man of letters and of Argentines as literati. He sent out copies of the work to libraries, foreign ministers, and even the Arcadia Romana, which had honored Longfellow for his translation just decades before. The enthusiastic response from those who received the work was overwhelming, and the great majority of letters that flooded in from at home and abroad praise Mitre's erudition and emphasize the honor his translation brought to the Argentine nation. Osvaldo Magnasco, an Argentine politician and jurist, wrote "congratulations for the honor that this noble monument reflects on your name and on our national literature."[36] The Academy of Arcadia in Rome congratulated him and wrote that the translation demonstrates that "the cult of the greatest Christian poet exists on the other side of the Atlantic, in a land hospitable to Italians who seek refuge far from the motherland."[37] As is clear from such responses, the prestigious translation added to the symbolic capital of Argentine letters, while sending a message of welcome to prospective Italian immigrants.

Conclusion

Apart from conveying glory and honor on himself and the Argentine nation, with the *Comedy* Mitre intended to promote a social message very different from that found in *Martín Fierro*. José Hernández had given voice to the oppressed figure of the gaucho and the rural community protesting against the Argentine political establishment, which he considered the cause of the gaucho's demise. The work strongly emphasizes the contrast between the rural, illiterate inhabitants of the pampas and the urban intellectuals who control their fate: "El campo es del inorante/el pueblo del hombre estruido."[38] His aim was to "listen to the most uncultivated of our countrymen," in hopes that they no longer be excluded from the political decisions of the elite.[39] Mitre, of course, disapproved of the social philosophy of Hernández's protagonist, who rebels against, and withdraws from, the "civilized" society. Mitre admitted as much to Hernández himself in the letter I quoted at the beginning of my analysis of their relationship:

> I am not completely in agreement with your social philosophy, which leaves in the depths of the soul a bitterness without the correction of social solidarity. It is better to reconcile antagonisms with love and the necessity to live together and united, than to ferment hatred which has as its cause, more than the nature of man, the imperfections of our social and political state. Nevertheless, as it is, I believe "it won't rain on the ranch" where people read your book.[40]

For Mitre, *Martín Fierro* was a work that would foster discord, unrest, and rebellion among the rural population. Furthermore, depicting the past life of the gaucho, prior to the country's modernization, as the golden days was counter to the progressive Argentina that Mitre was working to establish. The *Divine Comedy*, on the other hand, was a work that not only was representative of European high culture (i.e., "civilization" in contrast to "barbarism"), but had also been a means for Italian Risorgimento thinkers to promote cultural cohesion. The literary endeavors of these two men, Hernández and Mitre, stand on opposing sides of the political and cultural divide in nineteenth-century Argentina. For the former, the national essence of Argentina was to be found in rural traditions and in the rough realities of the pampas; for the latter, nation-building and cultivating a future Argentine civilization meant turning to the country's European ancestry via translation.

THREE

Leopoldo Lugones on Immigration and Argentine Identity

In the twentieth century, the influence of Dante on Argentine writers and literary scholars remained paramount. In fact, rewriting Dante became a way for influential Argentine authors to comment on and develop the national literature. As will be discussed in chapter 4, both Leopoldo Lugones (1874–1938) and Jorge Luis Borges (1899–1986) were heavily influenced by the *Divine Comedy*, and both wrote creative adaptations of *Inferno* V. But before we can understand their reasons for rewriting Dante, we must understand how great influxes of immigration in the late nineteenth and early twentieth centuries resulted in a rapidly changing demographic that made defining what it meant to be Argentine all the more imperative for Argentine authors. In this chapter I will discuss the shift in the perception of the Italian immigrant and the growing sentiments of xenophobia and nostalgia for the past among the creole population.

As we have seen in chapter 1, Mitre's generation viewed immigration as an essential component of national development, along with building railways, improving the shipping industry, and developing Argentina's economy. In order for Argentina to become a major exporter of grains, meat, and wool, the country needed large numbers of laborers. In addition to powering Argentina's growing economy, immigrants were expected to import the values necessary for cultural transformation. According to Juan Bautista Alberdi, Bartolomé Mitre, and Domingo Faustino Sarmiento, immigrants would set a positive example for the existing population by means of their industriousness and high ethical standards. In 1845 Sarmiento had written in *Facundo* that "the principal ingredient toward order and moralization in the Argentine Republic is immigration from Europe."[1] He depicts the European immigrants as upright individuals, living in clean, orderly, and picturesque houses, while the lazy native inhabitants of Buenos Aires wallow in filth and poverty. European immigration was largely envisioned as the cure for Argentina's state of "barbarism."

Furthermore, during the nineteenth century immigration was seen as a way for the country to break away from the cultural influence of Spain. In 1818 Bernardino Rivadavia had proclaimed that immigration "was the most efficient means . . . of destroying the degrading Spanish habits and of creating a homogeneous, industrious and moral population, the only solid base for Equality, Liberty, and consequently, the Prosperity of the nation."[2] Apparent in Rividavia's proclamation is the Hispanophobia of the nineteenth century, as well as the belief that the immigrant was to be the agent of a cultural transformation that would bring about economic, political, and moral "progress."

The dreams of the nineteenth-century liberals to "populate the desert" with European immigrants became a reality toward the turn of the century. The actual immigrants who came, however, did not correspond to the idealized version of the future immigrant envisioned by Argentina's forefathers. First of all, fleeing the desperate poverty of their home country, they came with a few tattered belongings rather than a great deal of capital. They were largely from southern, rather than northern, Europe, where wages tended to be higher than those offered in Argentina. They were often poor and illiterate, and therefore hardly the importers of high "culture." Their presence certainly did not generate a homogeneous population of new Argentines, but rather a racially mixed population of foreigners, most of whom did not acquire citizenship.[3] Furthermore, they arrived at rates that proved alarming to the existing population, in particular the landowning elite. Between the second national census of 1895 and the third of 1914, the population rose from 3.9 million to 7.8 million. The population of Buenos Aires alone increased sharply from 660,000 to more than 1.5 million.[4]

Although mass immigration was already under way during Mitre's presidency, it increased sharply during the presidency of Nicolás Avellaneda (1874–80). Unlike Mitre, who advocated spontaneous immigration, Avellaneda, Sarmiento's successor, was a firm believer in artificial immigration. In 1876 Congress passed the Avellaneda Law, which set up immigration offices in Europe to offer European farmers and workers subsidized passages, temporary lodging, and free transportation inland upon arrival. This law nearly doubled the number of immigrants willing to make the journey to Argentina. Between 1870 and 1914, 5.9 million immigrants came to Argentina, and approximately half of them were from Italy.[5]

The flood of recent immigrants meant major changes for the rapidly developing country. As regards economic growth, their presence proved positive. Agricultural production increased and Argentina became the third-largest world exporter of grain. She was also a major exporter of wool and beef to industrializing economies in Europe, and an importer of manufactured goods. Economic booms took place from 1884 to 1889 and 1905 to 1912.[6] Economically speaking, then, it could be said that the influx of immigrants did indeed bring about the desired "progress." But such large-scale immigration was not without problematic consequences.

One major consequence of the mass immigration was an accelerated urbanization. Although the Immigration and Settlement Act of 1876 sought to promote colonization of the interior, many of the immigrants had difficulty acquiring land and chose instead to settle on the coast and in the cities, namely in Buenos Aires.[7] This led to rapid urbanization and the exponential growth of an urban middle class. Jeane Delaney in her article "Making Sense of Modernity: Changing Attitudes toward the Immigrant and the Gaucho in Turn-of-the-Century Argentina" explains how the Argentine intellectuals at the time tended to blame the social consequences of rapid modernization on the immigrant population alone. She identifies this tendency to make the immigrants into scapegoats as a distinct feature of Argentine antimodernism.[8] The creole inhabitants of Buenos Aires, especially the elite, felt threatened not only because of the sheer number of immigrants pouring into the country, but also because these immigrants occupied an "intermediary" social standing:

> In contrast to the other nations formed by immigration such as the United States, where most nineteenth- and twentieth-century immigrants occupied the stratum below the native white working class, most immigrants to Argentina occupied an intermediary place in Argentine society, above the traditional popular classes but below the native elite and professional groups.[9]

Indeed, in Argentina, where previously a clear social hierarchy had existed, the social status of inhabitants became increasingly blurred. Although it was difficult for most immigrants to acquire land, which was a huge economic asset for agricultural production, there was a substantial amount of social mobility.[10] The small elite, which constituted about 5 percent of the population in comparison with the working classes, became increasingly hostile toward the newcomers, whom they perceived as encroaching on their hegemony.

Not only did they blame immigrants for social problems in rapidly growing cities, they also were concerned about their lack of social integration and naturalization. The population was racially mixed and culturally segregated to an extreme degree. In addition to the Spanish and Italians who made up the great majority, there were Slavs, French, Germans, Russians, Irish, and other ethnicities. But very few of these many immigrants acquired citizenship. Between 1850 and 1930 fewer than 5 percent of immigrants took Argentine citizenship.[11] Argentina was populated, but it remained "un país sin ciudadanos," as reads the title of a book by Lucio Mansilla published in Paris in 1907.[12]

Although immigrant workers without citizenship could not vote, they were not entirely politically powerless. They brought with them political movements from their European countries of origin, such as labor unionism, anarchism, and socialism. Worker strikes and anarchist and socialist activism increased as workers tried to improve their economic condition. The anarchists, who controlled much of Buenos Aires's unskilled laboring class, quickly became the most powerful element in the Argentine labor movement.[13] Osvaldo Bayer shows how Italian immigration played a direct role in the anarchist movement in Argentina, specifically emphasizing the roles of Errico Malatesta and Pietro Gori, two figures of Italian anarchism who had a definitive influence in the formation and consolidation of organized Angentine anarchism.[14]

Also disconcerting to the creole population was the fact that the racially mixed immigrant population was not, as Rivadavia had imagined, becoming "homogeneous." The immigrant workers did not share a common past or a common language. In Buenos Aires, many of them lived in *conventillos*, urban collective housing known for being overcrowded and unsanitary, where several different languages were spoken at any given time. The great majority of the workers were men, who came on their own before sending for their families. Among the foreign-born population of Buenos Aires, there were three times as many men as women.[15] The densely populated immigrant areas of Buenos Aires were associated with squalor, brothels, and crime. The polyphonic, predominantly masculine, and racially mixed masses appeared, in the eyes of the native population, to produce a degradation of language, morals, and tradition.

The negative stereotyping of the immigrant by the intellectual elite can be seen in works of literature from the period. Luis Pascarella's 1917 novel, *El conventillo* (The tenement), for example, depicts the Italian immigrant as a man who has forgotten his history and who is only concerned with material gain:

> [The immigrant's] mind, free of memories of the past, is filled now with only one phrase: earn, earn money. This and no other was the chatter [*retintín*] which circulated from morning to night around the patio [of the *conventillo*]. When someone was mentioned . . . or when two people met, the first thing they would ask was how much he earned, how much he had saved, how much he had, how much had been sent back to Italy.[16]

In addition to being associated with materialism, immigrants were frequently depicted as shrewd and lacking in ethical standards. Delaney explains that the common image of the immigrant that appeared repeatedly in both fiction and journalistic writings of the period was that of a "grasping, greedy individual whose sole purpose in coming to Argentina was to enrich himself."[17] This is a far cry from the moral and hardworking individual that Mitre's generation had envisioned.

The lack of cultural cohesion in early twentieth-century Argentina generated a frenzy of discourses regarding national identity in which important writers sought first to delineate what was uniquely "Argentine" and secondly how to impart these qualities and traditions to the immigrant masses.[18] In other words, they sought to foster a sense of nationalism. As Carl Solberg demonstrates in his book *Immigration and Nationalism: Argentina and Chile, 1890–1914*, the uneasiness regarding the immigrant population ultimately led many intellectuals to question the liberal cosmopolitanism of the previous generation: "After 1905 influential writers in both republics [Argentina and Chile] were rejecting the positivist and cosmopolitan-oriented ideologies invoked by the elites since the 1850's to justify liberal immigration policies. In place of cosmopolitanism, these intellectuals began to formulate nationalistic ideologies."[19] Although Solberg's book looks specifically at Argentina and Chile, nationalism was a phenomenon characteristic of all of Latin America. But in Argentina the topic of national identity was particularly pressing, given that for forty years the number of persons born abroad exceeded the population of those born in the territory. As such, there was an acute urgency to delineate a national identity, an urgency which is reflected in the country's literature.[20] If I may take the liberty of using a term from personal psychology to refer collectively to the nation, Argentina underwent an identity crisis of sorts.

Both Lugones and Borges dedicated much of their writing to inventing a literary tradition for their country. In particular, I will examine how Dante factors into their endeavors to articulate a uniquely Argentine type of literature. While Mitre believed the *Divine Comedy* to be the ideal epic for his new nation (given that in his eyes Argentina was too young to produce its own), Lugones argued that no epic of another culture and time could possibly serve as a substitute literary tradition for a new nation. He sought to establish an existing Argentine work as the national epic, a work that was written at precisely the same time that Mitre began translating the *Comedy*: José Hernández's *Martín Fierro* (1872, 1879).[21]

As previously noted, Mitre did not even mention this work in his 1887 letter on the state of South American literature, as it represented for him the rural barbarism he was trying to eradicate. The book enjoyed immediate popular success, although it was not until Lugones gave a series of lectures on the work in 1913 that it was raised to the status of a classic. I will examine Lugones's reasons for choosing this work as the reflection of national essence, as well as his own rendition of an episode of the *Divine Comedy.*

Leopoldo Lugones, belonging to the generation following Mitre's, was born on June 13, 1874, to Santiago M. Lugones and Custodia Argüello. He grew up during the so-called wave of immigration that brought about an ever-changing demographic. The Lugoneses perceived themselves as a family of ancient lineage, with creole ancestry dating back to sixteenth-century Perú. His grandparents belonged to the first generation of Argentines after the nation's independence, and therefore his family considered themselves among the original citizens of the nation, as opposed to the children of recent immigrants.[22]

Leopoldo was schooled in the conservative and Catholic city of Córdoba before moving to the more cosmopolitan city of Buenos Aires in 1896. It was there that the young Lugones met Rubén Darío, whose book *Azul* (1888) gave rise to what would later be known as *modernismo*, the artistic movement of which Lugones was the primary Argentine exponent.[23] His first major publication, *Montañas de oro* (1897), is an exemplar of this aesthetic, as is his most significant work of poetry, *Lunario sentimental* (1909). It is at the end of this collection of poetry that we find Lugones's creative reinvention of the story of Dante's Francesca of Rimini.

Although Lugones considered himself first and foremost a poet, he was also a journalist, orator, polemicist, and minister of public education. Politically he was a socialist in his early years, a traditionalist later on, and finally a supporter of Fascism. He supported the 1930 coup d'état of General José Félix Uriburu that ousted President Hipólito Yrigoyen.[24] The coup marked the start of what would later be referred to as the "Infamous Decade." During these dark years when Argentina was hit hard by the global Great Depression, Lugones himself fell into a depression from which he never recovered. In 1938 he committed suicide by ingesting a mixture of whisky and cyanide at the resort town of El Tigre just outside Buenos Aires.

Lugones on Immigration and Nationalism

> ¡Feliz quien como yo ha bebido patria,
> En la miel de su selva y de su roca!
>
> —LEOPOLDO LUGONES, "Oda a los ganados y a las mieses"[25]
>
> (Happy the man who like me has drunk homeland,
> In the honey of its forest and its rock!)

Lugones, like many creole intellectuals, worried about the future of Argentina in view of the massive changes brought on by the influx of immigration. In 1930 he articulated his anxieties regarding immigration in *The Great Argentina.* His xenophobic views reflect the fears of much of the creole population at the time, including racial prejudices, fear of colonization, and fear of growing labor movements. At the onset of his discourse, Lugones seeks to make clear that he is not opposed to immigration in general. He declares it to be a function of internal markets, and outlines its many benefits, including increases in labor, production, and consumption. More services offered means lower prices, therefore "a growing density of the population makes it easier to ensure that everyone has a comfortable and inexpensive life."[26] He acknowledges Argentina's need to attract immigrants to further the country's economic progress.

He does not, however, see unbridled immigration as beneficial to the nation. His first concern is that society may become overburdened by a rapid influx of immigrants, and he insists that measures should be taken to "prevent a rushed and crowded congestion."[27] Further, he sees all instances of mass immigration as colonization attempts by the countries of origin:

> Given the formation of the European mind and consciousness, which is simply the natural consequence of such events, every mass immigration is a movement of colonization. This is proven by the spiritual state revealed in Rome by the Conference on Emigration, and by the law of double citizenship in force in Germany and incorporated into the current project of the Spanish constitution.[28]

Here Lugones refers to the international conference on emigration and immigration which was held in Rome in 1924. Several countries at the time, in response to increased international migration, were adjusting citizenship requirements in order to allow emigrants to maintain their original citizenship when they acquired citizenship in their new country.[29] Lugones sees dual citizenship as inherently problematic, as it permits the country of origin to maintain its ties with the recently emigrated, thereby hindering their full integration in the new society and potentially presenting a conflict of interests.

Unlike Mitre, who advocated spontaneous immigration, Lugones felt that the exact conditions of the plan of immigration should be well publicized in the countries of origin and that economic and political agreements should be established with the appropriate governments.[30] Such agreements, in addition to Argentina's vigilance, he claims, would help prevent the "transplantation of people predestined to misery from unemployment or incompetence." It was also in Argentina's common interest, he argued, to prevent the entrance of delinquents, agitators, Marxists, and anarchist communists. Likewise, he did not support a proletarian immigration, which he claimed would overburden the urban population and artificially increase "the sectarian elements and the domestic services—the servile condition being itself parasitic and depressing."[31]

In addition to productivity, political beliefs, and profession, race is another essential criterion by which Lugones believes potential immigrants should be evaluated. The goal in his view is to achieve "an organic unity" rather than a racial heterogeneity, for "there is no greater destructive anarchy than the millenary conflict of the races."[32] The preventive solution is to "adopt preferences, not only concerning the economic capacity and the health and civic state of the immigrant, but also with regard to his ethnic character."[33] Although Lugones does not here specify which ethnicities should be avoided, it can be inferred that he is referring to the so-called new immigrants from the poorer nations of southern and eastern Europe, who, fleeing poverty in their own lands, constituted the bulk of immigration to Argentina in the early decades of the twentieth century, and who were perceived as culturally and ethnically distinct from the northern European immigrants desired by Argentina's forefathers. He may also be referring to the many Jews who came from Eastern Europe (mainly Russia and Poland), fleeing Tsarist persecution. In any case, he underscores the fact that Argentina is by no means obliged to open its doors to those fleeing harsh conditions or religious persecution: "Our country is not a refuge or a shelter, but an association of people living in agreement. No one has a right to turn our homeland into a source of charity."[34]

To explain what he feels might be misconstrued as an inhumane stance, he makes a distinction between homeland and humanity. The homeland, unlike humanity, is a political entity, which does not have obligations to human beings. To pretend, he says, that "the homeland be host to all of humanity is a paradox that inverts to the point of the absurd the relationship between continent and content."[35] For its overall benefit and survival, he argues, the homeland is obligated to restrict residence and citizenship, which are native privileges or ones bestowed uniquely on those deserving of residing in the homeland. Argentina must be concerned not with performing charity but with safeguarding its interests: "The morality of the homeland demands that she not harm anyone but it does not force her to do good to anyone who is not her son." Lugones's rhetoric is obviously problematic. In the same moment that he makes a distinction between humanity and homeland, he conflates the two by personifying the homeland and employing the terms "morality" and "son." One could make the same argument in regard to humanity in general. Could it not be said of humans that they should act in their own interest if performing charity means risking their own survival?

A further problematic aspect of Lugones's argument is the lack of clarity regarding what constitutes an Argentine, or rather a "nonimmigrant." He says of the Argentines,

> We belong to the Latin race, and it is to our benefit that we do. Naturally because we are. But also because in this manner we belong to the most noble of civilizations. When Sarmiento pronounced that profound sentence declaring that "we form an integral part of the Roman Empire," he formulated our true destiny with brilliant precision.[36]

Placed at the end of a discourse arguing against what he considers the overzealous admission of immigrants from southern Europe, this comment is decidedly ironic. The majority of newly immigrated, as it were, came from Italy, but yet according to his logic their admission must be restricted in order to ensure Argentina's brilliant destiny to form a part of the Roman

Empire. In mentioning the noble past of the Roman Empire, he indulges in a fiction regarding Argentina's heroic past and heroic destiny, but yet he warns, "We must form a homeland with those people who are a benefit to us, *not* with those whom we may like for some sentimental or ideological satisfaction." The Argentines are descendants of the Italian people, but the Italians are not Argentines.

Further stressing his fear of colonization, Lugones insists that the "Argentines," as opposed to the "foreigners," must be in control of the nation's affairs: "The Republic of Argentina is not a condominium or an experimental colony of more or less prestigious ideologies. It belongs to Argentines, and only Argentines can administer her toward her stated goal."[37] In other words, the current hegemony of the oligarchy must be maintained, and foreigners distinguished from the true sons of the nation. While the first native generation he claims belongs to Argentina "heart and soul," this does not guarantee that the newly immigrated will in one generation's time become fully integrated Argentines, for the nation's "digestive capacity" has its limits. His solution to what he clearly views as a foreign invasion is to make the immigration process far more selective, citing the Johnson-Reed Act in the United States (1924) as a "valuable example." This legislation, responding to fears concerning the mass immigration from southern and eastern Europe (especially of Jews) and from Asia, established a quota system in the United States which limited the number of immigrants from certain regions.[38] Lugones strongly advocates a more selective immigration policy for Argentina, one which regulates "the selection of the elements that we are to incorporate, with attention paid to their productive efficacy and fecundity, and the correlative determination of its race."[39]

As becomes apparent from Lugones's nonfictional writing on immigration, he viewed national identity as something that existed previously but which was threatened by the ever-increasing racial and cultural heterogeneity of the population. Like many other creole writers at the time, he viewed modern society as decadent and sought to distinguish the "creoles" from the "gringos." From Mitre's generation to Lugones's, the word "criollo," a theoretically neutral term referring to a native of a locality, had acquired entirely new connotations. As James R. Scobie demonstrates, in Argentina's early years, the word was practically pejorative: "During the nineteenth century in the texts of foreign travelers as well as Argentine essayists, the word criollo became a synonym for incompetence and idleness."[40] As time went on, however, it came to be used both as a noun and as an adjective with increasingly positive connotations. By the time of Lugones, who proudly considered himself a "viejo criollo," the word was frequently used in association with certain values and virtues, in opposition to the term "gringo," associated with certain vices such as greed and materialism. As Beatriz Sarlo and Carlos Altamirano explain,

> While the word "criollo" was identified with positive attributes such as generosity, impartiality, and even a certain disposition for heroic life, "gringo" came to signify industriousness with no higher aim than personal profit. Literature and theater dramatize this semantic and ideological opposition.[41]

In literature, the operation of denigrating the qualities of the "gringos" while exalting the virtues of the "criollos" is known as *criollismo*, a nationalistic preoccupation with native scenes and types. The term was employed as early as 1902 by Ernesto Quesada in the essay *El "criollismo" en la literatura argentina*, and subsequently was used to refer to literature that represented the national culture, as opposed to that of the immigrant masses.[42] Just two years before, in 1900, Quesada had deplored the corrupting influences of Italian immigration on the Spanish language in *El problema del idioma nacional*. He was one of many turn-of-the-century Argentines who lamented the linguistic and cultural changes brought about by mass immigration.

Although *criollismo* refers to regionalist tendencies that occurred in all of Spanish America in the first decades of the twentieth century, I will be limiting my discussion to *criollismo* in Argentina, which specifically took the form of gauchesque literature, wherein the figure of the gaucho, previously despised by Mitre's generation as an impediment to civilization, is represented as the embodiment of Argentine virtues. This shocking transformation of the formerly "barbaric" plainsman into the heroic "civilizer" of the pampas was possible because the gauchos at the time had all but disappeared from the Argentine plains and were no longer a threat to the modernization advocated by the liberal intellectuals of the nineteenth century. Because the gaucho was an obvious "nonimmigrant," and because he was associated with the land and the past, he was converted into a mythological national symbol around which the creole elite could converge.

As mentioned previously, I consider national identity as something constructed by the intellectuals who concern themselves with writing "guiding fictions" or "inventing traditions" to foster nationalism. I can think of no better example of a clearly invented tradition than gauchesque literature, which does not describe the real conditions of the historical gaucho, nor reflect the poetry of the *payadors*.[43] Rather, it presents an idealized, romanticized version of the gaucho, while eruditely poeticizing an imagined golden era of Argentine history, pre–mass immigration. The gauchesque was, for many authors, the preferred means to locate the essence of the "native" population in the creole past.

Three major Argentine thinkers whose nationalistic responses contributed to elevating the status of the Argentine gaucho are Ricardo Rojas, Manuel Gálvez, and Leopoldo Lugones.[44] All three claimed gauchesque literature to be the literature that best represented the historical essence of Argentina. Rojas, author of the eight-volume *Historia de la literatura argentina*, begins his work with a chapter on *Los gauchescos*. Gálvez saw the native creole as the preserver of the spiritual and moral values essential for the nation. He argued that these values, embodied in the figure of the gaucho, must be safeguarded against the corruptive influence of the immigrant. In 1913 he wrote of *Martín Fierro*: "It synthesizes the profound and permanent aspects of the spirit of the American race."[45]

But arguably the intellectual most responsible for the gaucho's conversion into a national emblem was Lugones. Unlike Mitre, who was pro-European as regards cultural production, Lugones sought a noble past for Argentina within Argentina's recent history, rather than outside it. Nonetheless, as I will discuss in chapter 4, in 1909 Lugones published the story "Francesca," a rewriting of an episode of the *Divine Comedy*, canto 5, which does not fall in line with his later *criollista* prescriptions of 1916. This led Jorge Luis Borges to write his own rendition of the same Dantean episode in "The Intruder," which satirizes many of Lugones's arguments regarding Argentine literature and creates a wildly original Francesca of the pampas.

Although Lugones's rewriting of Dante is anything but gauchesque, his first book, *La Guerra Gaucha* (1905), does in fact belong to his genre. It is a book of poems about the gaucho guerrilla war commanded by Martín Miguel de Güemes against the Spanish royalists during the Argentine War of Independence. In preparation for this patriotic book, Lugones traveled to Salta Province to visit the battlefields and to record the oral traditions of the locals. Filled with lengthy poetic descriptions of the Argentine pampas, the work is clearly an endeavor to create a glorified portrait of the land and its "heroes" responsible for her liberation. Most episodes center around the valor of the gaucho characters. "Carga," for example, describes a gaucho raid on the Spanish camp, while in "Al rastro" one gaucho single-handedly fights a royalist battalion, and in doing so loses his life. The work, an obvious idealization, is far from a realistic representation of gaucho life. It is filled with the fictional gaucho slang of the time, which renders the work somewhat cryptic and artificial for those not versed in this style of writing. Nevertheless, the book was successful during its day, and years later (1942) was made into a movie of the same title, directed by Lucas Demare, which is considered to be a classic of Argentine cinematography.[46]

More important for the reevaluation of the gaucho than Lugones's own gaucho poetry is the book *El payador*. Published in 1916, the book is a modified version of a series of lectures given at the Odeón theater in Buenos Aires in 1913. It consists of ten sections, including a discussion of the function of epic poetry, a heroic portrait of the gaucho and his habitat, an examination of gaucho poetry, an argument that *Martín Fierro* is an epic poem, and a detailed study of *Martín Fierro*.[47] Thus, like Sarmiento's *Facundo*, it is a heterogeneous, nonfiction work offering a particular interpretation of Argentine landscape, people, and history. Like *Facundo*, it is now considered a foundational text of Argentine literature. Both works engage in describing the Argentine national character and in explaining the effects of Argentina's geographical conditions on the inhabitants. Both authors were profoundly concerned with national identity. Already in 1883 Sarmiento had proclaimed: "Are we a nation? A nation without an amalgam of accumulated materials, without adjustment or foundation? Argentines? To what end and since when? It's important to be aware of this."[48] But Lugones's generation felt more acutely the need to define "argentinidad," particularly around the time of the centenary of Argentine independence. It was a time when nationalistic sentiments ran high, and there were a number of rituals, festivities, exhibitions, and monuments commemorating the occasion. It was also, as the historian José Luis Romero has pointed out, a moment of cultural reevaluation, national affirmation, and the generation of new cultural myths. The publication of *El payador* (1916) coincided with the centenary of the Argentine declaration of independence (July 9, 1816).

As regards the vision of the gaucho, *Facundo* and *El payador* are antithetical. While Sarmiento paints a negative portrait of the gaucho Juan Facundo Quiroga in order to show the "barbaric" nature of nineteenth-century Argentina if left uncivilized by European cultural ideals, Lugones presents a glorified picture of the gaucho, emblem of a former civilization threatened by immigration. The striking reversal of the civilization/barbarism dichotomy has been noted by a number of scholars, including Altamirano and Sarlo, who in their seminal essay "La Argentina del Centenario" write:

> The symbolic gaucho, the desert, the wagon are no longer the representatives of a "barbarous" reality that must be left behind in the march toward "civilization"; rather, they are the symbols used to construct a national tradition that "progress" threatened to dissolve.[49]

Immigration, formerly associated with progress, had come to be seen as the new form of barbarism. Although it may seem surprising that the gaucho (a troublesome figure in the eyes of the founding fathers of the nation) could be chosen by many twentieth-century intellectuals as the symbol of Argentine national essence and gaucho poetry as the expression of her people, we must remember that writers at the time sought a regional literary genre unique to Argentina alone. As Ángel Rama points out, gaucho poetry developed without a European model.[50] Instead it pretends to mimic Argentine rural orality and describe a gaucho-way-of-life which came to be seen as "traditional."

For Lugones, the gaucho is not only a heroic figure, but also the "prototype of present-day Argentines,"[51] and the *payador*, who poeticizes gaucho life, the most significant agent in the formation of the Argentine race:

> The title I have chosen for this book is the name of the old errant singers who roamed our countryside looking for romances and laments, because they were the most significant figures in the formation of our race. Just as happened in Greek and Latin cultures, this phenomenon began with a work of beauty.[52]

In the first chapter, Lugones explains that a race is defined by its epic poetry: "epic poetry is the expression of the heroic life of a race: of this race and of no other."[53] Hence, no epic poem from another culture can represent a new race. In following with Lugones's definition of the function of epic poetry, the *Divine Comedy* could only serve as the epic of the Italian people. For Lugones, an epic poem does not just sing for justice and liberty in a general sense, but shows how a particular people fought for these ideals. Having established his definition of epic, he states that his primary objective is to prove that *Martín Fierro* is the Argentine national epic.

His selection of *Martín Fierro* as Argentina's national epic accomplishes several important objectives. First of all, it is an attempt to immediately assuage the widespread anxiety regarding national identity, or rather the perceived lack thereof. One need look no further than its covers for the "secret to her [Argentina's] destiny." As he clearly explains in the 1916 prologue:

> The aim of this book is to define from this angle epic poetry, to demonstrate that our *Martín Fierro* belongs to this genre, to study it as such, and to determine, simultaneously, on account of its natural characteristics, the formation of our race and its destiny.[54]

In other words, all the answers to the questions which plagued the intellectuals of the turn of the century were to be found just within its pages.

Secondly, *El payador* is an assertion that Argentina is already a civilization on par with ancient Greece, whose epics Lugones refers to as a model in his discourse on the function of epic poetry. Argentina, no less than ancient Greece, has a unique artistic expression of her land, race, and language. Finally, because gaucho poetry has no European model, and because *Martín Fierro* was written in 1872, before the influx of immigration, his definition of Argentine identity is a rejection of the culture of the immigrant population.[55] While offering a point of convergence for the *criollo* citizens, it excludes the immigrant masses.

Scholars such as Carlos Altamirano, Beatriz Sarlo, Richard W. Slatta, and Rafael Olea Franco have emphasized the exclusionary nature of Lugones's intentions, not only as regards race, but also in respect to social standing. The 1913 lectures were attended by prominent members of the oligarchy, including the president of the republic, Roque Sáenz Peña, and his cabinet.

In his remarks to the audience, Lugones insists upon the cultural hegemony of the upper class:

> I am happy to have been the agent of an intimate national communication between the poetry of the *pueblo* and the cultivated minds of the upper class; the spirit of the homeland is formed in this way. . . . My words are only the pollinating bee that transmits the message from the wild flower to the noble rose of the garden.[56]

Although gaucho poetry pertains to "el pueblo," the "spirit of the homeland" can only be cultivated by the elite.

As Altamirano and Sarlo have argued, Lugones's advocacy of *Martín Fierro* affirms, "through the myth of origin, the guiding right of the elite 'criollos viejos' over the country. A right that the recently immigrated seemed to challenge."[57] Similarly, Olea Franco has argued that Lugones wanted to create a myth which would legitimize the power of the creole elite.

> What actually happened was that the gaucho, ineffectual for the capitalist aims of the oligarchy of the 19th century, was used at the beginning of the 20th as an instrument of opposition toward the growing power of the immigrant masses.[58]

In conclusion, both Mitre's translation of the *Divine Comedy* and Lugones's reevaluation of Hernández's *Martín Fierro* are attempts to fortify a sense of national identity via epic poetry. Mitre's choice of translating the *Divine Comedy* was a means to embrace incoming immigrants, especially Italians, and promote national cultural cohesion for present and future generations, including the recently immigrated. Although *Martín Fierro* was written before Mitre published his translation, he did not consider it a representative epic. Nor did he believe that Argentine society at the time was mature enough to produce one. Furthermore, what he sought was a cosmopolitan, Old World epic that would have a "civilizing" effect on the undeveloped rural population.

Lugones, on the other hand, argues that no epic borrowed from another culture can serve the same formative role for another nation. The possession of an epic poem indicates the existence of a national identity. Not only did he see Argentina as developed enough to produce her own epic, if anything, he saw her as a civilization on the decline. In his view nationality must be preserved in the face of foreign invasion. The goal for both Mitre and Lugones is "civilization," but while Mitre saw civilization as something brought about via immigration, Lugones sees a uniquely Argentine epic, one which was written before Mitre's translation, as proof of her already extant culture. Mitre's endeavor was cultural cohesion for the recently immigrated. Lugones offered a point of conversion specifically for the creole elite.

FOUR

Hypermedievalizing and Demedievalizing Dante: Leopoldo Lugones's and Jorge Luis Borges's Rewritings of *Inferno* V

Both Leopoldo Lugones and Jorge Luis Borges, two authors intent on developing Argentine national literature, wrote innovative adaptations of the fifth canto of Dante's *Inferno*.[1] While Lugones accentuates and romanticizes everything medieval in his version, Borges eliminates medievalisms entirely by setting the tale on the Argentine pampas in the nineteenth century. I will discuss their individual motives for choosing to embrace or reject medievalisms in their rewritings of the Francesca episode in relation to their ideas on how to develop a uniquely Argentine literature.

In canto 5 we encounter Francesca and her lover Paolo (who remains unnamed) in the second circle of hell, where the lustful are blown about by violent winds in punishment for their inability to control their passions. Francesca and Paolo in particular are guilty of adultery, although Dante does not explain to us the exact circumstances, which the reader is assumed to know—that Francesca was married to Giovanni Malatesta ("Gianciotto," or "crippled John") circa 1275, that she committed adultery with Paolo Malatesta, and that she and Paolo were both murdered by Gianciotto, most likely in the 1280s. Dante tells us only that Francesca was born where the river Po meets the Adriatic, that she and her lover are related by marriage, and that their killer will be punished in *Caina* (a place in lower hell named after Cain, who slew Abel) following his death.[2] The focus of the episode is on their unbridled love for one another and their consequential suffering in the afterlife. Francesca, with great rhetorical skill, tells the story of how they fell in love, seeking to win her auditor's compassion. There are no details or place descriptions that might lead us to locate the story in the Middle Ages, other than the inference that the two lovers succumbed to their lust while reading the story of Lancelot.[3] Apart from this reference to a quintessential medieval tale, Francesca's declarations of love could be described as timeless, and her and her lover's subsequent suffering is eternal rather than linked to any temporal period.

Leopoldo Lugones's reworking of the fifth canto was first published in *Lunario sentimental* (1909) as a short story entitled "Francesca."[4] *Lunario sentimental* is Lugones's third major work, after *Las montañas del oro* (1897) and *Los crepúsculos del jardín* (1905). In *Lunario* he seeks to revive and modernize poetry by radically reworking age-old poetic tropes of western Europe—most notably, odes to the moon. Lugones, along with other leading proponents of *modernismo* at the time, saw Western models as a point of departure upon which to effect innovations. The goal was to borrow exotic elements from other cultures and to rework archetypal patterns in unorthodox ways to produce a poetry unique to Latin America, ideally a poetry which would rival the classics of Old World Europe. In *Lunario* Lugones employs unexpected metaphors and imagery and pointed irony to call into question traditional views of poetic beauty. The short story "Francesca" is the concluding piece of the collection, and he no doubt included it on account of its status as a classic Western love story. However, "Francesca" lacks the shock value present in many of the poems that proceed it in the collection; rather, it is a romantic, tender, innocent, and highly medievalized retelling of Dante's classic.

Lugones makes his reverence for the great Italian author clear from the outset of the book when he claims in the first poem of *Lunario* that he learned his own verse from Dante, "Arduous and concise ancestor / Through whose

Paradise/No pedant ever passed."[5] But he chooses to rewrite Francesca's story in prose rather than poetry. At every turn Lugones adds medieval elements and plays with the dichotomy of literary fiction versus historical reality.

The protagonist of the story is a young traveler, who finds himself in Forli and who plans to visit Rimini "because a visit to the hometown of Francesca fit right in with my program as a young traveler."[6] There are no markers to indicate that the young traveler is Argentine or from the New World. He may be European, for all we know. But since the story is written in Argentine Spanish by an Argentine author, it is more likely than not that the protagonist is indeed intended to be Argentine. He meets an Italian student with whom he converses about the schedule of the train going to Rimini. The poor but "exquisitely courteous" traveler offers to sell him a parchment manuscript which he claims contains the true story of Francesca. The two young men are said to share a fervor for the medieval heroine, and for this reason there is a fellowship ("confraternidad") between them. Thus the brotherhood established between the strangers of likely different origins is based on common interest in this medieval subject.

The unnamed protagonist claims to have acquired the manuscript without great enthusiasm, since he is little inclined to historical investigations, but the moment it is in his hands, it has a special power over him, and he remains in Forli for seven days trying to decipher its pages. Lugones dedicates approximately one-fourth of the tale to the detailed description of the thirteenth-century manuscript, which is the real protagonist of this section of the story. The deteriorated document is written in Latin, in beautiful gothic calligraphy characteristic of the thirteenth century. It is graced by an intricate nine-sided *signum tabellionis* of the notary Balzarino de Cervis, dated June 12, 1292. Deciphering the text proves difficult due to its innumerable abbreviations and symbols, which make the collaboration of a paleographer (a medievalist, in other words) indispensable. Both the manuscript and the medievalist, then, are vital links to the past, and although the medieval script inhibits easy comprehension, the narrator calls it "precious" proof of the document's authenticity. The paleographic paragraph in which Lugones describes in detail the abbreviations and signs that make it datable to the supposed lifetime of Francesca is worth quoting:

> The *o* crossed by an oblique line that descends from right to left, signifying *cum*, a peculiar sign characteristic of the last years of the 13th century, at the beginning of which, just as in the ones before and after, took on other forms; the 2, crowned by a *b* like an algebraic exponent (2b), meaning *duabus*, and adding by means of its presence one other fact, given that Arabic numbers did not become common in Europe until the 13th century; the 7, represented by an A without the crossbar, as if to mark the said transition; the word *corpus* abbreviated to its first syllable and crowned by a 9 (cor9) and the word *fratibus*, abbreviated to *ftbz* with an *a* superimposed on the *f* and an *i* on the *t*; and amen to various signs that I omit here. I don't want to forget the initials of our heroine, that F and that R, again so characteristic and similar to the handwritten PP of our calligraphy, except for the crossbar that cuts them.[7]

So far in the story, we have not yet begun to know the content of the manuscript. The prolonged focus on the manuscript itself as a physical artifact produces various effects: (1) it creates suspense, (2) it sensationalizes the decodification process, (3) it stresses the fact that the medievalist/paleographer is a vital and necessary link to the past, and (4) it emphasizes the authenticity of the manuscript.

Lugones's insistence on this historical record of Francesca's existence is all the more noteworthy, given that no trace remains of the historical record that Dante the poet could have appropriated in telling the story of the lovers.[8] It is wishful thinking, perhaps, that one day a medievalist might chance upon a parchment that will validate the historicity of Dante's tale. There is a clear fascination in Lugones's story with material realities that have survived from the time. The medieval world, which becomes tangible and decipherable through its fragments, is both enigmatic and worthy of investigation.

Like any good medievalist, the narrator does not neglect the information that is found in the margins of the manuscript—in this case, the coats of arms of two different families.

> In addition, in the margin of the text there are, as an apostille, two coats of arms: one in a wide almond shape, also characteristic of the 13th century, and the other rhomboidal, that is, a lady's crest, except for some rare exceptions like those of the Visconti; but the Visconti were from Lombardy, and in the epoch of my document, they had only recently conquered the sovereignty of Milan.

> Furthermore, the two coats of arms were overlapping, which indicates marital union. Unfortunately, their country does not conserve anything except a few specks of the pieces and heraldic colors.[9]

Again, this detail is provided as a testament to Francesca's historical reality. Perhaps the only thing we do know for sure about Francesca was that her marriage was political: born into the Polenta family that ruled Ravenna, she married Giovanni Malatesta, lord of Rimini. One can hardly think of something more symbolically medieval to represent their union than the two coats of arms. From Old French, "*cote a armer*," coats of arms were originally used to adorn the shields, helmets, and armor of knights so that the wearer could be easily identified in knightly tournaments. Heraldic designs came to be used among the Western nobility in the twelfth century to denote the prestige of a family, publicly mark their property, provide commentary on their occupation, and trace family membership across time. Since this system of visual identification of rank and pedigree developed in the European Middle Ages, it is closely associated with courtly culture, Latin Christianity, and the crusades. Here the two coats of arms are said to be used "a manera de apostilla," as an apostille to certify the authenticity of the document.

At this point in the narrative, approximately one-fourth of the way through, Lugones shifts gears. After having provided the reader with meticulous details of its authenticity up to this point, he suddenly announces that he will not translate the actual contents of the document because the rough and curial Latin, he claims, would inhibit interest for the reader. He plans, therefore, to provide a retelling "as free as I please,"[10] leaving the original at the disposal of the meticulous (the medievalists?) to be examined in "our National Library." If we assume that the narrator is Argentine, and that the national library in question is perhaps the Biblioteca Nacional de la República Argentina, founded in 1810 by Mariano Moreno in Buenos Aires, then this is an interesting detail and also the key to interpreting how Lugones at that time felt Argentines should go about interpreting, drawing upon, and building from the Western medieval literary models—to acknowledge their authenticity and importance and to use them as a point of departure for innovation. Lugones and the modernists viewed Western models and medieval elements as material at their disposal for subsequent modification.

His version of the Francesca story diverges greatly from Dante's—Francesca is not guilty of adultery: "Paolo and Francesca never had any relationship beyond *exalted friendship*. Even their hands were free of guilt; and their lips did nothing more than tremble and become pale in the sweet anguish of unconfessed passion."[11]

Lugones transforms the adulterous love of Dante's Paolo and Francesca into unconsummated, courtly love. Courtly love, or "*fin' amor*," is a medieval European literary conception of love that emphasizes nobility and chivalry and which began with the troubadour poetry of Aquitaine and Provence in southern France toward the end of the eleventh century. As we will see, Francesca and Paolo's love affair as described by Lugones meets the primary criteria of courtly love elaborated by the poets of the Middle Ages. First and foremost, courtly love is a literary phenomenon, and Lugones emphasizes the fictionality of the story that follows when he tells us that he will offer us a translation "as free as I please."

Second, it is a love which is noble, and which takes place in a courtly setting. When we first meet Francesca, she is standing in the window of a noble palace, watching as the nuptial procession arrives. It is a lady in waiting who points out to her the brave knight, whom she assumes to be her future husband. The knightly gallantry of Paolo is emphasized continuously throughout the tale. He is described as handsome, courteous, and a man of letters.

Third, it was one of the assumptions of courtly love that the lady in question was married and unattainable. This means that the meetings between lovers had to be conducted in an atmosphere of secrecy and danger. The absolute discretion of the lover was indispensable if the honor of the lady were to be preserved. Francesa and Paolo, we are told, meet only during the light of day, when Giovanni is occupied with his black magic. In contrast to the beautiful and courteous Paolo, Giovanni is portrayed as a cruel hunchback and monster who takes advantage of Francesca's virginal faith. Thus, we have the typical love triangle of courtly love—the courteous lover, the honorable lady, and the jealous husband.

Fourth, courtly love is ritualistic. The lover/knight must follow elaborate conventions of etiquette, showering his lady with gifts and tokens of love such as songs, poems, bouquets, and sweetmeats. Paolo does this to make a solitary existence in the castle more enjoyable for Francesa, who appreciates his gifts and attentions on account of her refined sensibility: "Paolo thought up every way possible to make the young girl's enclosure in the gloomy castle more tolerable. And his exquisite courtesy, as well as his dignified tenderness, melted the heart of the woman whose refined ways, still Byzantine from her natal city, had deepened her sensibilities."[12] Paolo is more than a knight—he is a troubadour: "Paolo was adept at composing enigmas, which the tastes of the epoch had elevated to high literature."[13] The manuscript itself transcribes some of his enigmas written for Francesca. For example, "the cross of love":

E C **A** T E
N E **M** E A
A M O R E
F U **R** I E
I M **E** N E

And another which reads from left to right and also in a V:

A N I M **E**
A **M** A **R** O
C U **O** R E[14]

These banal love crossword puzzles are a parody of the *trobar clus*, a complex and obscure style of poetry characterized by difficult language and metrical complexity and written for an elite audience, able to decode their meaning. A parallel is drawn here between the decoder of the enigmas and the decoder of the medieval manuscript (the narrator, the medievalist).

Lugones poetically describes the romantic scene when Francesca and Paolo read the notorious story of Lancelot, which in Dante's account is the catalyst to their sinning. He claims, however, that Dante was mistaken: "*Galeoto* was the book . . .—said the poet. Oh no, my God! It was the moon."[15] Finally, Lugones's tale corresponds to the tenets of courtly love while differing from Dante's version in that Francesca and Paolo are beyond a doubt not guilty of adultery: "Physically, they did not sin, for they did not touch, or even speak; but her husband *saw* adultery in their eyes with such vertiginous clarity, as the acknowledgment of rebellion and crime, that he severed their hearts without hesitating a bit. And the manuscript agrees with him, on my word."[16] Thus, the tale ends with the manuscript's testimony to Francesca's innocence. Dante's Francesca, on the other hand, is beyond a doubt guilty, as is evidenced by her just condemnation to the second circle of hell for all eternity. She may be a dazzling rhetorician who seeks to blame everything but herself for her fate—Love ("ch'a nullo amato amar perdona"), her gentle heart, and even a book—but she is still guilty, and it is questionable as to whether the pilgrim's pity is warranted. Lugones's Francesca, on the contrary, is a picture of innocence. She has been mercilessly deceived and tortured by Giovanni, but yet remains Christ-like in her innocence. Instead of focusing on the climactic moment of Dante's fifth canto—the kiss ("la bocca mi basciò tutto tremante")—Lugones emphasizes Francesca's innocent, tear-filled eyes: "those black eyes like two swallows of the Passion. What sacrifice of tenderness plunged in the heroism of her silence."[17] The mention of Christ's Passion here is another key to interpreting Lugones's retelling of the Francesca story—Francesca is more akin to Dante's Beatrice than to Dante's Francesca. It was Dante, after all, who revolutionized the phenomenon of courtly love by heightening the spiritual element. Prior to Dante, the love that a knight/troubadour felt for his lady might make him a better person by inciting him to fight in a crusade, but the lady figure in courtly love poetry was not associated with Christ himself until Dante's *Vita nuova* and the *Divine Comedy*.

The irony then is that Lugones rewrites the story of Francesca according to Dante's own innovations within the literary genre of courtly love poetry. He is at once hypermedievalizing the text and redoing Dante according to Dante. The result is innovative, but the text still possesses a decidedly western European flair. Could the poems in *Lunario* and the short story "Francesca" be said to be uniquely Argentine? Not in an easily identifiable way. It was precisely this uniqueness that Lugones and other Argentine authors were looking to establish at the time via verbal play with foreign models.

Just seven years later, in 1916, Lugones would completely reverse tactics, embracing the realism commonly rejected by modernist poets and turning to rural rather than cosmopolitan elements, poeticized with a patriotic rather than an ironic tone. In one of his most famous texts, *El payador*, he sought to establish a rural, gauchesque poem—Hernández's *Martín Fierro*—as the national epic of Argentina. As discussed in the previous chapter, prior to the turn of the century, and most notably in Sarmiento's *Facundo*, the gaucho was a figure associated with the "barbaric" nature of nineteenth-century Argentina. Lugones revindicates the gaucho and argues that the *payador*, who poeticizes gaucho life, is the most significant agent in the formation of the Argentine race. Because gaucho poetry had no European model, and because *Martín Fierro* was written in 1872, pre-influx of immigration, his definition of Argentine identity offered a point of convergence for the *criollo* citizens, while excluding the newly immigrated population.[18]

In conclusion, with both *Lunario sentimental* and *El payador*, Lugones was seeking to establish a uniquely Argentine literature. While in the former book, his strategy for doing so involved embracing and innovating upon medieval western European models, in the latter he eliminates the medieval entirely in order to elevate the status of the gaucho, the uniquely Argentine errant poet of the pampas. Obviously his hypermedievalization of the episode of Francesca stands in stark contrast with his later *criollismo* proscriptions of 1916. This did not go unnoticed by Jorge Luis Borges, who decided to parody what Lugones advocates in *El payador* by creating a version of the Francesca story that takes place on the pampas.

Borges was well acquainted with Lugones's story "Francesca." In fact, he wrote the prologue to the collection of Lugones's short stories entitled *La estatua de sal*, in which "Francesca" was republished in 1985. In that prologue Borges acknowledges the various ideological shifts of Lugones's lifetime: "diverse sincerities of a man interested in the same problem, who gives, over time, contradictory solutions."[19] Although here Borges was referring to Lugones's political fickleness (morphing from anarchist, to socialist, to fascist), this observation can also be applied to the drastic shifts in strategy to be seen in Lugones's literary productions. *Modernismo* and *criollismo*, although contradictory tendencies, were at different times seen by Lugones as the ideal means for arriving at a uniquely Argentine literature.

Before analyzing Borges's parody, it is important to state that Borges himself went through a *criollismo* phase early in his career, when he felt that sticking to local themes was the surest way to create a unique national literature. His nationalistic 1926 essay, "El tamaño de mi esperanza" (The size of my hope), is no less an exaltation of creoles and an exclusion of immigrants than Lugones's *El payador*. In the opening, Borges addresses himself to a specifically creole audience.

> It is to the *criollos* that I wish to speak—to the men who feel their life and death inextricably linked to this land, not to those who think the sun and the moon are in Europe. This is a land of born exiles, of men nostalgic for the far-off and the foreign: they are the real gringos, regardless of their parentage. With them my pen does not speak.
>
> I wish to speak to the others, to our own boys attached to this earth who do not belittle the reality of this country. My topic today is the patria: her present, past, and future.[20]

The patriotism of this paragraph is not without the xenophobic tendencies common among many creole authors at the time.

A more mature Borges, however, rejected the idea that Argentine authors should limit themselves to local themes. He confesses that his "happily forgotten" book *Fervor de Buenos Aires* does indeed abound in local color and words such as "*cuchilleros*," "*milonga*," and "*tapia*." But this he sees as a mistake of his youth, an overzealous attempt to appear Argentine. He later saw his earlier attempts at writing a uniquely Argentine type of literature as extremely artificial, and his change in opinion is also evidenced by his omission of "El tamaño de mi esperanza" (1926) and "El idioma de los argentinos" (1928) from *Obras completas* (1974). In 1951, in his essay "El escritor argentino y la tradición," he countered Lugones's arguments regarding gauchesque poetry and *Martín Fierro*. In this essay, originally prepared for a lecture given at the Colegio Libre de Estudios Superiores, he questions the validity of the so-called problem of the Argentine writer and tradition: "I would like to formulate and justify some skeptical proposals concerning the problem of the Argentine writer and tradition. My skepticism does not relate to the difficulty or impossibility of solving this problem, but rather to its very existence. I believe we are faced with a rhetorical topic which leads to pathetic elaborations, rather than with a true mental difficulty. I understand that we are dealing with an appearance, a simulacrum, a pseudo problem."[21]

If the question of the Argentine writer and tradition is, as Borges says, a "pseudo problem," then all attempts to resolve it must therefore be "pathetic."

Borges follows this pronouncement with a debunking of various theories, most notably that of Lugones. Borges refutes the assertions that Argentine literary tradition exists in gauchesque poetry and that *Martín Fierro* is for Argentines what the Homeric poems were for the Greeks, all the while taking great care not to slight *Martín Fierro*, which he calls "the most lasting work we Argentines have written."[22] Although he recognizes the literary merit of the work, he does not believe that it can be considered the canonical book of all Argentines. According to Borges, Lugones is making a nationalistic argument and erroneously seeking a national epic to fulfill the role of a *Don Quixote* or *Divine Comedy*. Even worse, in Borges's view, are the conclusions of Ricardo Rojas, who claims that gauchesque poetry is a continuation or expansion of the poetry of the *payadores*. Borges sees this affirmation as fundamentally flawed. He suspects that Rojas made this "skillful error" in order to give the gauchesque poetry a popular basis.

As Nicolas Shumway rightly points out, Borges's intention was to "depoliticize the gauchesque for which Argentine nationalists were making quite extravagant claims."[23] In his book *The Invention of Argentina*, Shumway documents the transformation of the term *gaucho* into "a nationalist rallying cry that in this century has made *gaucho* synonymous with *authentic Argentine*."[24] He outlines the process by which the term came to label "one of Argentina's principal guiding fictions."[25] Lugones's *El payador*, of course, played a major role in this process. But where Lugones had argued for authenticity, Borges emphasized artificiality: "gauchesque poetry . . . is a literary genre as artificial as any other."[26]

To highlight the genre's lack of correspondence to the poetry of the gauchos, Borges points out that gauchesque poetry is composed in hendecasyllables, a meter which was not used by the *payadores*, whom he claims could not perceive its harmony. He also contrasts the vocabulary and themes of the *payadores* (whom he claims to have heard in person) with those of the gauchesque poets. While the *payadores* employ a general vocabulary to sing of abstract themes like time, space, the sea, and night, the gauchesque poems feature a forced preoccupation with local color and abound in *criollismos*. In other words, gauchesque poetry is extremely *recherché*: "The proof is this: a Colombian, Mexican, or Spaniard can immediately understand the poetry of the *payadores*, of the gauchos, and yet they need a glossary in order to understand, even approximately, Estanislao del Campo or Ascasubi."[27]

In Borges's view, not only do nationalist theories such as that proposed by Lugones lead to erroneous conclusions as regards literature, they also greatly limit the creativity of authors: "the nationalists pretend to venerate the capacities of the Argentine mind but want to limit the poetic exercise of that mind to a few impoverished local themes, as if we Argentines could only speak of *orillas* and *estancias* and not of the universe."[28] Obviously, Borges finds the idea of limiting oneself to supposedly "Argentine" themes ridiculous. If Lugones himself had advocated this theory from the very beginning of his career, it would have greatly reduced his poetic oeuvre, and *Lunario sentimental* would not exist. What would happen, we might imagine, if his rewriting of Dante's "Francesca" included nothing of the medieval and instead only rural Argentinian elements? Borges cleverly does just that in his short story "The Intruder" ("La intrusa," 1966), which, I argue, is both a rewriting of Dante's Vth Canto of *Inferno* and a parody of the ideas posited in *El payador*.

As aforementioned, Borges wrote the prologue and selected the tales included in a 1985 edition of Lugones's stories published under the title *La estatua de sal* for the La Biblioteca de Babel series. Although he was no fan of *Lunario* in general, he seems to have genuinely admired the story "Francesca," of which he writes in the prologue, "In 'Francesca' Lugones dares to compete with the fifth canto of *Inferno* and the discovery of this adventure is in an intimate tone."[29] Furthermore, Lugones's story seems to have influenced Borges's writing of the poem "Infierno, V, 129," which begins:

> They let the book fall, when they know
> that they are the ones in the book.
> (They will be in another, greater,
> but what can that matter to them.)
> Now they are Paolo and Francesca,
> not two friends who are sharing
> the savor of a fable.
> They gaze at each other with incredulous wonder.
> Their hands do not touch.[30]

The line "their hands do not touch" is likely inspired by Lugones's story, which emphasizes three times that they do not touch, focusing specifically on their hands.[31] Whether Borges was conscious of this influence is difficult to say. What is without a doubt, however, is that in his second rewriting of the Francesca episode, "The Intruder," Borges demedievalizes Lugones's version to create a nineteenth-century, Argentine adaptation that is devoid of courtly love and its conventions.

"The Intruder" (1966) is the story of two rough-and-tumble brothers, Eduardo and Cristián, living on the outskirts of Buenos Aires. When it comes to women, they usually frequent whorehouses after one of their drunken outings, but one day the elder brother, Cristián, brings home a girl, Juliana de Burgos, to live with them. Eduardo falls in love with her, and Cristián agrees to share her. This love triangle leads to dissension between the brothers, and they agree to sell her to a whorehouse to save their relationship. Both, however, continue to secretly visit her, until one day they run into each other while waiting their turn. This leads them to buy her back, but her renewed presence in the house revives the former jealousies. In the end, Cristián kills her, and the brothers bury her together on the pampa.

At first glance, it would seem that "La intrusa" has little to do with the fifth canto of *Inferno*, but as has already been noted by Sylvie Davidson, the story is "diametrically opposed" to that of Dante.[32] Both stories involve a love triangle. In the fifth canto, two cousins are in love with the same woman, who loves the younger of the two in return. The jealousy of the elder cousin, Giovanni, causes him to murder both Paolo and Francesca. In "The Intruder" we have two brothers in love with the same woman, mutually jealous, and she is the only one who loses her life. In Dante, lust overpowers reason; and in Borges, fraternal bonds prove stronger than lust or love.

The character of Juliana de Burgos is the antithesis of Francesca. In Dante, Francesca is the only figure who has a voice. She is the one who eloquently narrates her story and defends her point of view. In "The Intruder," not only does Juliana have no voice, but she has virtually no control over anything that happens throughout. She is treated as a servant and whore who "attends both men's wants with an animal submission."[33] Nothing is said of her reaction to the suffering she is forced to endure, and we know nothing of her feelings except that she had "a certain preference, probably for the younger man."[34] As Borges himself clarifies, Juliana is not a main character of the story: "Really there are only two characters: the two brothers.

Of them, we are allowed to hear only what the elder brother says; it is he who takes all the decisions, even the last one."[35] Thus the elder brother, Cristián, takes on the role of Francesca who speaks on behalf of Paolo (Eduardo).

The story is also clearly in opposition to Lugones's "Francesca." Lugones's version of Dante's story is a tender tale of innocent love, characterized (in the words of Borges) by "an intimate tone." It is also markedly European, taking place in Italy and involving a medieval palimpsest, a castle, and a moonlit balcony. Borges, on the other hand, writes a callous tale of the cruelty of two "hard-bitten men living on the edge of Buenos Aires before the turn of the century."[36] Herein lies the key to the story: the idea behind Borges's "The Intruder" was to rewrite Lugones's "Francesca" in accordance with Lugones's nationalistic theories regarding Argentine literature. Lugones had proclaimed the gaucho to be the "archetype" of "argentinidad," and Borges's playful objective is to write a Francesca of the pampas featuring two gaucho outlaws. The story abounds in local color to humorously "argentinize" this medieval Western love story by filling it with mate, horses, whorehouses, and hides.

The story starts off with the narrator's explanation of how he first heard the story, "between one sip of mate and the next."[37] This mention of Argentina's national drink immediately locates our story. Like Lugones's narrator who confesses his version will be told "as free as I please,"[38] the narrator of the "The Intruder" admits that he will "give in to the writer's temptation of emphasizing or adding certain details."[39] These details serve to paint a picture of the way of life of the Nilsens. He begins by describing the meager dwellings of the two brothers. They live in a rambling old house of "unplastered brick," "sleep in bare rooms on cots," and own only one book, a worn Bible with names and dates written on the back flyleaf: "the roaming chronicle of the Nilsens."[40] In true gaucho fashion, their luxury consists in their freedom, and "their extravagances were horses, silver-trimmed riding gear, the short-bladed dagger, and getting dressed up on Saturday nights, when they blew their money freely and got themselves into boozy brawls."[41] The tale holds true to all of the characteristics of the gaucho outlaw, detailed in Sarmiento's *Facundo*. The brothers are said to be "drovers," "teamsters," and "horse thieves," and like Juan Quiroga Facundo, they have a propensity for gambling and violence, heightened by excessive drinking. They are hardly the noble picture of the gaucho promoted by Lugones.

As regards their amorous habits, they usually satisfy themselves "in darkened passageways or in whorehouses."[42] Frequent reference is made to the rampant prostitution in the outskirts of Buenos Aires at the turn of the century, including mention of the forbidden dance that is said to have originated in the brothels of poor neighborhoods—the tango, the preferred pastime "at those dingy parties held in tenements, where suggestive dance steps were strictly forbidden and where, at that time, partners still danced with a good six inches of light showing between them."[43] It is a rough, chauvinistic society "where drudgery and neglect wear women out."[44] Far from showering their lady with poems and gifts, as was customary of the troubadour/lover engaged in courtly love, Cristián and Eduardo treat Juliana as a servant and sexual slave. When Cristián decides to share his possession (Juliana), he says to his brother: "if you want her, use her."[45] Rather than exalting their beloved lady, they view love as something which is shameful: "In tough neighborhoods a man never admits to anyone—not even to himself—that a woman matters beyond lust and possession, but the two brothers were in love. This, in some way, made them feel ashamed."[46]

These rough gauchos are incapable of dealing with feelings, and instead take them out on others: "on strangers, on dogs, on Juliana." After selling her to the whorehouse, they go back to "their old life of men among men . . . to cardplaying, to cockfights, to their Saturday night binges." In true gaucho fashion, they prize their horses more than anything else. Their excuse for eventually buying Juliana back from the madame is so as to not "wear out the horses" running back and forth to the whorehouse.[47]

The climax of the story takes place under a starry sky out on the pampa where our protagonists set out to bury Juliana's corpse. The burial scene is worthy of any gauchesque novel. They pack up her body with a bunch of hides, and once arrived at a secluded spot, Cristián throws down the cigar he has just lit and says matter-of-factly, "Let's get busy, brother. In a while the buzzards will take over."[48] The tale ends in the middle of the pampa with the brothers embracing.

Borges accomplishes multiple objectives in this brief tale. Instead of hypermedievalizing Dante's version, as Lugones had done in "Francesca," he hyper-Argentinizes it, parodying and unromanticizing the picture of the gaucho that Lugones had declared to be the "archetype" of the Argentine. He playfully pokes fun at Lugones's nationalistic theories and his failure to have followed them in his retelling of the fifth canto. His strategy here is *reductio ad absurdum*—establishing a claim by showing the opposite scenario in an extreme form; the point being made is that Argentines need not limit themselves strictly to local themes in order to appear Argentine. As he explains in "El escritor argentino y la tradición," great authors such as Racine and Shakespeare are no less French and English, respectively, on account of setting their stories in different time periods and geographical locations: "I think Racine would not even have understood a person who denied him his right to the title of poet of France because he cultivated Greek and Roman themes. I think Shakespeare would have been amazed if people had tried to limit him to English themes, and if they had told him that, as an Englishman, he had no right to compose *Hamlet*, whose theme is Scandinavian, or *Macbeth*, whose theme is Scottish. The Argentine cult of local color is a recent European cult which the nationalists ought to reject as foreign."[49]

To further prove his point he gives the now famous example of Edward Gibbon, who in his *Decline and Fall of the Roman Empire* had remarked upon the lack of camels in the Koran. Borges believes the absence to be sufficient proof that the work is indeed Arabian: "It [the Koran] was written by Mohammed, and Mohammed, as an Arab, had no reason to know that camels were especially Arabian; for him they were a part of reality, he had no reason to emphasize them; on the other hand, the first thing a falsifier, a tourist, an Arab nationalist would do is have a surfeit of camels, caravans of camels, on every page."[50] It is for this very reason that Dante (unlike Lugones) does not need to put castles and palimpsests on every page of his *Divine Comedy*. There is no mention of anything we associate with the medieval in canto 5, apart from the reference to the story of Lancelot. He didn't have to fill his tale with medievalisms because he is inherently medieval. Similarly, Argentine authors are still Argentine, whether or not they have gauchos riding across every page. Borges confesses that in his "happily forgotten" book *Fervor de Buenos Aires* he was guilty of this error. This early work of his abounds in local color and words such as "*cuchilleros*," "*milonga*," and "*tapia*." But this he sees as a mistake of his youth, an overzealous attempt to appear

Argentine, hence his omission of "El tamaño de mi esperanza" (1926) and "El idioma de los argentinos" (1928) from *Obras completas* (1974).

The second solution to the "pseudo problem" that Borges counters in "El escritor argentino y la tradición" is the belief that Argentine writers should adhere to Spanish literature. This is very easily argued against given that "Argentine history can be unmistakably defined as a desire to become separated from Spain."[51] In conclusion, he dismantles the assumption that Argentina is in essence cut off from the past. Belief in a discontinuity between Argentina and Europe leads to the opinion that searching for European themes is an error. He argues that it is reasonable for Argentines to be cosmopolitan and to recognize their European roots.

> What is Argentine tradition? I believe we can answer this question easily and that there is no problem here. I believe our tradition is all of Western culture, and I also believe we have a right to this tradition, greater than that which the inhabitants of any other Western nation might have.[52]

Being non-European, in fact, provides a certain advantage when reworking Western themes. Because Argentines act within Western culture, but yet are not tied to it by any special devotion, it is easier for them to effect innovations. He interprets the frenzy of discourses related to the "problem" of Argentine tradition as nothing more than a fad, "a contemporary and passing form of the eternal problem of determination."[53] In conclusion, he declares the Argentine patrimony to be the universe and encourages authors to essay all themes:

> We cannot limit ourselves to purely Argentine subjects in order to be Argentine; for either being Argentine is an inescapable act of fate—and in that case we shall be so in all events—or being Argentine is a mere affectation, a mask.
>
> I believe that if we surrender ourselves to that voluntary dream which is artistic creation, we shall be Argentine and we shall also be good or tolerable writers.[54]

Ultimately, Borges considered himself to be, like Dante, an author of the universe, and as such he believed that he and other Argentines had just as much a right to medieval European themes as medieval Italian authors themselves. For this reason, he praised Lugones's highly medieval reworking of canto 5, while satirizing *El payador* in his wildly original and "gauchesque"

Francesca of the pampas. However, a closer examination of Borges's *oeuvre* reveals that "The Intruder" was not the first nor the only time that Borges drew inspiration from Dante in order to cleverly critique Lugones and weigh in on the polemic regarding Argentine literature. In the next chapter, we will discuss how in an earlier and more famous short story of his, "The Aleph," Borges likens himself to Dante while portraying Lugones as a failed Dante with the character of Carlos Daneri.

FIVE

Rewriting Dante to Parody Lugones: Borges's "The Aleph"

> Lugones, a poet reminiscent of Hugo, a critic more devoted to intimidation than persuasion, has simplified to a monstrous degree our literary debates. He has postulated a moral difference between marking pauses with rhyme and choosing not to do so. He declared light to those who make use of this device, and darkness and perdition to those who don't.[1]

The above citation is from Jorge Luis Borges's essay "Roberto Godel: Nacimiento del fuego" (1932), a response to the polemic started by Leopoldo Lugones's prologue to his book *Lunario sentimental* (1909). In his essay, Borges imagines Lugones in the role of Dante, determining the afterlife of his contemporaries. Similarly, in "The Aleph" ("El aleph," 1945) we find Lugones mascarading as Dante in the figure of Carlos Argentino Daneri. "The Aleph" is one of Borges's most popular stories. It evidently held a special place in the author's estimation as well, given that "The Aleph" is also the title story of the collection in which it was reprinted in 1949. In "The Aleph," Borges rewrites Dante in order to engage in the literary polemic regarding Argentine identity.

Dante was one of Borges's favorite poets. His influence is omnipresent in Borges's work, and a thorough study of Dante in Borges would provide enough material for many books.[2] I will limit myself to examining Dante parallels in works pertaining directly to the question of national identity and those which are a veiled critique of Leopoldo Lugones. According to Borges himself, the first time he read the *Comedy* was shortly before the dictatorship. He chanced upon a bilingual edition with an English translation by Thomas Carlyle. He would pore over it on the long tram ride from his home to the library at Avenida La Plata and Carlos Calvo where he worked at the time. First he would read the text in English, then in Italian, until finally at the moment in the text when Dante is abandoned by Virgil in Paradise, he found that he was able to read the Italian directly, only occasionally referring to the English. He had never formally studied Italian, and learned it primarily from Dante and later Ariosto. Subsequently, he reread the work many times, "in all of the editions I could find."[3]

Mentions of the *Comedy* occur frequently in Borges's nonfiction. In 1949 he wrote essays on Ulysses, Ugolino, and Beatrice as part of an introduction to a Spanish translation of the *Commedia* ("Estudio preliminar"). Between 1948 and 1962 he wrote several more essays, including one on the fifth canto of *Inferno* ("El verdugo piadoso") and one on Dante's limbo ("El noble castillo"). His essays were later published as *Nueve ensayos dantescos.*[4] The number of essays in this collection is no coincidence. It had to be nine, a miracle, like Beatrice. Nine essays with a prologue brings the total parts to ten, the perfect number.

In various essays and interviews he identifies the *Divine Comedy* as one of his favorite books, and his opinion did not change over the course of his lifetime. In his 1943 essay "Sobre el 'Vathek' de William Beckford," he proclaims the work to be "the most justifiable and the most solid book of all literature."[5] In 1977 when he was asked to give a series of seven lectures on various cultural themes in Buenos Aires (later published as *Siete noches*), he dedicated his first lecture to Dante: "I have chosen the *Commedia* for this first talk," he explains, "because I am a man of letters and I believe that the apex of literature, of all literature, is the *Commedia*."[6] In an interview with Roberto Alifano in the early 1980s, when asked if he still considered the *Comedy* the greatest work of literature, he responded:

> Yes, certainly. The *Comedy* has given me highly intense aesthetic emotions; it is a book that all of us must read. Not to read the *Comedy* is to deprive ourselves of the greatest gift that literature can give us. Dante, moreover, is one of the most extraordinary personages in all of literature. I always say that I read for pleasure, that I seek emotion in books. The emotion that I felt in my many readings of the *Comedy* will be with me until my end; it is an emotion that goes beyond my wakeful hours.[7]

From Borges's response, we can see that the primary reason he praised the *Divine Comedy* was for the emotional response it engenders.

His works of fiction are a further testament to his great admiration for Dante. Among the poems inspired by the *Comedy* are most notably the "Poema conjectural" and "Inferno, V, 129." He also wrote the parables "*Inferno*, I, 32" and "*Paradiso*, XXXI, 108," published in *El hacedor* (1960). His short stories also abound with allusions and references to Dante. One of the challenges Borges constantly posed himself as a short story writer was how to capture the universe in words, a feat which he believed Dante had somehow miraculously accomplished. In the "Estudio preliminar" to the *Divine Comedy* he compares the book to an intricately painted panel "whose edges enclose the universe":

> Imagine, in an Oriental library, a panel painted many centuries ago. It may be Arabic, and we are told that all the legends of *The Thousand and One Nights* are represented on its surface; it may be Chinese, and we learn that it illustrates a novel that has hundreds or thousands of characters. In the tumult of its forms, one shape—a tree like an inverted cone; a group of mosques, vermilion in color, against an iron wall—catches our attention, and from there we move on to others. The day declines, the light is wearing thin, and as we go deeper into the carved surface we understand that there is nothing on earth that is not there. What was, is, and shall be, the history of past and future, the things I have had and those I will have, all of it awaits us somewhere in this serene labyrinth. . . . I have fantasized a magical work, a panel that is also a microcosm: Dante's poem is that panel whose edges enclose the universe.[8]

Many of Borges's stories involve similar attempts to describe the universe or recall what is infinite in words. In "Tlön, Uqbar, Orbis Tertius," the protagonist and other intellectuals attempt to reconstruct the entire history, culture, and languages of an imaginary world. In "La esfera de Pascal," Hermes Trismegistus is said to have dictated books "in whose pages all things were written."[9] Mention, of course, is made of Dante who long before him "preserved Ptolemaic astronomy, which for 1,400 years governed the imagination of man."[10] In "Funes el memorioso" the main character possesses the capacity to remember everything that ever happened to him and everything he ever read. Funes could reconstruct what he did on any given day, but doing so would take him the course of an entire day.[11] There is always in Borges the problem of enumeration, the impossibility of conveying the infinite and simultaneous through language, which necessarily requires a sequential order.

Borges's most notable attempt to capture the infinite within the confines of a story is "The Aleph." The Aleph is "one of the points in space that contain all points," or in other words, a point in the in the universe where "without admixture or confusion, all the places of the world, seen from every angle, coexist."[12] Its contents cannot be related in their entirety:

> I come now to the ineffable center of my tale; it is here that a writer's hopelessness begins. Every language is an alphabet of symbols the employment of which assumes a past shared by its interlocutors. How can one transmit to others the infinite Aleph, which my timorous memory can scarcely contain? . . . What my eyes saw was *simultaneous*; what I shall write is *successive*, because language is successive.[13]

Borges's eventual description is partly inspired by Dante the pilgrim's vision of God in the Empyrean, the realm of pure light. Like God's intolerable brightness, the Aleph is "a small iridescent sphere of almost unbearable brightness."[14] And like Dante the poet, Borges the protagonist in the above passage laments the impossibility of describing what he saw. Borges's descent into the cellar mirrors Dante's descent into hell. Also in parallel with the *Divine Comedy* and *Vita nuova*, Borges is both author and protagonist of his story.

Another obvious parallel with the *Divine Comedy* is Borges the protagonist's love for an unattainable lady, Beatriz Viterbo, a more awkward, unidealized version of Dante's Beatrice.[15] Although Beatriz is said to have passed away in 1929 (the story takes place in 1941), Borges's unrequited love is stronger than ever. Every year on her birthday he visits her house in Calle

Garay, still inhabited by her cousin, Carlos Argentino Daneri. Every year Borges stays a little longer: first only for twenty-five minutes, then (thanks to a fortuitous downpour) for dinner, and finally, by the time the story takes place, he has become the sole person whom Daneri entrusts with a great secret. In desperation Daneri discloses to Borges the existence of the Aleph hidden in his cellar, which risks being demolished as a pair of businessmen plan to expand their already enormous café. He insists upon Borges's descent into the cellar and guides him through the process, thereby taking on the role of Virgil in this Dantean catabasis. Although Borges does in fact see the Aleph, he pretends otherwise in order to make his arch-nemesis Daneri doubt its existence and believe himself to be mad.

Some critics who have glossed the allusions to Dante throughout "The Aleph" have read Carlos Argentino Daneri as a parody of Dante. This hasty conclusion is arrived at by combining the first three letters of *Dan*te with the last three letters of Alighi*eri*.[16] This is hardly sufficient evidence for such a sweeping conclusion. Such an interpretation ignores both the definition of parody and the details of the story. To parody is to deliberately exaggerate the particular style of an author for comic effect, and a close look at Daneri's verses, as we shall see, reveals no sign of similarities with Dante's. Furthermore, a great majority of the story is dedicated to the derision of this character. The predominant emotion in the tale is not love for Beatriz, but spite directed against Daneri, her first cousin. As the story progresses, this spite escalates to bitter hatred and ends with Borges the protagonist enacting his revenge against this figure ("instantly I conceived my revenge")—leading Daneri to believe himself to be mad.[17] But revenge for what? And why would Borges seek revenge upon a character associated with Dante, one of his favorite authors whom in all other instances he praises? Jon Thiem has suggested that this is a case of Bloomian "anxiety of influence" in regards to Dante.[18] But a close examination of the story (and the reason behind Borges's protagonist's derision of Daneri) reveals that Borges's anxiety is on account of one of his more immediate precursors: Leopoldo Lugones—the true alter ego of Carlos Argentino Daneri.[19]

Prior to Lugones's death, Borges was actively antagonistic toward Lugones's poetry and also toward his theories regarding Argentine literature laid out in *El payador*. Following Lugones's death, however, decorum and tact required Borges to write humble homages in the place of biting critiques.

At this juncture, Borges's fiction, and specifically "The Aleph" (written eleven years after Lugones's death), became an outlet for his pent-up hostility. His animosity is the expression of what he could no longer voice through criticism. In her 2007 article on Borges's literary criticism on Lugones, Marisa Martínez Pérsico takes a close look at Daneri's verses and the critique of them waged by Borges the protagonist. She demonstrates striking parallels between these fictional criticisms and the ones Borges as an esayist launched against Lugones's *Lunario sentimental* and *Los crepúscolos del jardín.* Borges's parody of Lugones's verses, the pedantic commentary of Daneri, and the ensuing critique by Borges as protagonist take up approximately three pages of the twelve-page story, whereas his description of what he saw within the Aleph (i.e., the entire universe) takes up little more than a page.

With this in mind, Borges's clever choice of Carlos Argentino Daneri's name makes more sense. Carlos is the name of Lugones's younger brother, Carlos Florencio Lugones, born in 1885. The middle name Argentino is significant because Lugones was considered the "primer escritor argentino," and the Day of the Argentine Author is celebrated on his birthday, June 13.[20] Finally, the surname Daneri is a distortion of Dante, perhaps because this pathetic poet does not live up to the great master's name.

The first thing we learn about Carlos Argentino is that he is a "gray-haired man of refined features" who holds "some sort of subordinate position in an illegible library in the outskirts toward the south of the city."[21] In 1915 Lugones became the director of the Biblioteca Nacional de Maestros, a public library that specialized in pedagogy.[22] Second, we are told that Daneri is "authoritarian, though also ineffectual"; Lugones, although fickle in his political views, ultimately defended an authoritarian state. We then learn that "until very recently he [Daneri] took advantage of nights and holidays to remain at home," and that his chef d'oeuvre was written "leaning always on those twin staffs Work and Solitude."[23] This depiction of Daneri as an eccentric and solitary man is much in line with Borges's characterizations of Lugones to be found in his literary criticism. In 1955, in collaboration with Betina Edelberg, Borges wrote a long essay intended as an introduction to Lugones's work, in which he describes him as a proud and solitary poet, unable to express true feeling. He declares that his introduction will leave to others the "exhaustive stylistic analysis and the history of a solitary, proud, and brave man whose books earned him admiration but not affection, and who died, perhaps, without having written a word that expressed himself."[24] Similarly, in the closing paragraph of the work he refers to Lugones as "a man who, without knowing it, rejected passion and laboriously erected tall and illustrious verbal edifices, until the cold and solitude caught up with him."[25] Likewise, the verses of the solitary Daneri, a parody of Lugones, are all verbal pomp and pedantism, devoid of passion.

Furthermore, Daneri is said to be obsessed with Paul Fort, whom he deems "the prince of the poets of *la belle France*."[26] Fort was associated with the symbolist movement, which was influential to the development of *modernismo* in Latin America, and therefore to Lugones, who was Argentina's most famous practitioner of this aesthetic. Lugones, a big fan of Fort, featured his poetry in not one but two of only seven issues of the *Revue Sud-Américaine*,[27] a journal published entirely under Lugones's direction. This seemingly ironically named journal (it was printed in Paris, in French) frequently featured French poets such as Fort, Emile Verhaeren, and Francis Vielé-Griffin.[28] Daneri, Lugones's literary alter ego, waxes defensive in response to Borges the protagonist's criticism of Fort's poetry: "You assail him in vain; you shall never touch him—not even the most venomous of your darts shall ever touch him." His polemical tone is not appreciated by Borges, who deems his observations and ideas so "witless," "sweeping," and "pompous in the way they are expressed" that he "immediately associates them with literature."[29] As is readily apparent from the first few pages, the Aleph is an extremely metaliterary text, and its characters Borges (Borges) and Daneri (Lugones) stand on opposite ends of the literary spectrum.

Daneri's masterpoem, *La Tierra* [*The Earth*], dedicated to the "terraqueous orb," is a jab at Lugones's masterpiece dedicated to a lesser orb, the moon (*Lunario*). An allusion to *Los crepúsculos del jardín* is to be found in Daneri's appellation of his work as "a broad garden of rhetorical devices, figures, charms."[30] A few verses from Daneri's work are presented and then ridiculed by Borges's protagonist in the same way that Borges criticized Lugones's poetry during his lifetime.

> He visto, como el griego, las urbes de los hombres,
> Los trabajos, los días de varia luz, el hambre;
> No corrijo los hechos, no falseo los nombres,
> Pero el *voyage* que narro, es . . . *autour de ma chambre*.[31]

I have seen, as did the Greek, man's cities and his fame,
The works, the days of various light, the hunger;
I prettify no fact, I falsify no name,
For the *voyage* I narrate is . . . *autour de ma chambre.*[32]

The obviously laughable lines are followed by Daneri's pompous explanation of their significance, which merits being quoted at length. It is a parody of what Borges perceives as the erroneous principles behind Lugones's poetics:

> "A stanza interesting from every point of view," he said. "The first line wins the kudos of the learned, the academician, the Hellenist—though perhaps not that of those would-be scholars that make up such a substantial portion of popular opinion. The second moves from Homer to Hesiod (implicit homage, at the very threshold of the dazzling new edifice, to the father of didactic poetry), not without revitalizing a technique whose lineage may be traced to Scripture—that is, enumeration, congeries, or conglobation. The third—baroque? decadent? the purified and fanatical cult of form?—consists of twinned hemistichs; the fourth, unabashedly bilingual, assures me the unconditional support of every spirit able to feel the ample attractions of playfulness. I shall say nothing of the *unusual rhyme*, nor of the erudition that allows me—without pedantry or boorishness!—to include within the space of four lines three erudite allusions spanning thirty centuries of dense literature: first the *Odyssey*, second the *Works and Days*, and third that immortal bagatelle that regales us with the diversions of the Savoyard's plume . . . Once again, I show my awareness that truly *modern* art demands the balm of laughter, of *scherzo*. There is no doubt about it—Goldoni was right!"[33]

Not only is Daneri's gloss of his own verses pedantic, it is also extremely elitist and condescending toward "would-be scholars" and "popular opinion." Daneri's commentary is Borges's way of poking fun at Lugones's well-known elitism, as well as his tendency to be classicizing. Lugones proudly considered himself a Hellenist, and his publications include *Prometeo* (1910), *El ejército de la Ilíada* (1915), *Las industrias de Atenas* (1919), *Estudios helénicos* (1923), and *Nuevos estudios helénicos* (1928). Borges acknowledges his well-known reputation as a Hellenist in the section "Lugones y lo Helénico" in his book *Leopoldo Lugones*, coauthored with Betina Edelberg.[34] Like the other sections of this introduction to Lugones's work, it is not without a pointed critique. First quoting Lugones to demonstrate his haughtiness, he follows up with a criticism of the laboriousness and insensitivity of his translation of the *Iliad*:

> "I am convinced"—wrote Lugones—"that my commentary is interesting and my translations good." Perhaps they seemed good to him because he continued to hear, in every word, the original text. This delusion is frequent among translators and almost inevitable. But this indirect clarification is not perceptible to the reader, who only sees the final result of the work.
>
> More focused on the meaning of the words than on their aesthetic value, Lugones combines them and squanders them with a strange insensibility. He constructed passages as laborious as this:
>
> *—Oh hermano, el raudo Aquiles te acosa grandemente*
> *Con pie veloz, en torno de la ciudad de Príamo.*
> *Maa, ea, detengámonos ya y hagámosle frente.*
> *Contestóle el grande Héctor del casco tremolente:*
> *—Siempre fuiste, Deífobo, mi hermano más querido*
> *Entre los que hijos de Hécuba y Príamo hemos sido;*
> *Pero aun sabrá mi estima crecer en adelante,*
> *Pues a dejar los muros por mí te has atrevido*
> *Al ver mi riesgo, mientras los demás se quedaron.*
> *Y la ojizarca Atena díjole:*
> *—Hermano, es cierto*
> *Que padre, augusta madre y amigos, abrazaron*
> *Mis rodillas rodeándome, y harto me suplicaron*
> *Quedase allá (pues todos de terror están yertos.)*
>
> (*Ilíada*, canto XXII)[35]

It is significant that this passage from the *Iliad*, which Borges decrees to have been produced according to flawed principles of translation and resultantly awkward, is the only thing he quotes from any of Lugones's Hellenistic works. The lines also serve as the closing to the section of the essay, providing a rather negative impression of Lugones as a Hellenist. Rather than mentioning any positive aspect of Lugones's many publications, Borges chooses to highlight his arrogance and cheapen his contribution.

In an interview with Fernando Sorrentino, Borges quotes Paul Groussac (a much-admired mentor of his), whose manner of articulating criticism was far more unabashed than Borges's. Borges relates that once when Groussac was asked in an interview what he had been doing as of late, Groussac quipped: "What can I do in a country in which Lugones is [considered] a Hellenist?"[36] Elsewhere Borges laments the Latin nostalgia found in Lugones's verses, such as "El hombre numeroso de penas y de dias" (Man abundant in days and sorrows), which Borges complains reads and feels like Latin.[37]

Returning to "The Aleph," Daneri is further depicted as a devotee to the "fanatical cult of form," baroque poetry. Borges disliked poets such as Quevedo and Góngora, whom he calls "vain, baroque people who wanted to dazzle the reader."[38] He lumped Lugones into the same category. In his literary criticism, Borges berated Lugones for his verbal pompousness, the baroque aspect of his writing (which lends itself to parody), and the selection of words based on rhyme and sound rather than meaning. For example, in reference to *Los crepúscolos del jardín*, Borges writes:

> With this book Lugones achieves a greater formal dexterity, but not a greater rigor. His goal is to be original, and he doesn't hesitate to sacrifice everything for this goal. Every adjective and every verb must be unexpected. This makes his writing baroque, and it is well-known that the baroque lends itself to parody.[39]

Finally, perhaps the clearest indication that Daneri is Lugones is his use of "unusual rhyme." In the prologue to *Lunario sentimental*, Lugones had declared rhyme to be the essential element of the modern strophe. In Borges's opinion, this strict adherence to rhyme often leads to ridiculous word choice and metrical clumsiness. Of *Los crepúsculos del jardín* he had written that "the lexical and metaphorical abundance surely aroused smiles."[40] Of Lugones's *Lunario sentimental*, Borges complains:

> Rhyme—says Lugones in the prologue—is the essential element of modern verse. This text abounds in unsual rhyme: apio—Esculpio, astro-alabastro, sarao-cacao, ampo-crisolampo, copos-Atropos, anda-Irlanda, garbo-ruibarbo, apogeo-Orfeo, oréganos-lléganos, insufla-pantufla, pícara-jícara, hongos-oblongos, orla-por la, petróleo-mole o, náyade-haya de, pretéritas-*in vino veritas* . . . [41]

Borges's ridiculous list of unusual rhymes has the same comical effect and intention of debasing Lugones's rhymes as do Daneri's verses.

Let us look first at Borges the protagonist's response to Daneri, followed by the literary criticism of Lugones, which is strikingly similar. Borges's protagonist reacts to Daneri's verses as follows:

> Carlos Argentino read me many another stanza, all of which earned the same profuse praise and comment from him. There was nothing memorable about them; I could not even judge them to be worse than the first one. Application, resignation, and chance had conspired in their composition; the virtues that Daneri attributed to them were afterthoughts. I realized that the poet's work had lain not in the poetry but in the invention of reasons for accounting the poetry admirable; naturally, that later work modified the poem for Daneri, but not for anyone else. His oral expression was extravagant; his metrical clumsiness prevented him, except on a very few occasions, from transmitting that extravagance to the poem.[42]

Daneri's poetry is then described as "laborious" and lacking "the relative agitation of the prologue," a further allusion to Lugones's polemical prologue to *Lunario sentimental*.[43] Later, when Daneri rereads four of five pages of his poem aloud, Borges has the same reaction:

> Then he reread four or five pages of his poem to me. Verbal ostentation was the perverse principle that had guided his revisions: where he had formerly written "blue" he now had "azure" "cerulean," and even "bluish." The word "milky" was not sufficiently hideous for him; in his impetuous description of a place where wool was washed, he had replaced it with "lactine," "lactescent," "lactoreous," "lacteal."[44]

On both occasions Daneri's lines leave Borges the protagonist cold. He finds them to be devoid of emotion, and coldly constructed according to a "perverse principle" of verbal ostentation. The word choice of "depravado" (depraved/perverse) is significant, as it indicates moral corruption. As Marisa Martínez Pérsico has shown, Borges makes similar condemnations of Lugones's poetry in his 1955 book written with Bettina Edelberg, criticisms which uncoincidentally coincide in some places word for word with those found in "The Aleph":

> In Lugones's hands the *mot juste* degenerates into the *mot surprenant* and proves to be a page from an anthology of sheer technical triumphs, less apt at conveying emotion or persuading than at simply dazzling. His literature, on

> account of its excess or perverse implementation, is tainted by vanity; behind the outrageous epithets and the alarming metaphors, the reader perceives, or believes to perceive, this grave moral defect. . . .
>
> For the dictionary *azulado*, *azuloso*, *azulino* and *azulenco* are strictly synonymous; and the same was true for Lugones. Mindful only of the meaning, he did not notice, did not want to notice, the distinct connotations. *Azulado* and perhaps even *azuloso* are words that can be included in a paragraph without standing out; *azulino* and *azulenco* sin of emphasis.[45]

The second strophe of Daneri's that appears in "The Aleph" serves as a further example of his unusual rhyme, audacious word choice, and ridiculous use of neologisms.

> Sepan. A manderecha del poste rutinario
> (Viniendo, claro está, desde el Nornoroeste)
> Se aburre una osamenta—¿Color? Blanquiceleste—
> Que da al corral de ovejas catadura de osario.[46]
>
> Hear this. To the right hand of the routine signpost
> (Coming—what need is there to say?—from north-northwest)
> Yawns a bored skeleton—Color? Sky-pearly.—
> Outside the sheepfold that suggests an ossuary.[47]

These laughable lines parody what Borges found to be most obnoxious about some of Lugones's poetry. In the pompous commentary that follows, Daneri praises himself for his originality and his "picturesque neologism" *blanquiceleste* (sky-pearly).

> "Two audacious risks!" he exclaimed in exultation, "snatched from the jaws of disaster, I can hear you mutter, but success! . . . The second half-line sets up the most animated sort of conversation with the reader; it anticipates his lively curiosity, puts a question in his mouth, and then . . . *voilà*, answers it . . . on the instant. And what do you think of that coup *sky-pearly*? The picturesque neologism just *hints* at the sky, which is such an important feature of the Australian landscape. Without that allusion, the hues of the sketch would be altogether too gloomy, and the reader would be compelled to close the book, his soul deeply wounded by a black and incurable melancholy."[48]

Daneri's commentary serves to reduce the lines (and by association Lugones's poetry) to mere pompous explanation of outrageous phrasing. Secondly,

Daneri's dialogue (or rather monologue) is a parody of Lugones as a poor conversationalist. In an interview with Osvaldo Ferrari, Borges confessed:

> I have talked to Lugones five or six times—he was a rather sad man who found conversation difficult. Or, rather, conversation was impossible with him.[49]

And in another interview with César Fernández Moreno, Borges described the difficulty of interacting with him socially:

> a solitary and dogmatic man, a man who did not open up easily . . . Conversation was difficult with him because he [would] bring everything to a close with a phrase which was literally a period. . . . Then you had to begin again, to find another subject. . . . And that subject was dissolved with a period. . . . What he wanted was to control the conversation. Everything he said was final.[50]

To parody this personal trait of Lugones, Borges ends Daneri's comments not with a period, but with an exclamation mark. Although Borges the protagonist is thoroughly at odds with everything Daneri asserts throughout the story, he realizes the futility of contradicting him. In response to Daneri's request that he persuade Lanifur of the "formal perfection" and "scientific rigor" of his work in order to elicit from him a prologue, Borges cannot but acquiesce: "I agreed, I agreed most profusely."[51]

Although in the case of Lugones Borges sees adherence to rhyme as the primary culprit of irreverent word choice, that is not to say that he disapproved of rhyme in general. In his criticism of Lugones's *Romancero* he makes a distinction between the rhyme and word choice of classical texts and Lugones's.

> If a poet rhymes in Spanish with words that end in *ía* or *aba*, there are hundreds of words available to finish off a stanza. . . . On the other hand, if he rhymes using a word ending in *ul*, as Lugones does, he has to *azular* (to blue) something right away and then arrange a trip so he can carry a *baúl* (suitcase) or other indignities. In the same way, someone who rhymes using *arde* commits himself to this ridiculous obligation: *I don't know what I'll say to you, but I commit myself to think awhile about the "brasero" (because it burns—"arde") and yet another while about five-thirty (afternoon, "tarde"), and yet another while about bragging (alarde), and still another about some yellowbelly (coward, "cobarde").*
>
> The classics felt that way, and if they ever rhymed *baúl* with *azul*, or *calostro* (colostrum) with *rostro* (face), it was in joking compositions where those rhymes are appropriate. Lugones does it seriously. Let's see, friends, what do you think

> of this little gem?: "illusion that its wings doth spread/ in a fragile bow of tulle/and in the sensitive heart doth stick/its insidious pin so blue."
>
> This quatrain is the last card in the deck, and it's terrible not only because of the *spiritual misery*, because of the *insignificance of its soul*. This say-nothing quatrain, silly and frivolous, sums up the *Romancero*. The *sin* of this book resides in its nonexistence, in its being almost a book of blank pages annoyingly dotted with lilies, ribbons, silks, roses, fountains, and other colorful consequences of gardening and tailoring.[52]

This caustic critique is from an article written in 1926, long before Lugones's death, after which Borges would creatively veil his criticism, as in "The Aleph." But as Sorrentino correctly affirms, "despite a bit of ambivalence and a certain repentant attitude (purely exterior), Borges would retain, till the end of his life, a generally averse and disdainful opinion of the literature of Leopoldo Lugones."[53]

It is interesting that on this occasion Borges happens to use Dantean vocabulary to condemn his rival. The "sin" of his book is the result of his "spiritual misery," the "insignificance of his soul." In "The Aleph," Lugones is depicted via the figure of Daneri as an anti-Dante. They are on opposite ends of the poetic spectrum. Daneri/Lugones's poetry is driven by the "perverse principle" of "verbal ostentation," and Borges disapproved of writers whom he deemed overly focused on form: "Rhetoric should act as a bridge, a road, but generally it is a wall, an obstacle. That can be seen in such different writers as Seneca, Quevedo, Milton, Lugones; in all of them, what they say comes between them and us."[54] Elsewhere Borges says that in Quevedo and Lugones "words came before emotions":[55]

> With both of them [Quevedo and Lugones] you feel that each poem is a sort of verbal object, a verbal structure. That gets in the way of these two poets and their emotions, yet creates its own emotion. In Lugones, for instance, there is no intimacy; Lugones was a proud man. Each of his poems is a verbal object that lives beyond the author's intention.[56]

Borges insists that it is important for a reader to feel that they are "receiving something fresh, not a labored structure, which is what always happens with Quevedo and Lugones."[57] Furthermore, he says that Lugones never created a symbolic character that will live in people's imaginations.

Borges labels Lugones as "a formalist writer whose main concern was words," and in Borges's opinion, such poetry was doomed to failure.[58] In an interview on poetry with Roberto Alifano, he emphasizes the importance of emotion:

> BORGES: For poetry to move us we must feel that it corresponds to an emotion. That is, if we read the poem as a linguistic exercise, if we believe that poetry is a mere word game, poetry fails.
>
> ALIFANO: What you have just said suggests that the only criterion for poetry is its affective quality, a hedonistic criterion, isn't it?
>
> BORGES: Yes! If a text gives us pleasure, moves us, that text is poetic. If it doesn't move us, it is a wasted effort to point out to us that it has novel rhymes, that the metaphors are unique to the author's style or that they fall within a certain poetic movement. All that is worthless.[59]

In contrast to the form-focused but failed poetry of Lugones is that of Dante. Borges considered Dante an affective writer who also achieved formal perfection. He certainly praises the metrics of the *Comedy* ("an element which is to me one of Dante's greatest virtues"), but what he most values in the work is its "tenderness."[60] His love for the *Comedy* is primarily because of the emotion it engenders: "The emotion that I felt in my many readings of the *Comedy* will be with me until my end; it is an emotion that goes beyond my wakeful hours."[61] In Dante it is the content and emotions that first and foremost drive the verse, not wordplay. When asked by Alifano if he agrees with Benedetto Croce's contention "that the *Comedy* sustains itself, never falters, mainly because of the unique narrative style created by Dante," Borges agrees and praises the "almost magical way" in which Dante introduces us to the narration. He continues, "As I've said, I have always let myself be carried by the act of reading the narrative, by the aesthetic emotion which every turn of the page gave me."[62] In Borges's opinion, Dante is so convincing as a poet that the illusion of reality he gives is "so vivid, so precise, that we come to suppose that he truly believed in his other world—in that world imagined by his poetic vision, by his poetic faith."[63]

Dante was for Borges the perfect synthesis of content and technique. It would hardly make sense that he would seek to parody him in the character of Daneri. As an author Dante earned nothing but praise from Borges, and it is clearly the character of Borges who is identified with Dante throughout the story. It is Borges who suffers the unrequited love and loss of Beatriz, Borges whose description of the aleph we are reading, and Borges whose reaction to his total vision is "infinite veneration, infinite pity," pity being a marked word that immediately associates him with Dante the pilgrim.

Lugones, on the other hand, is envisioned as the anti-Dante. A devotee of the "fanatical cult of form" and a stranger to emotion, in Borges's eyes he has no right to rewrite the story of Francesca. An author as cold as Borges imagines Lugones to be couldn't possibly understand a heroine who submits all reason to desire. Lugones is the poet who "died perhaps without ever having written a word that expressed himself,"[64] the poet who always subjected emotion to form. He is simultaneously the anti-Francesca, the anti-Dante, and the anti-Borges. Indeed, it could be said, perhaps, that Borges developed his particular style of writing to counter that of Lugones, to come out from behind his shadow. As Harold Bloom argues in *The Anxiety of Influence*, poets must develop an original poetic vision in order to guarantee their survival into posterity. The influence of precursor poets results in a sense of anxiety in living poets.[65] This anxiety can be seen in both "The Aleph" and the prologue to *El hacedor*, which he dedicated to Lugones.

In "The Aleph" Borges the protagonist feels increasing resentment toward Daneri. Apart from finding Daneri's verse appalling, Borges's protagonist is frustrated by Daneri both because he fears having to write prologues for a poet he despises ("deep down, we had always detested one another") and because he is envious that Daneri gets all the recognition despite his bad poetry. When Daneri decides to publish the first cantos of his poem, he calls up Borges and suggests they meet to "imbibe the milk of the gods together in the nearby salon-bar." Daneri tells Borges that he desires a prologue written by another author, "an accolade penned by a writer of stature, of real import."[66] Borges protagonist, mortified, suddenly realizes the purpose of the invitation: "the man was about to ask me to write the preface to that pedantic farrago of his."[67] His fears turn out to be unfounded, for instead Daneri asks him to persuade a friend of his, Alvaro Melián Lafinur, to write the called-for foreword. This is a further slight to Borges's ego, given that he initially imagined himself to be the "writer of stature, of real import," but instead finds himself as nothing more than a middleman. Daneri instructs Borges to speak to Lanifur "on behalf of the poem's two incontrovertible virtues: its formal perfection and its scientific rigor—'because that broad garden of rhetorical devices, figures, charms, and graces will not tolerate a single detail that does not accord with its severe truthfulness.'"[68] Borges, between a rock and a hard place, weighs his options. He could "(a) speak with Alvaro and tell him that that first cousin of Beatriz' . . . had written a poem that seemed to draw out to infinity the possibilities of cacophony and chaos"; or "(b) not speak with Alvaro." He opts for the second and, dreading the inevitable follow-up phone call from Daneri, finds to his dismay that the telephone becomes "a constant source of anxiety."[69]

In my opinion, "The Aleph" is a nightmarish literary expression of the situation Borges found himself in following Lugones's death, when he was asked to write not only prologues but also tributes to his rival. As Estela Canto explains, despite his humbler homages following Lugones's passing, Borges continued to have a dismal opinion of his poetry.

> Borges *decided* to admire Lugones and in his *Obras completes* of 1972 he mentions him with admirable humbleness. It was a canonically established attitude. . . . A November night of 1985 . . . I had with me a copy of Lugones's *Lunario sentimental.* I have wanted for some time to discuss these poems with you, I told him. I read a few poems at random. Borges blushed and moved about uncomfortably in his seat. Finally he said, "Yes, it is certain. They are horrible. Go on, read some more." I read others. His impression was confirmed. When we left the restaurant he said something that I had heard him say various times, but this time with a new intonation/haughtiness: Can you believe that my generation considered good writing to be writing like Lugones! This time the sentence sounded like a pretext. He added, reflectively: You know something, Estela? In these verses there is not one real idea. His only purpose is the rhyme. There is nothing heartfelt, nothing lived.[70]

Here we can see essentially the same criticism of Lugones's writing found first in his literary criticism, and later in the parodic critique in "The Aleph." We can see the similarity between Borges and the literary version of himself, who upon rereading his rival's verses has the same gut reaction and confirmation of his first impression. Borges feels dumbfounded that such verses could be considered good writing by his generation. In "The Aleph" Borges the protagonist likewise feels incomprehension and envy as a result of

Daneri's popularity. After the demolition of Daneri's home, he writes, "Procrustes Publishers, undaunted by the length of Carlos Argentino Daneri's substantial poem, published the first in its series of 'Argentine pieces.'"[71] This specification that Daneri/Lugones's work is particularly Argentine is all the more frustrating for Borges. While Daneri's poem earns him second place in the National Prize for Literature, Borges the protagonist's work does not even receive a single vote: "Once more, incomprehension and envy triumphed!"[72]

A poem entitled "La luna" published in 1960 in *El hacedor* is a further expression of the anxiety of influence Borges felt toward Lugones. At the opening of the poem Borges imagines a man who desires to "cifrar el universe / En un libro y con ímpetu infinito" (to record the universe / in a book and with the energy of the infinite). He creates an "alto y arduo manuscrito" but ultimately fails at this task because he forgets the moon.[73] This made-up story, Borges writes, encapsulates the dilemma of writers, who must "cambiar en palabras nuestra vida. / Siempre se pierde lo esencial" (change our life into words / The essential is always lost). Again we see Borges's Dantean desire to capture the universe in words, and the linguistic impossibility of such a task. What is interesting is that the poet (Borges) fails precisely in regard to Lugones's greatest success: *Lunario sentimental.* Borges openly admits to his anxiety of influence when divulging the story of his personal relationship with penning the orb of poets:

Cuando, en Ginebra o Zürich, la fortuna
Quiso que yo también fuera poeta,
Me impuse, como todos, la secreta
Obligación de definir la luna.

Con una suerte de estudiosa pena
Agotaba modestas variaciones,
Bajo el vivo temor de que Lugones
Ya hubiera usado el ámbar o la arena.[74]

(When, in Geneva or Zurich, fortune
Desired that I too become a poet,
I assumed, as all poets do, the secret
Duty to define the moon.

In a studious struggle
I exhausted all modest variations,
Living in intense terror that Lugones
Had already employed amber or sand.)

His response to this anxiety is, in line with Bloom's theory, to forge an original poetic identity in order to ensure his survival into posterity. Although Borges had once sought to imitate Lugones, he later came to disdain Lugones's extravagant vocabulary and constant invention of new metaphors. Contempt for Lugones's creativity in this respect was made possible by interpreting Lugones's focus on formalism as pompous and lacking in sincerity. The birth of Borges's new poetic identity, which allowed him to step out from behind the shadow created by the gleaming moonlight of Lugones, is described in the latter half of the poem:

Y, mientras yo sondeaba aquella mina
De las lunas de la mitología,
Ahí estaba, a la vuelta de la esquina,
La luna celestial de cada día.

Sé que entre todas las palabras, una
Hay para recordarla o figurarla.
El secreto, a mi ver, está en usarla
Con humildad. Es la palabra *luna*.

Ya no me atrevo a macular su pura
Aparición con una imagen vana;
La veo indescifrable y cotidiana
Y más allá de mi literatura.[75]

(And while I sounded the depths of that mine
Of all the moons of mythology,
There it was, at the turn of the corner,
The everyday celestial moon.

I know that among all the words,
There is one that can rightly represent it.
The secret, in my opinion, is to use it
With humility. It is the word *moon*.

Now I shall never dare to stain
Its pure appearance with a futile image;
I see it indecipherable and daily
And out of reach of my literature.)

These lines describe the formation of a distinct poetic theory—a process that was in fact a slow evolution—as a sort of instantaneous revelation. Rather than trying to beat Lugones at his own game of writing extravagant metaphors employing all the words in the dictionary, Borges recognizes the path to originality as a return to the everyday. Rebelling against the "fanatical cult of form" he parodies in "The Aleph," a more mature Borges focused on content, employing straightforward vocabulary with so-called humility. This change in strategy can be seen by comparing the original edition of *Fervor de Buenos Aires* (1923) with his later rewriting of the work for *Obras completas*. In the prologue written in 1969 he explains that he made substantial changes in order to eliminate the "baroque excesses." One of the tendencies that the elder Borges laments in his earlier career was his preoccupation with discovering "the metaphors that Lugones had already discovered."[76] In his later work he would eliminate not only "baroque excess," but also neologisms and forced attempts to appear Argentine. Commenting on his literary transformation, he writes:

> A writer's fate is strange. At first he is baroque, vainly baroque, as the years pass, he can achieve, if the stars favor him, not simplicity, which is nothing, but modest and secret complexity.[77]

Having developed his own literary theories, which in many ways are diametrically opposed to those of Lugones, and having achieved enormous success, a sixty-year-old Borges continued to fear how his works would fare in the future. Would posterity perceive him as the greater author, or would his literary legacy be confused with that of his greatest rival? These fears are voiced in his famous foreword to *El hacedor*, "A Leopoldo Lugones," written eleven years after "The Aleph." Dedicating the prologue of one of his own books to Lugones would seem to be an extremely honorific gesture, but Borges's mixed feelings toward his predecessor are in full evidence. The prologue can be read as an attempt to come to terms with his influence.

Borges imagines himself entering the library where Lugones works. To the left and right, he sees the profiles of readers in the light of "studious lamps, as in Milton's hypallage." This reflection in turn reminds him of one of Lugones's lines from *Lunario*, "the arid camel,"[78] which leads him to cite the hexameter from the Aeneid "Ibant obscuri sola sub nocte per umbram." Borges was not fond of Milton, whom he considered, like Lugones, a formalist writer void of feeling. But sandwiched between Milton's line and that of Virgil, Lugones's "arid camel" appears particularly absurd, and would lead one to believe that Lugones should leave aside trying to imitate the literary devices of the classics, just as elsewhere he had criticized Lugones for his "Latin nostalgia."[79]

With these reflections in mind (i.e., reflections on what he deems failed versification), he enters Lugones's office and presents him with a copy of *El hacedor.*

> Si no me engaño, usted no me malquería, Lugones, y le hubiera gustado que le gustara algún trabajo mío. Ellos no ocurrió nunca, pero esta vez usted vuelve las páginas y lee con aprobación algún verso, acaso porque en él ha reconocido su propia voz, acaso porque la prática deficiente le importa menos que la sana teoría.[80]
>
> (Unless I am mistaken, you didn't dislike me, Lugones, and you'd have liked to like some work of mine. That never happened, but this time you turn the pages and read a line or two approvingly, perhaps because you've recognized your own voice in it, perhaps because the halting poetry itself is less important than the clean-limbed theory.)[81]

We can only assume that the "sana teoría" refers to Borges's poetics, which in this imagined scenario Lugones is said to prefer over his own "prática deficiente." Andrew Hurley, in his English translation, makes an interesting translational choice of giving further indication of what these theories are: "perhaps because the halting poetry itself is less important than the clean-limbed theory."[82] Borges's version is more ambiguous on this point but establishes a clearer dichotomy between good and bad: "sana" and "deficiente." Thus we see that the prologue is really not laudatory at all. Just as in his introduction to Lugones's work written in collaboration with Betina Edelberg, an obstensively honorific text is ultimately a vehicle for insults.

In the next paragraph Borges admits that all of this has been imagined:

> My vanity and my nostalgia have confected a scene that is impossible. Maybe so, I tell myself, but tomorrow I too will be dead and our times will run together and chronology will melt into an orb of symbols, and somehow it will be true to say that I have brought you this book and that you have accepted it.[83]

The underlying cause of Borges's imagined scenario is his anxiety that the two of them will be confused by posterity. Perhaps it was a way for him to come to terms with Lugones's influence, while at the same time attempting to exert his own influence over posterity's vision. Lugones was Borges's precursor, but here he is acknowledging Borges talent.

In "Kafka and His Precursors" Borges also inverts the order of influence. He recognizes Kafka in Kierkegaard, Robert Browning, and other authors. Although chronology would have it the other way around, Borges insists that after Kafka, our readings of his precursors are forever altered.

> In the critic's vocabulary, the Word "precursor" is indispensable, but it should be cleansed of all connotation of polemic or rivalry. The fact is that every writer *creates* his own precursors. His work modifies our conception of the past, just as it will modify the future.[84]

Borges no doubt hoped to exert his influence over our impression of Lugones's legacy. As we have seen, his literary criticism provides a stark critique of Lugones's poetics and refutes his nationalistic theories put forth in *El payador.* In the last two chapters we have examined how Borges not once, but twice, rewrites Dante in order to parody Lugones. With "The Intruder," he rewrites both Dante's Francesca and Lugones's version while unromanticizing the picture of the gaucho that Lugones declared to be the "archetype" of the Argentine. He makes use of the polemic regarding the Argentine author and tradition to fuel his literary creation. With "The Aleph" he likens himself to Dante by attempting to describe the universe, while parodying Lugones in the figure of Carlos Argentino Daneri. Thus, we can see that for Borges, rewriting Dante in the form of a short story became a clever way to weigh in on the discussions involving Argentine literature, much in the same way that in Dante's day, lyric poetry was a vehicle for debating the meaning of love with poet friends and rivals. We might even liken the tension between Borges and Lugones to that between Dante and Guido Cavalcanti, the "best friend" of the *Vita nuova*, from whom Dante needed to distinguish himself.[85]

The practice of rewriting Dante to critically comment on the state of Argentine literature did not end with Borges. In the following chapters, I will examine a similar operation on a much larger scale. Leopoldo Marechal, with his novel *Adán Buenosayres* (1948), rewrites Dante while at the same time parodying the divergent viewpoints in the literary polemics concerning "argentinidad," including that of Borges (Luis Pereda). The result is a polyphonic novel of epic proportion that seeks to convey the complexity of Argentine identity.

SIX

Leopoldo Marechal on Immigration and Argentine Identity

Thus far in our journey through Dante's afterlife in Argentina we have learned that in order to understand a particular Argentine author's motives for translating or rewriting Dante, we must first understand (1) his political leanings; (2) his attitude toward immigrants (especially Italian); (3) his views on *Martín Fierro*; and (4) his rivalries with other Argentine authors (Mitre/Hernández; Lugones/Borges). No less is true for Leopoldo Marechal, whose novel of epic proportions, *Adán Buenosayres* (1948), marks the most profound engagement with Dante herein discussed. Before turning to the book itself in chapters 7–8, I will here include information on Italian immigration to Argentina in the age of Juan Domingo Perón; biographical information on Marechal that is necessary to an understanding of his political position as a supporter of Perón; and an analysis of Marechal's nationalistic poetry in which he personifies Argentina as a young girl in a difficult stage of coming of age, a stage in which her identity is not yet fully formed. This poetry with its militaristic sentiments depicts Argentina as a nation in need of a new spiritual order.

Italian Immigration to Argentina after World War II

Another wave of Italian immigration to Argentina occurred after World War II. Italy had a pro-emigration stance at that time. In fact, emigration came to be perceived as a safety valve—a way to mitigate the high unemployment rate and lack of resources.[1] In 1946, with unemployment in Italy estimated at over two million, Italians began emigrating both to other European countries and further abroad. Approximately 7.5 million Italians left Italy from 1946 to 1976. Over 70 percent came from the northeastern and southern areas of Italy. While 59 percent emigrated to other European countries, the rest opted for destinations overseas. Following the Italian economic boom (1958–63), emigration came mostly from the south.[2]

Argentina proved a particularly attractive overseas destination, given that Perón's government had launched a program of industrialization in 1946 and needed immigrant workers. The Italian and Argentine governments signed two agreements in 1947 and 1948. These agreements differed notably from those between Italy and other European countries. Argentina promoted permanent settlement of the immigrants and did not specify a limit to the number that would be accepted. Additionally, the degree of kinship needed for family reunion was expanded.[3] Furthermore, Perón's Argentina proved a safe destination for fleeing fascists.[4] In addition to spontaneous immigration and immigration organized by the state, Federica Bertagna notes another mechanism of post–World War II Italian expatriation that was new in comparison to the nineteenth and early twentieth centuries: the emigration of technicians and general labor force managed by the dozens of Italian private companies that moved to Argentina with all their workers in tow.[5] In total, almost 300,000 Italians emigrated to Argentina between 1947 and 1950, which is equivalent to 60 percent of all Italian overseas emigration at that time.[6]

This migratory boom lasted until Argentina's economic crisis of the 1950s.[7] In the years that followed, the devaluation of the Argentine currency meant that Italian workers had increasingly less money to send home to their families. At the same time the Argentine government placed limits on how much money could be remitted. These two factors made Argentina increasingly less attractive as a destination.[8]

Leopoldo Marechal's inclusive views on immigrant workers were largely in line with those of Perón, of whom he was a staunch supporter. Marechal was born in Buenos Aires in 1900 to Lorenza Beloqui and Alberto Marechal, a self-taught mechanic. His mother was Argentine and his father Uruguayan of French descent. In 1910 the family moved to Monte Egmont 280, a neighborhood of Villa Crespo. Every summer Leopoldo traveled to Maipú, in the province of Buenos Aires, and these summers of his childhood would always be remembered with nostalgia. As the only child from Buenos Aires who traveled there every summer, he earned the nickname "Buenos Aires."[9]

Marechal had his first job in 1913 at the young age of thirteen, working in a factory. He had socialistic sentiments from an early age, and was fired from this job for having incited the employees to ask for better wages. In 1919 his father fell ill with the flu. When he was still convalescing, he was forced to return to work to maintain his wages. On July 7, he died. The death of his father would mark Marechal's political outlook, as his support of workers' rights and populist government stemmed from very personal experiences. Alberto's passing left the family in a difficult financial situation. Nevertheless, they decided that Leopoldo should continue his studies. He also began working as a librarian at the Biblioteca Popular Alberdi. In 1921 he became a schoolteacher.[10]

Although Marechal did not, like many other Argentine authors such as Lugones and Borges, have the privilege to focus primarily on literary pursuits, he did somehow find time to publish even from a young age. In 1922, at the age of twenty-two, he published his first book of poems, *Los aguiluchos*. In 1923 he became involved with the journal *Proa* and was part of the *martinfierrista* avant-garde movement. He also collaborated with the journal *Martín Fierro*, publishing poems and essays.[11]

In 1925 Marechal decided to travel to Europe, and his mother and siblings began to help save for the trip, which took place the following year. During his travels he was active in the cultural life of the cities he visited. In Paris he met Picasso, Unamuno, and the Argentines Horacio Butler, Héctor Basaldúa, Antonio Berni, and Raquel Forner, among others. In 1929 he returned to Europe, and in the following year he began writing *Adán Buenosayres.* It was at this time (1930) that he traveled to Italy and became an avid reader of Dante.[12] His fascination with Florence and its most famous author would have a lasting effect on his writing, especially on *Adán Buenosayres*, which was published in 1948. After a return from Europe in 1949, he was shocked at the hostile reaction the work had generated among his friends and fellow men of letters.[13]

Perhaps the main factor that led to Marechal's later ostracization from the intellectual elite was his political views. He was an active supporter of Perón from the 1940s onward. He endorsed Perón's "doctrina justicialista" known as "Justicialismo," which was, according to Perón, "a new philosophy of life, simple, practical, popular, profoundly Christian and profoundly humanist."[14] Perón proposed a more even distribution of wealth and appealed especially to the working class. His popular appeal during the years following the 1943 coup d'état led to his first presidency in 1946.

Critics of Perón and his administration could not accept the president's subversion of freedoms through actions such as nationalizing the broadcasting system, centralizing the unions under his control, and shutting down opposition newspapers such as *La Prensa.* Perón's supporters saw his more antidemocratic moves as acceptable because they conceived of Perón as the incarnation of the will of the people, and as the leader who best organically expressed their desires.[15] Marechal was one of the latter who strongly felt the fervor of this charismatic leader perceived as a godlike figure chosen by the people.

Under Perón's government, Marechal held a number of important positions. First he was president of the Consejo General de Educación and director of the Schools of Santa Fe. Later he was appointed "Director General de Cultura de la Nación." He was also the national director of Enseñanza Superior y Artística. During these years he wrote *Adán Buenosayres* (1948) and the play *Antígona Vélez* (1951), which received much acclaim. In the same year, it was performed at the Teatro Cervantes (directed by Enrique Santos Discépolo) and won the Primer Premio Nacional de Teatro. After the fall of Perón in 1955, however, Marechal's literature suffered a decline in popularity. Many of the intellectual elite could not forgive his support of Perón, and the late '50s and '60s were for Marechal a period of solitude and intellectual isolation. In the years following 1955, his works were not taught in schools and were largely ignored, most likely because of Marechal's Peronist views. Since then, however, his work has been reevaluated and *Adán Buenosayres* has emerged as one of Argentina's most important novels.

The novel is set in the 1920s, and the protagonists correspond to important members of Argentina's literary elite: Borges (Luis Pereda), Xul Solar (the astrologer Schultze), Francisco Luis Bernárdez (Franky Amundsen), and Jacobo Fijman (Samuel Tesler), among others. By parodying their viewpoints throughout the novel, Marechal shuts down anti-Peronist perspectives, puts into evidence the contradiction of trends among the Argentine literati, and ridicules previous attempts to create literary identity via figures such as the *gaucho* and *compadrito*. In their place he offers a totalizing novel (620 pages) whose cast of characters takes into account the vast demographic and complex identity of *porteños*, who tend to define themselves more by their *barrio* (neighborhood) than by their city or country.

As regards structure, *Adán Buenosayres* can be divided into three main parts: the "Indispensable Prologue," which opens with the funeral of Adán; books 1–5, which recount the adventures of the protagonist and his closest friends during the last days of his life; and books 6 and 7, which are said to be manuscripts by Adán himself. Book 6 is "The Blue-Bound Notebook," dedicated to Solveig Amundsen, the Beatrice figure in the novel. Book 7 is the infernal journey, the "Journey to the Dark City of Cacodelphia," in which Adán, guided by the astrologer Schultze (Virgil), descends through limbo ("un arrabal" [slum]) and then through nine circles of hell (an inverted cone), which are divided into sectors, or *barrios*. During his journey Adán will encounter historical figures, contemporary politicians, invented characters, beasts, and even his former friends (the aforementioned members of the literary "grupo martinfierrista"), who occupy the lowest circles. The book ends abruptly with Adán and Schultze in the ninth circle, almost as if Adán's manuscript dropped off when he died.

In books 1–5 there are numerous Dantean references and wonderful parodies of Argentine intellectuals, with their contrasting viewpoints regarding what direction their literature should take. However, I will limit my discussion in chapters 7–8 to books 6 and 7, which are direct rewritings of the *Vita nuova* and the *Inferno*, respectively. In the rest of this chapter, I will provide an overview of Marechal's views on Argentine identity, to help explain how and why he draws from Dante.

Patria—the Need to Define National Identity

La Patria es un dolor que aún no sabe su nombre.
(The Homeland is a pain that does not yet know its own name.)
—LEOPOLDO MARECHAL, "Descubrimiento de la patria"

Marechal's poem "Descubrimiento de la patria" (Discovery of the homeland) is about a poet grappling with Argentine national identity and how to express it. It is the first part of a two-part poem, *La patriótica*, first published in 1960 and later included in Marechal's book of poems *Heptamerón* as "Segundo día," the second day of the seven. The poet narrator describes the metaphysical pain of being an inhabitant of a country that has not yet reached an understanding of its essence or found its means of expression. He writes from Buenos Aires, "Ciudad de la Yegua Tordilla" (City of the Dapple Gray Mare), declaring "La Patria es un dolor que aún no tiene bautismo" (The Homeland is a pain, not yet baptized).[16] This line is taken from an earlier poem, "De la patria joven," which Marechal wrote in 1929.[17] In this earlier poem, which has as its epigraph a line by Juan Chassaing, "Melancólica imagen de la patria" (Melancholic image of the homeland), Marechal also defines the homeland as a pain that must be borne without the possibility of expression: "un dolor que nuestros ojos/no aprenden a llorar" (a pain that our eyes/have not learned to cry over) (5–6).[18] The unshed tears signify that there is no release and no expression of this suffering. In this poem Argentina is personified as a young girl whose identity is not yet fully formed: "un pie arraigado en la niñez y el otro/ya tendido a los bailes de la tierra" (one foot rooted in childhood and the other/already stretched out to the dances of the earth). The narrator wants to immortalize her through his writing, but his efforts are deemed premature:

Y quisiera grabar en el día su sombra,
y decir las palabras
que castigan al tiempo
como a un noble caballo.

Pero vacila su talón ardido:
"¡No es hora!" canta el año junto al Río.[19] (11–16)

(And I would like to engrave in the day her shadow,
  and say the words
  that punish time
  like a noble steed.
But her burning heel falters:
"It's not time!" sings the year by the River.)

The speaker is denied his desire, even though he believes himself to be more passionate than other countrymen, and therefore perhaps more apt at expressing his nation's destiny. But as the last stanza explains, despite the zeal of the poet, the infancy of the *Patria* is destined to continue long after his death.

La infancia de la Patria se prolonga
más allá de tus fuegos, hombre, y de mi ceniza.
  La Patria es un dolor
  que aún no tiene bautismo:
  sobre tu carne pesa lo que un recién nacido.[20] (26–30)

(The infancy of the Homeland continues
beyond your fires, man, and my ashes.
  The Homeland is a pain
  not yet baptized:
  the weight of your flesh is but that of a newborn.)

The poet, then, must bear the existential angst in silence.

The idea of the difficulty to define a land in its infancy (first articulated in "La patria joven") is then further elaborated in the aforementioned poem "Descubrimiento de la patria." Throughout the poem the poet distinguishes himself from those responsible for the material progress of the country: in the first stanza these are the immigrant cobblestone layers who stare at him blankly as they devour their bread and onions.

Dije yo en la ciudad de la Yegua Tordilla:
"La Patria es un dolor que aún no tiene bautismo."
Los apisonadores de adoquines
me clavaron sus ojos de ultramar;

y luego devoraron su pan y su cebolla
y en seguida volvieron al ritmo del pisón.[21]

(I said in the city of the Dapple Gray Mare:
"The Homeland is a pain that is not yet baptized."
The cobblestone layers
fixed me with their overseas eyes;
and then they devoured their bread and their onion
and then they returned to the rhythm of the hammer.)

The construction workers, with their "overseas eyes," are clearly immigrants who remain indifferent to (or who perhaps simply do not comprehend) the poet's cry. Their reaction calls him to question his vocation and his timing.

¿Con qué derecho definía yo la Patria
bajo un cielo en pañales
y un sol que todavía no ha entrado en la leyenda?[22]

(What right did I have to define the Homeland
under a sky in diapers
and a sun that had not yet become a legend?)

Rather than attempting to define the Patria still in its infancy, he continues to distinguish himself from the immigrants.

y en sus pies forasteros ya moría una danza.
"Ellos vienen del mar y no escuchan," me dije.
"Llegan como el otoño: repletos de semilla,
vestidos de hoja muerta."
Yo venía del sur en caballos e idilios:
"La Patria es un dolor que aún no sabe su nombre."[23]

(and on their foreign feet a dance was already dying.
"They come from the sea and don't listen," I told myself.
"They come like autumn: full of seed,
clothed in dead leaves."
I came from the south on horses and idylls:
"The Homeland is a pain that does not yet know its name.")

His first instinct is to separate himself from the newly immigrated, whose autumn contrasts with the birth of the nation and his own horses and idylls.

But subsequently, he admits that after all he really is an immigrant too, as he wonders how immigrants from different European nations will fit in to this new landscape dominated by livestock:

> Una lanza española y un cordaje francés
> riman este poema de mi sangre:
> yo también soy un hijo del otoño,
> que llegó del oriente sobre la tez del agua.
> ¿Qué harían en el Sur y en su empresa de toros
> un cordaje perdido y una lanza en destierro?[24]
>
> (A Spanish spear and a French rope
> rhyme this poem of my blood:
> I too am a child of autumn,
> That came from the east on the skin of the water.
> What would they do in the South and in the company of bulls
> a lost rope and a spear in exile?)

In the next stanza, he returns to emphasizing the youth of the country, this time poeticizing the tilling of the land in the countryside. He continues the contrast between himself (a poet concerned with the metaphysical) and the other men of his lineage (concerned only with the physical).

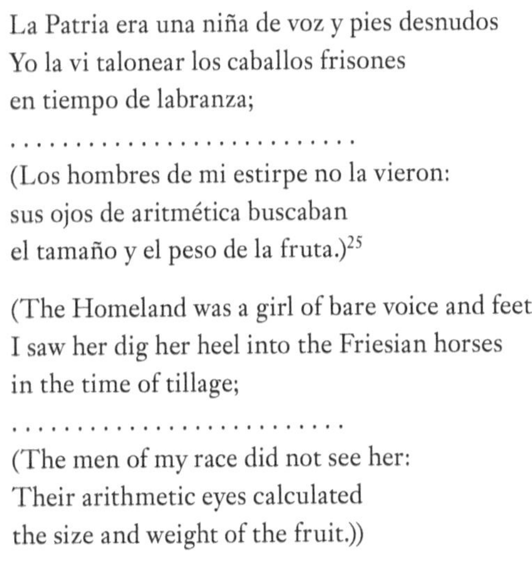

> La Patria era una niña de voz y pies desnudos
> Yo la vi talonear los caballos frisones
> en tiempo de labranza;
> . . . .
> (Los hombres de mi estirpe no la vieron:
> sus ojos de aritmética buscaban
> el tamaño y el peso de la fruta.)[25]
>
> (The Homeland was a girl of bare voice and feet
> I saw her dig her heel into the Friesian horses
> in the time of tillage;
> . . . .
> (The men of my race did not see her:
> Their arithmetic eyes calculated
> the size and weight of the fruit.))

The distinction between the speaker and other men is interesting because it is not, as was usually the case, a distinction between the second-generation immigrants and the newly immigrated, who were frequently stereotyped as materialistic. Rather, it is a contrast between poets and non-poets.

In the fifth stanza, the established pattern repeats: (1) The first line emphasizes the youth of the Homeland: "La Patria era un retozo de niñez" (the Homeland was the frolicking of childhood). (2) The body of the stanza paints a picturesque image of an aspect of the Patria, in this case sheep shearing in the countryside, accompanied by the melodic music of guitars. (3) And the last lines of the stanza relate the indifference of workers to the poet's song. This time the "hombres de mi clan" (men of my clan) do not notice the glorious frolicking of the young Patria because "sus ojos verticales se perdían / en las cotizaciones del Mercado de Lanas" (their vertical eyes were lost / in the prices of the Wool Market).

As the poem progresses, the personifications of the Patria mature from an infant to a nearly pubescent girl. While in the first stanza he mentions "un cielo en pañales" (a sky of diapers), by the time we reach stanza 6 the Patria is "dormida y con los pechos no brotados aún" (asleep and with her breasts not yet sprouted). The poet considers her with a paternal uneasiness as regards her imminent development. In stanza 8 he expresses the solitude of his encounter with the Patria and the resultant existential angst.

la descubrí yo solo allá en Maipú.
Y de pronto, en el mismo corazón de mi júbilo,
sentí yo la piedad que se alarmaba
y el miedo que nacía.
"La Patria es un temor que ha despertado,"
me dije yo en el Sur y en su empresa de toros.
. . . .
El temor de la Patria y su niñez
me atravesó encostado (la cicatriz me dura).[26]

(I discovered it by myself there in Maipú.
And suddenly, in the same heart as my joy,
I felt the pity that was alarming
and the fear that was born.
"The Homeland is a fear that has awakened,"
I told myself in the South and in the company of bulls.
. . . .

The fear of the Homeland and her childhood
pierced me through the side (the scar remains).)

The side wound is an obvious reference to Christ, who suffers for the sins of his fellow men. The poet returns to Buenos Aires with the pain of his discovery and tries to communicate (to no avail) what he has seen to the architects and the businessmen. He explains that "the eyes who look at her will not sleep." In other words, those conscious of the Homeland (the poets) will not sleep, much like Adán and his other literary-minded friends in *Adán Buenosayres*, the group that Marechal in another essay calls the creators of culture (as opposed to the consumers). But here the would-be consumers of culture, the cobblestone layers, continue to chew their bread and onions, oblivious to the anguished song of the poet. He tries yet again to communicate, this time addressing his poetry to the builders (*albañiles*).

La Patria es un peligro que florece.
Niña y tentada por su hermoso viento,
necesario es vestirla con metales de guerra
y calzarla de acero para el baile
del laurel y la muerte.[27]

(The Homeland is a danger that blooms.
A girl tempted by her beautiful wind,
it is necessary to dress her with metals of war
and shoe her with steel for the dance
of laurel and death.)

The militarization of the State suggested by these lines contains echoes of Italian fascism and especially of futurist poetry. These lines also suggest that the Patria is being courted by an unknown destiny and must be prepared for a future of war but also poetic glory. The poet seems to suggest that this tender age is crucial, but his cries continue to fall on deaf ears. Marechal's depiction of the workers as unresponsive seems to indicate that they are incapable of thinking for themselves. A similar attitude toward the masses emerges in *Adán Buenosayres*:

It's poor old Demos . . . our great *majority*, equally inclined to good and to evil, who go whichever way the wind blows. These days, it's clear from their actions

> and words that the majority is wooed by contemptible winds. But with his very clay, a Neogogue will work wonders.[28]

"Neogogo" is a neologism that combines *neo*, meaning new, and *demogogo*, or demagogue, a political leader who seeks support by appealing to popular desires and prejudices rather than by using rational argument. Given Marechal's political stance, one can hardly read this passage without thinking of Perón. The metaphor of Perón as a godlike figure molding clay can also be found in Marechal's essay "Proyecciones culturales del momento argentino," in which he wrote that Perón "worked the real material of the country with an exact knowledge of its essence."[29]

Returning to the poem, the following stanza contains the solution to the problem of poetic national expression. This time the poet speaks to the blacksmiths.

> "No solo hay que forjar el riñon de la Patria,
> sus costillas de barro, su frente de hormigón:
> es de urgencia poblar su costado de Arriba,
> soplarle en la nariz el ciclón de los dioses.
> La Patria debe ser una provincia
> de la tierra y del cielo."[30]

> ("It is not only necessary to forge the kidney of the Homeland,
> but also its mud ribs, its concrete forehead:
> It is urgent to populate its upper side,
> Blow into its nose the cyclone of the gods.
> The Homeland must be a province
> of earth and heaven.")

The verb "forjar," meaning to forge, to create (nation), or to invent, emphasizes that the Homeland is being constructed. It is a metaphysical construction of which he speaks, which runs parallel to the physical construction of the city by the builders and blacksmiths. It is a metaphysical construction that, according to Marechal, must take place with spiritual direction: "de Arriba," "dioses," "de cielo." But the blacksmiths too pay him no heed: "me clavaron con sus ojos en ausencia" (they fixed me with their absent eyes). In fact, no one in the city hears his words, for he comes from the South, an idyllic place of horses and eclogues. As Fernanda Bravo Herrera points out,

Marechal's "Sur" is not that of the criollistas Marechal parodies in *Adán Buenosayres.*

> The South assumes authentic elegiac and heroic characteristics which contrast with the empty and false stereotype of the *criollista, malevo,* and *orillero* parodied in the nocturnal excursion to Saavedra in *Adán Buenosayres* (1948).[31]

The extended lament ends with the poet giving up because he concludes that it is simply too early to sing of the Patria.

> Y descubrí en mi alma: "Todavía no es tiempo:
> no es el año ni el siglo ni la edad.
> La niñez de la Patria jugará todavía
> más allá de tu muerte y la de todos
> los herreros que truenan junto al río."[32]
>
> (And I saw in my soul: "It is not time yet:
> It is not the year, not the century, nor the age.
> The childhood of the Homeland will still play
> beyond your death and that of all
> the blacksmiths who thunder by the river.")

The argument made by the poet narrator in "Descubrimiento de la patria" is very similar to the opinion Mitre articulated in his letter to Señor don Miguel M. Ruíz in 1887: that true poetic expression of nation in the early years of nationhood is premature. In Marechal's poem, through the use of repetition, we see five main points driven home: (1) the Patria is yet in her infancy, and will be for quite some time; (2) the Patria must be militarized for her glorious destiny; (3) the inhabits of the Patria are immigrant workers from Europe; (4) the poet too is an immigrant, and he comes to recognize other immigrants as "his clan," although this "clan" yet lacks self-expression; (5) the majority of Argentines are concerned only with material progress and do not experience the existential angst of the poet. They are not conscious of the Argentine identity crisis. It is for this reason that the poet must suffer in silence and solitude his inability to sing of the Patria. It must remain

> un miedo inevitable
> y un dolor que se lleva en el costado
> sin palabra ni grito.

Por eso, nunca más
hablaré de la Patria

(an inevitable fear
and a pain that in the side
without a word or a scream.
Therefore, I will never speak of the
Homeland)

Here his suffering is Christ-like. The poem ends in metaphysical pain due to the failure to grasp the essence of the Patria and successfully express it.

This same idea of pain resulting from failed national expression can be found in a letter from Marechal to Eduardo Mallea regarding the latter's *Historia de una pasión argentina* (1937). In this letter Marechal writes of "the metaphysical struggle of being Argentine," transcribing the concluding verses from the aforementioned poem "La patria joven":

La Patria es un dolor
que aún no tiene bautismo:
Sobre tu carne pesa como un recién nacido.[33]

(The Homeland is a pain
not yet baptized:
the weight of your flesh is but that of a newborn.)

He refers to Mallea's description of America as a continent that had not yet found its expression, and likens Mallea's book to Dante's *Divine Comedy*:

> Your story is the story of a soul, and thus it is the story of an awakening, like my story, like the story of all the awakened: once Dante awakens spiritually and finds himself in a dark wood. . . . What we can declare with direct language is that our Argentina will continue to rise up as the number of awakened among the sleeping, and the number of the "sober" among the "inebriated" increases.[34]

Marechal laments that the majority of Argentines are ignorant of their own perdition and lack of self-expression, much like the workers in "Descubrimiento de la patria" who remain deaf to the poet's cries. What is needed, in his opinion, is a spiritual awakening (hence his mention of Dante). In fact, he ends his letter by proclaiming Mallea's idea of a spiritual reorientation as worthy of further study:

> There are other interesting observations in your book. For example, the idea that our country must reintegrate itself in a spiritual trajectory that it once had and then lost, seems to me an idea worthy of further study.[35]

The idea that Argentina has strayed from her spiritual path is also at the heart of a talk entitled "Fundación espiritual de Buenos Aires" (Spiritual foundation of Buenos Aires) that Marechal gave in 1936 for the fourth centenary of the founding of Buenos Aires. The title is clearly a reference to Borges's 1926 poem, "The Mythological Foundation of Buenos Aires." Marechal begins by asking the question "where is the city going, toward which course do its feet so solidly shod in metal and stone march?"[36] He laments that this great city in full growth lacks the spirituality to guide its greatness:

> We see the forehead of the city getting higher and higher; the feet of the city deeper and deeper; the body of the city, bigger and bigger; the city causes us to ache, for we do not see the spiritual form of its body, the form of its life, and because we know that without this spiritual form, no live body can have authentic life, but only a frozen mechanism that ends up, as do all mechanisms, as *a sad parody of life*.[37]

Argentines feel an existential pain as they watch their city grow aimlessly. It is a city that has not yet reached its full potential, is not yet fully formed.

> Instead, what predominates in our love for Buenos Aires is a rare paternal anxiety, as if we were the builders of the city that grows at our side, as if the infancy of the city will go on long after our death. It is for this reason that we can't take our eyes off its stature, and for this reason that we contemplate it as we would contemplate a child, that is to say as an enigma, with suspicion and hope.[38]

Essentially this paragraph is the prose version of what he expresses poetically in "Descubrimiento de la patria." Argentines who are aware experience something of a paternal uneasiness at thinking of their daughters' eventual coming of age, something which will happen after their deaths. This paternal metaphor conveys a sense of powerlessness, but also that as "fathers," they are responsible for Argentina's guidance.

Marechal's words of concern are addressed above all to those who "suffer the city like an intimate pain," and he speaks to them of the spiritual vocation of Buenos Aires, its "spiritual calling."[39] To begin, he specifies that the lack of spirituality is not unique to Buenos Aires, but is a widespread problem pertaining to the century. But according to Marechal and his spiritually oriented friends, the effects are worse in Buenos Aires than elsewhere, "perhaps because its traditional foundation is not as ancient or as strong as that of other cities."[40] The inhabitants of Buenos Aires lack a history to anchor them. Detached from their spiritual vocation, they wander aimlessly in a world of rampant materialism.

> Modern history, faithful to its century, only moves in the plane of the natural and the temporal, totally detached from the supernatural and the eternal, that is the cause of the causes. It is such that history, by not getting beyond the circle of the second causes, becomes more and more unintelligible.[41]

The citizens of Buenos Aires have lost their way and have found themselves in a dark wood, so to speak. Marechal laments that the city, "consecrated, from its origin, to the loving labors of the spirit," has forgotten its noble birth. The solution is a spiritual reorientation.

"Didáctica de la patria"—A Spiritual Itinerary

The second part of the second day of *Heptamerón* is the poem "Didáctica de la patria," which follows "Descubrimiento de la patria." The poem offers a solution to the problem of Argentine poetic expression presented as a lament in the previous poem. It is a call for a spiritual reorientation. Marechal begins the poem by stating, as in the "Fundación espiritual de Buenos Aires," that the problem pertains to the whole century: "conozco a los varones de mi tierra y mi siglo: / inciertos en el mal y en la virtud" (I know the men of my land and my century: / uncertain in evil and virtue).[42] This is of particular cause for concern because Argentina is a young country: "es fatal en esta Patria joven." As in "Descubrimiento de la patria," the infancy of the country is predicted to last far beyond the years of the poet: "la infancia de la Patria jugará todavía" (the infancy of the Homeland will play on).[43] Because poetic expression of the infant nation is premature, and because of the lack of spiritual direction, no poetic greatness is possible: "nos legaron / un tiempo sin destino que merezca un laurel" (they bequeathed us / a time without a destiny that merits a laurel). Just a few lines after this mention of a lack of destiny, Marechal alludes to Dante's *Paradiso*:

> Nos enseñaron que la Patria era
> no sé yo qué juicioso paraíso
> de infalibles trigales y vacas repetidas.[44]

> (They taught us that the Homeland was
> I don't know what judicious paradise
> of infallible wheat fields and numerous cows.)

Argentines are the direct inheritors of the ideas from Western culture (in this case a judicious paradise such as Dante's). These traditions are then melded with national particularities such as the landscape and livestock. Although there is no current possibility of poetic greatness, the poet declares, "algo debemos hacer en esta infancia" (we have to do something with this childhood). The rest of the poem provides a spiritual and moral itinerary to be followed for the benefit of future generations. The dichotomy tierra/cielo (earth/heaven) is repeated throughout: "yo siempre fui un patriota de la tierra / y un patriota del cielo" (I was always a patriot of earth / and a patriot of heaven).[45] Whereas "Descubrimiento de la patria" is an anguished lament at the lack of current expression, here, thanks to the spiritual itinerary, the poet is hopeful for the future provided that Argentines look to the heavens in order to realize their destiny.

> El nombre de tu Patria viene de *argentum*. ¡Mira
> que al recibir un nombre se recibe un destino!
> En su metal simbólico la plata
> es el noble reflejo del oro principal.
> Hazte de plata y espejea el oro
> que se da en las alturas,
> y verdaderamente serás un *argentino*.[46]

> (The name of the Homeland comes from *argentum*. Mark
> that when you receive a name you receive a destiny!
> In its symbolic metal, silver
> is the noble reflection of the main gold.
> Become silver and mirror the gold
> that occurs in the heights,
> and you will truly be an *Argentine*.)

The poem is about the individual moral work necessary to elevate the Patria: "Hazte pilar, y sostendrás un día/la construcción aérea de la Patria" (Become a pillar, and you will sustain one day/the aerial construction of the Homeland). This effort of today will yield the fruit of tomorrow: "hazte carozo de la Patria en ti mismo,/y otros verán arriba la manzana/que prometiste abajo" (Grow the seed of the Homeland inside you,/and others will see above the apple/that you promised below).[47] Subsequently, there will be poetic glory among the generations to come: "otros recogerán, a su tiempo laureles" (others will reap, in time, laurels).[48]

The population of "recién venidos" (newcomers, i.e., recently immigrated) must realize their spiritual vocation individually through Christ.

> Josef, si como pueblo no trazamos la Cruz,
> porque la Patria es joven y su edad no madura,
>   la debemos trazar como individuos,[49]

> (Josef, if as a people we do not draw the Cross,
> because the Homeland is young and its age is not mature,
>   We must draw it as individuals,)

What follows is similar to the *Divine Comedy* in that it features the motif of the journey and is intended to deter sinners from sinning. The poet warns of certain sins that plague the population, namely Envy and Gluttony. He also explains how to avoid cowardice, temptation, and robbery, and what to do if chosen as a political leader: "Si acaso gobernaras a tu pueblo,/no has de olvidar que todo poder viene de Arriba" (If you were to rule your people,/you must not forget that all power comes from Above).[50] In addition to the Dantean theme, there is reference to Dante's cosmology: "Imita, si gobiernas, a ese Motor Primero/que hace girar al cosmos/y es invisible y a la vez inmóvil" (Imitate, if you rule, this Primum Mobile/that makes the cosmos rotate/and is invisible and at the same time immobile). The conclusion of the poem is that if the itinerary of inner development is followed, then the Homeland will grow as consequence.

> Es mejor construirse y apretarse uno mismo
>   (ya te hablé del pilar y la semilla),
> y crecer por adentro lo que afuera se poda
> y ganar por arriba lo que se pierde abajo.
>   Si así lo hicieras, crecerá la Patria,[51]

(It is better to build and solidify oneself
(I already told you about the pillar and the seed),
and grow inside what outside is pruned
and win from above what is lost below.
If you do this, the Homeland will grow,)

As we have seen from Marechal's poetry, it is the spiritual component that Marechal feels is lacking in his generation of poets. Their lack of spiritual direction goes hand in hand with a lack of community. In a talk given in 1936 for the fourth centenary of the founding of Buenos Aires, Marechal highlighted the lack of cohesion among his literary colleagues:

> I don't think there is a community of common direction among the writers of my epoch. There are some spirits worthy of attention, but their efforts are isolated and of a disconcerting diversity.
>
> We don't know each other. What is lacking is this spiritual bond of community that permits an exchange of values and which serves to discipline and stimulate young people.[52]

In *Adán Buenosayres*, Marechal chose to parody the discordancy among Argentine authors because he believed them to have lost the spiritual direction necessary to produce great works of art. The *Divine Comedy* functions as a metaphor for the whole nation that has strayed from the spiritual path. Another reason for his use of Dante is because he considered Dante part of the rightful Argentine cultural patrimony. In a letter written in 1949 to Dr. Atilio Dell'Oro Maini, Marechal writes:

> We have inherited the "intellectual substance" of Europe as their legitimate and direct heirs. Alighieri, Cervantes, and Shakespeare belong to me just as much as they do to an Italian, a Spaniard, or an Englishman. Aristotle and Saint Thomas are just as much mine as Jacques Maritain. We are the legitimate heirs, professors, and continuators of Western civilization; and with an advantage in our favor: that which we gain from "the American condition," which amounts to "no rhetoric" and no national bias.[53]

Argentines are the rightful inheritors of European intellectual history. They will continue Western tradition but yet have the advantage of not being tied down to any one ideology.

In an essay entitled "Sobre la inteligencia argentina" (1941), Marechal defines Argentine intelligence as "Hispanic," "Mediterranean," and "classical."[54]

Politically speaking, this classical intelligence translates into an intellectual minority who decide for the majority; in other words, it is "aristocratic":

> classical intelligence works on things, it understands them and classifies them in a harmonious order: it is a realistic and hierarchical intelligence. . . . There is inequality and from it a principle of hierarchy is born between the man who understands (the intellectual man) and the man who assents (the sentimental man).[55]

The defining moment of independence, he says, was when Argentine intelligence gained the opportunity to "flower and bear fruit on its own within this tradition." This moment coincided with the French Revolution, and unfortunately, in the opinion of Marechal, on account of romantic sentimentalism, Argentine intelligence "renounced an inheritance that meant its liberty" and fell into "the servitude of bad imitators."[56]

The problem of foreign imitation is at the heart of discourses on Argentine literature. Argentines, it seems, were always either trying too hard to imitate, or trying too hard to be original. Borges, as we have seen in chapter 3, eventually concluded that the question of how to be uniquely Argentine in writing was a "pseudo problem," and that all Argentine authors were inherently Argentine regardless of the subject matter of their literary creations.[57] For Marechal, the expression of Argentine identity is a very real problem, the crux of which lies at the intersection of the indigenous and the foreign.

The Indigenous and the Foreign

In a conference talk titled "La poesía lírica: Lo autóctono y lo foráneo en su contenido esencial" (Lyric poetry: The autochthonous and the foreign in their essential content), given on June 23, 1949, Marechal elaborated on the difficulties of being Argentine and an author. He characterizes being an Argentine author first and foremost as being plagued by anxiety over lack of national expression:

> Let us imagine, in the first place, a poet, surrounded by the natural forms of his country; living together with his fellow citizens in this province of land we

> call our "homeland"; involved in relationships of love and hate, joys and tears, that stem from a communal life in the same land, under the same sky, bearing the stamp of traditions and modalities that ought not, cannot, and should not be forgotten or violated. Imagine the poet faced with this world of forms and feelings that make up a "homeland," and imagine the poet goaded by the yearning to elevate the splendor of the forms or the intensity of the feelings, an irresistible yearning, a craving for music, in which any poetic inclination worthy of that name is ultimately decided.[58]

Marechal laments that it would be a great shame if in lieu of poeticizing this world around him, the poet instead took up foreign elements. For art to be authentic, he argues, it must affirm itself within its cultural context and not be a grotesque and subservient imitation of the foreign. Furthermore, he continues, the poet should address an audience who is close to him, meaning those who inhabit the same land and share the same traditions. And how could he address these listeners, Marechal asks rhetorically, through exotic forms that would fall on deaf ears? Foreign elements, in his opinion, would not foster the vital relationship that must occur between the creator and the contemplator of his work.

Unfortunately, according to Marechal, the tendency to imitate the foreign was a continuous crutch of Argentine literature. Many authors explicitly set out to imitate foreign works, looking to European cultural centers such as Paris for their every inspiration. Although they had gained political independence, this did not mean immediate cultural independence:

> Our political sovereignty consolidated and our economic sovereignty reached, the problem of cultural sovereignty is currently being debated in the consciousness of our intellectuals.Very certain is (and no one can deny this fact) that the tyranny of the foreign often managed to lead our art to the most grotesque mimicry.
>
> I remember a time when many Argentine painters didn't dare take up a palette if they were not previously informed of how painting was in Paris at that very instant.[59]

Marechal does not believe that this slavish imitation has occurred because Argentines lack talent, but rather because they suffer from an inferiority complex, the consequence of which is blind mimesis. In his explanation of this tendency, Marechal returns once again to the image of the Homeland as a young girl:

> What really happened (and in all honesty it has to be admitted), is that an inferiority complex regarding the foreign weighed down on Argentine authors. . . . In a word, these artists traveled in French carriages and Russian troikas while our national soul, fresh and childlike, galloped alone to the drumming sounds of our native horses.[60]

He concludes that although strict imitation of the foreign is undesirable, so too is the overzealous inclusion of the indigenous.

Marechal contra Criollismo

In 1926 Marechal wrote an article entitled "El gaucho y la nueva literatura rioplatense" intended to warn against what he considered a "disease" that was spreading throughout Argentine letters, namely a literary nationalism consisting of the pseudo-archetype of the gaucho and other forced localisms:

> The literature of Río de la Plata, following the debatable aim of literary nationalism, is at the point of coming down with two specific diseases: the *gaucho* and the *arrabal*. There wouldn't be anything objectionable if this were about the present-day farmer, who mounts a colt with the same indifference as he drives a Ford, but this is about the gaucho, exalted by bad literature, this cardboard superman who, abandoning his poor legend, wants to become our archetype.[61]

Essentially he deems the sustained imitation of gauchesque literature no better than imitation of the foreign. He points out that in foreign countries with a secular tradition rich in episodes and types, new art tries to forget the past, rather than prolong it. It is all the more ridiculous, he explains, that Argentina, with such a meager past, should latch on to "a tradition that is not ready to be one yet, and we start crying over the disappearance of a pseudo-archetype or moaning poems by second-hand-clothes dealers about ponchos, *chiripás*, and other pieces of junk in disuse." He pleads with fellow writers to "forget the gaucho. On the threshold of new days another greater legend will grow that is worthier of our verse, given that it is within us and is nourished by our years."[62]

In *Adán Buenosayres*, he parodies these *criollista* tendencies to poeticize the gaucho and the *arrabal* in books 1–5, in particular through the scenes that take place at the social gatherings at the Amundsen house and also in the group's nocturnal excursion to Saavedra. In a key scene that takes place after the characters decide to embark on an "aventura criolli-malevi-fúnebri-putani-arrabalera,"[63] the omnipresence and the problems of *criollismo* are elaborated upon by our narrator who describes the adverse reaction of Samuel Tesler (the philosopher) to the phenomenon and his uneasiness regarding his friend Franky Amundsen's unbridled enthusiasm for the gaucho and the arrabal. When Franky Amundsen exclaims, "We'll get down and dirty on the outskirts of town and up to our balls in *criollismo*!"[64] Adán and Tesler do not jump on the bandwagon as concerns *criollismo*:

> A look of irritation mixed with pity suffused the face of the philosopher from Villa Crespo. He was not unaware of the harm suffered by the current generation due to a doctrine of heretical principles and dubious ends. Concocted in the impure crucible of some irresponsible coterie, it had taken off in a manner unprecedented in the history of our national metaphysics, fully justifying the cries of alarm being heard on all sides. *Criollismo* was the name of this obscure heterodoxy, and whether it was inspired by Old Nick himself, we'll only know on Judgment Day toward nightfall. Upon dissecting that body of doctrine with the zealous scalpel of inflexible orthodoxy, one quickly came to realize that it was all about taking certain shady characters from suburban Buenos Aires, whose deeds were memorialized in police files, and raising them to the level of Olympian gods.[65]

One of the most notable things about this lengthy explanation of *criollismo* is the profusion of religious vocabulary: "doctrina herética" (heretical doctrine), "cenáculo" (Last Supper), "oscura heterodoxia" (obscure heterodoxy), "Mandinga" (Devil), Día del Juicio (Judgment Day), "ortodoxia" (orthodoxy), "dioses olímpicos" (Olympian gods). In labeling the tendency a heresy, he implies that the *criollistas* have strayed from the true path. Inspired by the dirty melting pot (*sucio crisol*) of Buenos Aires, the *criollistas* glorified outlaw personages such as the gaucho and the *malevo* whose stories belong in the criminal records of the city rather than in her literature. But while

Marechal was decidedly against the glorification of the gaucho authors of his generation, that is not to say he was against *Martín Fierro* itself. In fact, he has nothing but praise for what he considers one of Argentina's greatest masterpieces.

Marechal on Martín Fierro

Like Lugones, Borges, and nearly every Argentine author concerned with the literary expression of Argentine national identity, Marechal publicly voiced his opinions of Hernández's *Martín Fierro*. The text, later published as "Simbolismos del *Martín Fierro*," was originally read as "La conferencia de Hoy" for LRA Radio del Estado in 1955, seven years after the publication of *Adán Buenosayres*.[66] Marechal begins by explaining that his will not be a critical study, as there are enough of those given the positive reception of the work. Instead of considering the book as art for art's sake, he explains that in light of the recent historical consciousness he will consider it in regard to "those values that transcend the limits of pure art and make it so that a literary or artistic work is established in the paradigm of a race or a people in the manifestation of its intimate power, in the image of its historic destiny."[67] His view of the role of great literature in society seems to echo Lugones's statement that great literature (and specifically *Martín Fierro*) expresses "the heroic life of our race."[68]

Marechal's essential question is this: Does Hernández's poem have the capacity of transcendence along the lines of classical epics? If the answer is yes, "*Martín Fierro* will not only constitute for us the material of a literary art, but also the material of an art we need to cultivate now more than ever: the art of being Argentines and Americans."[69] Marechal does more than just praise the work as a good book; he calls it a miracle, "at once outside of and above natural laws and ordinary circumstances.[70] It is a "grave and solitary monument," unlike any other literature created at its time. It cannot be compared to the simple folkloric poetry nor to the *poesía erudita*, which, he claims, suffered from an "inferiority complex." While the *poesía erudita* imitated French romanticism and pseudo-Spanish classicism, *Martín Fierro* was a unique creation that did not bow down to foreign predecessors.

Marechal focuses on three main aspects that make it a truly unique Argentine literary creation: (1) its freedom from an inferiority complex, (2) its timeliness, (3) its lack of imitation:

> Without any hang-up, and "with all the voice it has," *Martín Fierro* ressembles a *free act* of national literature, produced, like all instructive miracles, in the precise moment when it was needed, that is to say, when the new and glorious nation, recently born of the war, and like everything that deserves to live, had to claim through its works its right to literary greatness, just as it had already claimed the right to exist as a free nation.[71]

Not only is *Martín Fierro* an exemplary work of literature, in Marechal's opinion, but it was also written at a crucial time in Argentine history, and was a reflection of the country's identity in this moment. Furthermore, he interprets the work as a message directed toward future generations and concerning the future of the nation. He calls the work "an invitation to greatness, written during the dawn of a nation that can, wants, and must merit her future."[72] Marechal's nationalistic view of the significance of the work shares many opinions with Lugones's discussion of its significance, while contrasting starkly with the antinationalistic views of Borges, who saw the work not as a reflection of Argentine national essence, but as the story of the changes in fortune of an individual gaucho. Of all the heroes of gaucho poetry, Borges explains, Fierro was "the most individual, the one that least corresponds to a tradition."[73] For Borges the story of *Martín Fierro* is not national, nor the story of a race, nor in any way related to the origins of a people.[74] For Marechal, on the contrary, the book is something akin to the voice of the people, which had previously been neglected by the ruling and intellectual classes. In the next section, he asks the question to whom the book is addressed, and the answer is to all members of the nascent nation:

> It is addressed to the national consciousness, that is to say, to the consciousness of a people who were born only recently to the life of books and who only recently began to exercise their liberty.[75]

In Marechal's antiliberal opinion, the leaders of the nation did not exercise well its newly gained liberty. He views the period immediately following independence as a time of alienation of the nation in its material, moral, and spiritual aspects. He interprets *Martín Fierro* as an alarm to citizens that the nation was going down the wrong path, claiming that the book expresses "a state of the national soul in the most painful moment of its consciousness."[76]

Marechal puts the blame for what he identifies as a loss of spiritual and moral values on the ruling and intellectual class: "with the actions of those two ruling classes began the alienation or the estrangement of the country from its spiritual and material values."[77] He points out that the elite sector of Argentine society either chose to ignore the book when it came out or accepted it as a literary work with little consequence other than its entertainment value:

> The dramatic message of the poem cannot reach the ruling class, who suffer from a considerable deafness when it comes to that which concerns the voice of our people, nor can it be heard by the intellectual class, who already look to foreign horizons for creative and meditative material.[78]

The *pueblo*, on the other hand, embraced *Martín Fierro* from the get-go, buying copies sold in the *pulperías*, rural stores. The message, ignored by the upper classes, thereby returned to the people from which it came. "Why did this unheard message return to its origin? To maintain itself there, alive and awake like a votive flame."[79] In addition to the word "votive," he also uses the word "occult" to describe the work. In short, *Martín Fierro* is the reflection of the "national essence," and being such, "it opens a path to the popular consciousness."[80] *Martín Fierro*, like classical epics, has symbolic meaning:

> *Martín Fierro* is, like the classical epics, the heroic song of a people, that is to say, it is the story of the notable deeds accomplished as the manifestation of its essence and the achievement of its heroic destiny. Already one can see that *Martín Fierro* is an epic *ad intra*, that is to say, an inward epic, that the Argentine essence is obliged by circumstances to observe. It is the interior epic produced by the seed, before projecting its creative potential in the world at large.[81]

He reads *Martín Fierro* on a literal and symbolic level. Literally, the book's hero is a gaucho of the pampas, but symbolically, he is "the national essence in a critical moment of its history: it is the people of the nation, just after the war of independence and civil wars, attentive to the organization of forces needed to realize its heroic destiny."[82] Thus, Fierro's journey into the desert is interpreted as an expulsion of the national essence. Fierro (i.e., Argentina's national essence) is no longer the protagonist of his own destiny and withdraws himself from the drama. His sojourn in the desert in Marechal's reading is the "suspension of its destiny."[83]

Marechal's views on *Martín Fierro* are typical of the Peronist populists, who, as Nicolas Shumway puts it, "made of Martín Fierro a battlecry against the abuses of Argentine liberalism."[84] A similar interpretation of the work was articulated by Raúl Scalabrini Ortiz in a lecture titled "The Enemies of the Argentine People" (1948): "the oligarchy governed the country with no concern beyond the ambition and selfishness of their own. . . . *Martín Fierro* is the tragedy of the entire pueblo."[85] Although fond of what he interpreted to be the original political message, Marechal did not approve of the frenzy of criticism and imitation the work spawned half a century later. Although he admits that he can pardon some of the early ethnographic criticism which focused on the gaucho as prototype of the two races destined to disappear, what he insists he cannot pardon is "the torrent of bad literature that came after, as a natural consequence."[86]

In summary, in Marechal's opinion, the Argentines do have and are capable of having national expression which is universal and transcendent. *Martín Fierro*, however, he sees as relevant to the birth of the nation, rather than as a reflection of its current identity. As we have seen in his poems on the Homeland, Marechal's solution to the problem of national expression is literature that provides a spiritual itinerary. With these considerations in mind, we can now understand why he chose to rewrite Dante. *Adán Buenosayres*, however, is not itself proposed as a work that will provide this spiritual direction. Rather it is a parody of the contemporary Argentine situation. What better way to highlight Argentina's lack of a guiding fiction like the *Divine Comedy* than to use it as an intertext to provide contrast?

Although Dantean references are to be found throughout the sprawling novel, I will limit my focus to books 6 and 7, which are rewritings of the *Vita nuova* and *Inferno*, respectively. Before doing so, however, I will provide a brief overview of important aspects of books 1–5 that are related to our theme. Marechal accomplishes two main objectives in regard to national identity and Argentine literature in books 1–5. The first is to aim for an all-encompassing depiction of the demographic of Argentina, and specifically of Buenos Aires, in all its complexity and ethnic diversity. It is a counteroperation to the works of literature that sought to define Argentines though a very narrow lens, or as one particular race. Second, in these books he parodies the lack of consensus among the Argentine literary elite regarding which direction their national literature should take. I will provide just a few salient examples to illustrate both, and we need not look far.

The first descriptions of the population of Buenos Aires are to be found when Adán ventures out from his apartment into Monte Egmont Street, which is described as "One hell of a street, or a street from hell! The melting pot of races. *argentinopeya?*"[87] This clever neologism is a combination of "Argentina" and "epopeya" or epic. In this interior monologue Adán goes from musing on the hodgepodge of races in their "barbarous dissonance" to questioning the very possibility of their literary expression. As a poet, he is inclined to ask himself how the epic of such a land can be written, epic being the genre believed to best express the values of a race. This is, in fact, the central question of the novel: How to write the epic of modern-day Argentina? The novel itself is the response. The only way to depict such diversity and dissonance is to strive for an all-encompassing work that includes the various personas and their divergent viewpoints as characters in polyphony.

One passage that demonstrates the degree of ethnic diversity to be found in Buenos Aires is when Adán witnesses a fight that breaks out in front of the grocery store La Buena Fortuna and joins the curious crowd. Standing in the midst of the mob, he finds himself marveling at the faces surrounding him:

> There were Iberians of thick eyebrows who'd left northern Spain and their dedication to Ceres to come here and drive orchestral streetcars; there were those who drank from the torrential Miño River, men practiced in the art of argumentation; those from the Basque countries, the natural hardness of their heads concealed by blue berets. Then there were the Andalusian matadors, abundant in guitars and brawls. And industrious Ligurians, given to wine and song. Neopolitans erudite in the fruits of Pomona, who now wield municipal brooms. Turks of pitch-black mustachios, who sell soap, perfumed water, and combs destined for cruel uses. Jews wrapped in multi-coloured blankets, who love not Bellona. Greeks astute in the stratagems of Mercury. Dalmations of

> well-rivetted kidneys. The Syrio Lebanese, who flee not the skirmishes of Theology. And Japanese dry-cleaners. In short, all those who had come from the ends of the earth to fulfil the lofty destiny of the Land-which-from-a-noble-metal-takes-its-name. *Adam studied those unlikely faces and wondered about that destiny, and great was his doubt.*[88]

Adán, whose vocation is poet, understandably feels a certain amount of anxiety when he is confronted with the diverse demographic which he must presumably represent via his poetry. Yet he views this diversity positively, as is indicated by the fact that he stands there marveling. What we see in Marechal's passage that we haven't seen in works previously discussed is a consciousness of ethnic diversity and an inclusionary attitude toward the immigrant workforce seen as responsible for carrying out Argentina's destiny, a stance for which Perón gained his support.

Adán's friends have hilariously contrasting viewpoints when it comes to what it means to be Argentine. They are introduced to us as Luis Pereda, "theoretician of *criollismo*"; Arturo del Solar, "activist of *criollismo* and acting leader of the seven"; Franky Amundsen, "radio host and animator, heretofore known as the man of the jesting voice"; the pipsqueak Bernini, "sociologist, the one we've been calling pint-sized"; and Lucio Negri who represents progress, positivism, and science.[89] Although the protagonists may be divided in opinion, they are united in their endeavor to observe the true *porteño* reality, from its center to the periphery, and their nocturnal wanderings expose a world that is neither the elegance of Europe nor the stomping ground of the gauchos.

In one of their identity-oriented and angst-ridden conversations, Adán is asked about his "position as an Argentine." He responds, "Very confused. . . . Unable to endorse the reality our country's currently living, I'm alone and motionless: I'm waiting, I'm an Argentine in hope."[90] As Norman Cheadle points out in the notes, Adán's words echo the title of Scalabrini Ortiz's *El hombre que está solo y espera* (1931);[91] but in contrast to Scalabrini's *Hombre* who cuts his ties with European tradition, Marechal's Adán wishes to reform them:

> As for me, the situation is different: if upon arriving in this land my grandparents cut the thread of their tradition and destroyed their table of values, it's up

> to me to re-tie that thread and reconstruct myself according to the values of my race. That's what I'm trying to do. And it seems to me that when everybody does the same, the country will have a spiritual form.[92]

As we shall see in the following chapters, this is the reason that Marechal turns to Dante, to reconstruct himself according to the values of his race, and to highlight the necessity of spiritual direction for the creation of great art. Furthermore, as already indicated, the central motif of the work is entirely Dantean: Adán's journey is a "vía penetencial" (penetential way).[93]

Another important motif is also Dantean: the *Mujer Celeste* or *Madonna Intelligenza*. The very nucleus of *Adán Buenosayres*, the "internal motor," is Adán's notion of Solveig Amundsen, the Beatrice figure in the novel. As Marechal himself explains in "Las claves de *Adán Buenosayres*," at first Adán mistakenly seeks the terrestrial Solveig, abandoning the unity of his interior world (and behaving as a lovesick poet). Thus he is exposed to risks, temptations, and battles of the street in the first chapters. Over the course of the novel, he realizes that possessing the terrestrial Solveig should not be the aim of his loving. Just as in the *Vita nuova*, when the hero realizes that the terrestrial woman will die, he dedicates himself to praising "Solveig Celeste." The result of this resolution is "The Blue-Bound Notebook," discussed in the next chapter, which is a philosophical reflection close in structure to the *Vita nuova*, and heavily influenced by the doctrine of the Fedeli d'Amore.

SEVEN

Dante's *Vita nuova* and Book 6 of *Adán Buenosayres*: Solveig as Beatrice, Solveig as Argentina

In "El cuaderno de tapas azules" (The blue-bound notebook), book 6 of *Adán Buenosayres*, Leopoldo Marechal draws extensively from Dante to tell the story of the poetic development and spiritual growth of Adán, the poet/lover. The book is modeled after Dante's *Vita nuova*, which tells the story of Dante's learning to love Beatrice properly. At first Dante feels physical love for his unattainable lady, but eventually, through a process of divinization, Beatrice becomes a Christ-like figure who leads him to God. In Marechal's version of the story, Solveig Amundsen is not only a Christ-like Beatrice figure, but also a national-allegorical figure for Argentina. The soul's journey of learning how to love is both spiritual and national.

The many parallels between book 6 of *Adán Buenosayres* and Dante's *Vita nuova* have been pointed out by scholars such as Washington Benavídez, Donald L. Shaw, and Fernanda Elisa Bravo Herrera, and more thoroughly examined by José Ignacio Gallardo Ballestero.[1] In each case, the work is an interior monologue of the lover divided into numbered sections. They are similar in tone, featuring a high style of prose. Both are philosophical reflections on the nature of love. While the prose of the *Vita nuova* is structured around thirty-one poems, "The Blue-Bound Notebook" is primarily prose, but does feature a few of Marechal's verses. Both are works about transcendent love for an unattainable, Christ-like female figure.

Adán's journey starts off much like Dante's with symptoms of lovesickness due to the inaccessibility of his lady. Early in the first book of *Adán Buenosayres* we are introduced to his love for Solveig and the longing and suffering he must endure on account of it: "That empty hopeless feeling and the sting of humiliation were mellowing into something like nostalgia for a cherished impossibility."[2] Adán loves her "in his role as poet without apparent prospects."[3] Thus Adán is immediately associated with the courtly love tradition. We learn more about his adoration of Solveig from afar when he explains to his friend Samuel Tesler that his love has "only the fragile essence of an ideal construct, although this was based on a flesh-and-blood woman."[4] Tesler asks if Adán is "making incursions into the realm of Celestial Aphrodite." He documents his hypothesis with examples from ancient literatures, and Adán is forced to admit that he is indeed creating a heavenly woman based on an earthly one:

> The Visited [Tesler] proceeded to convince him of his happy hypothesis by means of an eloquent display of examples he claimed to have drawn from ancient literatures, both Oriental and Occidental, wherein discourse on divine love was so frequently couched in the language of human love that it bordered on gibberish. Convinced by such solid documentation, the Visitor admitted he was fashioning a heavenly woman on the basis of an earthly woman. The Visited, attentive to the metaphysical work of the Visitor, asked if the terrestrial woman was still indispensable to his labours of sublimation.[5]

What Tesler is referring to is the tradition of poets in both Eastern and Western literature to write of their love for God in terms of human love. Adán makes clear that his specific model is Dante. When Tesler asks Adán how he defines love, Adán says, "I'm looking for something transcendental, a definition in three bound volumes."[6] Marechal too was very clear about the influence of Dante and the Fedeli d'Amore. In "Claves de *Adán*

Buenosayres" he calls Dante "mi terrible maestro," and explains that he exerted his "great" and "definitive" influence not as author of the *Comedy*, but as the leader of the "Fedeli d'Amore."[7] Marechal continues to give a brief description of the fundamental principles of the Fedeli d'Amore in order to shed some light on *Adán Buenosayres*:

> I will limit myself to the following, in synthesis: a) the "fieles de Amor" celebrated, in the language of love, an enigmatic Lady; b) this woman, despite the different names given to her by each of her lovers (Beatrice, Giovanna, or Laura) is, in the end, a single and symbolic Woman; c) the notion of this woman is clarified in Dino Compagni when this "fiel de Amor" designates her by the name *Madonna Intelligenza*; d) Madonna symbolizes the transcendent Intellect through which man unites or can unite himself with God, and which is symbolized in her "passive or feminine perfection"; e) therefore, *Madonna* is the *Janua Coeli* (Gate of Heaven) and the *Sedes Papientae* (Seat of Wisdom) that Christians understand as the Virgin Mary.[8]

Marechal was familiar with the writings of Luigi Valli, poet and scholar of Dante, whose membership in the secret sect of the "Fedeli d'Amore" he theorized. In fact, Marechal owned five of Luigi Valli's texts, which today are kept in his personal library.[9] In 1968 he mentioned one of these texts in particular (*Il linguaggio segreto di Dante e dei "Fedeli d'Amore"*) and the influence it had on his work. In 1969 he explained in a public conference that Dante, along with Guido Cavalcanti, Cino da Pistoia, and a whole group of "metaphysical poets," belonged to a "secret organization."[10] Valli had a very esoteric reading of Dante influenced by Gabriele Pasquale Giuseppe Rossetti and Giovanni Pascoli. He believed that there existed a secret language of the Fedeli d'Amore that Dante knew, and that words such as *Amore*, *Madonna*, *Salute* had secret meanings which were known only to the initiates of the group. He also believed that all the women in the lyric poems of Dolce Stil Nuovo were the personification of Divine Wisdom, and that every word of Dante's *Vita nuova* has a symbolic meaning.[11]

So too book 6 of *Adán Buenosayres* has symbolic meaning; Solveig can be read as a national-allegorical figure for Argentina. Such a reading has already been suggested by Pedro Luis Barcia, although only in the form of a brief note in his edition of *Adán Buenosayres*, a note which accompanied a key passage in which Solveig is described as a girl coming of age: "With one foot still in childhood and the other in the dance of the world."[12] This is, as Barcia points out, a reference to Marechal's poem "De la patria joven," in which he says of the Patria: "Un pie arraigado en la niñez y el otro/ya tendido en los bailes de la tierra."[13] In the poem, discussed previously in chapter 6, the youthful Argentine nation is equated to a young girl at a crucial point of maturation. Now, considering that Solveig is declared to be "the primordial matter of any ideal construct,"[14] and that the entirety of *Adán Buenosayres* makes clear that the construction of Argentina is the work of poets/intellectuals, it follows that Solveig may be associated with Argentina.

In both cases, the actual entity does not correspond perfectly to the ideal construct it inspires. Adán fears greatly that he will no longer recognize the physical Solveig after having elaborated to such an extent the metaphysical Solveig:

> Sliding down the same old slope of his imagination, Adam hit a final doubt concerning himself both as lover and artist. After so much distance, after having transubstantiated the girl with his poetry, would *he* recognize the ideal Solveig of his notebook with he saw the flesh-and-blood Solveig?[15]

Furthermore, his ideal construction of Solveig is somewhat fragile considering that when she laughs at one of his verses, her laughter "detonate[s] the collapse of a poetic construction and the ruin of an ideal Solveig."[16] But ultimately, he knows his love for her is good, as it encourages him to effect reality with his spiritually driven good deeds: "What exemplary acts, what Franciscan gestures would he bring to bear against the thoughtless cruelty of Monte Egmont Street?" His love for Solveig makes him want to be a better person and causes him to reason in spiritual terms: "Looking critically at this latest wave of spiritual schmaltz, Adam understood it was linked to his anticipation of transcendental events in Saavedra."

Argentina, too, then could profit spiritually from such an ideal construction. But the Argentina described throughout the novel is chaotic and complex, and her inhabitants are described as lost, confused, and lacking consensus. We could read Adán's journey of how to love properly as the explanation of how to love his country properly, and as a guide for how poets should find the spiritual direction needed to create cultural cohesion.

The first indication that this book of love is also about Argentina and not just about a woman occurs in the first seven sections, which contrast with Dante's *Vita nuova*. Dante begins his story with the famous lines:

> In quella parte del libro de la mia memoria dinanzi a la quale poco si potrebbe leggere, si trova una rubrica la quale dice: *Incipit vita nova*. Sotto la quale rubrica io trovo scritte le parole le quali è mio intendimento d'assemplare in questo libello; e se non tutte, almeno la loro sentenzia.[17]

> (In that part of the book of my memory before which little can be read, there is a heading, which says: '*Incipit vita nova*: Here begins the new life.' Under that heading I find written the words that it is my intention to copy into this little book: and if not all, at least their essence.)[18]

With these words he informs his readers that in this book they will find everything he remembers pertaining to his new life, that is, pertaining to his love for Beatrice. True to his word, the first chapter details his first encounter with his love when she was but nine years old. He includes no information about his life prior to this fateful encounter.

"The Blue-Bound Notebook," on the other hand, begins: "My life, for the first ten years, offers nothing that merits the honour of the pen or the exercise of memory."[19] Marechal also begins with the idea of memory, and although he claims that the first ten years of his life are of no interest, goes on to describe early childhood memories of his homeland. In these first seven sections he does not follow the plot of the *Vita nuova*. He does, however, say that he writes "in the hope that my story, should it one day be published, may give consolation and support to those who follow the paths of Love."[20] We could interpret these lines as directed at those who will love women, or, given the content of the following pages, those who love Argentina.

The first part of book 6 is, according to Adán, "the story of my soul in its abstract aspect." He writes of the time when he had "one foot still in childhood":

> My childhood universe was the prairie of Maipú, open from horizon to horizon, and the house built in the lowlands, where the ever-present water attracted an avian world whose myriad black, white, and pink wings cut the air and furled back the light at the slightest provocation—the sudden intrusion of a horseman making his way through the trees, or the movement of an otter hunter setting his traps in the glade.[21]

In addition to describing the "infinitude of the countryside," he also describes the family house, and the rooms, faces, voices, and objects that were dear to him. Overwhelmed by his surroundings, he burst into tears, and his tears were not understood by the others of his lineage, "who laughed and cried for concrete reasons only."[22] His strong emotions are the foreshadowing of his vocation as poet, and the accompanying anxiety and yearning for expression. What causes him the most anxiety is the way things come into being and then decay. What he desires through poetry is a stability of Time and Space.

A formative memory of the protagonist that is described in detail is the wedding party held in the big house at Maipú. On this joyous occasion, in the midst of dancing a mazurka with his whole family, he has a macabre vision:

> I seemed to see time racing ahead in those women and men entwined in dance; I saw time working on them, making faces wrinkle, eyes grow sunken, gums deteriorate; I saw all of them twitching and curling like leaves in a burning tree; and I saw as well how the walls cracked, how the rooftops blackened, how the house in Maipú crumbled to dust.[23]

In other words, he realizes that his loved ones will die, and that even their beloved home is not eternal. This passage corresponds to Dante's vision of Beatrice's death in the *Vita nuova* (chap. 23). Adán, who has yet to mention Solveig, is distraught because Argentina as he knows it will die.

In parallel, the notion of Space brings him sorrow, "a perception enhanced by the prairie, whose expanse is measured in the lather of horses, and where east and west, north and south were roads sliding away to absence, points where eyes searched longingly for someone's return." The great expanses cause him to sob "like a child lost in a wood."[24] Recalling his childish tears, he remarks that "many children must still weep on the prairie, beneath the oppressive weight of southern nights, in order that joyous ascending pathways might be opened up in the pure sky of the Argentine fatherland."[25] It makes sense, then, that when he says he writes the work to "give consolation and support to those who follow the paths of Love" he is referring to fellow Argentines who deeply love their country.

Luckily the splendor of the forms on the prairie (the spikes of wheat, horses, and flowers) do not die. He dreams of the stability they will enjoy when he is able to immortalize them in the language of beauty. "And I knew that my destiny was to pursue beauty according to the movement of love."[26] He understands his vocation as poet. The emotions he feels at watching the passing of the seasons on the prairie awaken in him the urge to express himself. At first, possessing no art whatsoever, he resorts to incoherent words or free-form phrases, but later "art succeeded chaos, and musical order replaced incoherence."[27] This leads to his teacher Don Bruno exclaiming "Adam Buenosayres is a poet" when he is fourteen years old.

At the beginning of the third section he explains to the reader the divergent quality of this book, which will not contain anecdotes, "for its purpose has been to trace the story not of a man, but of his soul."[28] The soul's journey begins when the "uncertainty of her [the soul's] destiny then began to afflict her in such a way that finally, in looking at herself, her eyes filled with tears."[29] In contemplating her sorrow and regarding herself one day "in the bitter mirror of her tears," the soul realizes that she is "alone and immobile."[30] This is another important clue that book 6 is really the story of the search for national identity and expression. This same phrase is used by Adán to describe how he views his position as an Argentine: "Very confused. . . . Unable to feel solidarity with the reality currently experienced by the country, I'm alone and motionless: I'm waiting, I'm an Argentine in hope."[31]

Adán continues to describe the soul as "lost," and "always alone in the group of gathered beings, always immobile in the circle of those who moved."[32] This recalls Adán's behavior at the end of book 2. While the other characters are "wheeling to the strains of the 'Blue Danube,'" Adán stands "immobile in the centre of the round, as he was yesterday, as always. Until when?"[33] Although Solveig is present at the *salon*, he has very little interaction with her. The focus of the chapter is on the discussions of national identity that take place between him and the other characters. Similarly, while book 6 may seem ostensibly to be about Adán's love for a lady, the true focus, at least for the first seven sections, is his inexpressible love for Argentina.

The soul's journey of learning how to love is not only national, but also spiritual. In section 3, his soul sprouts a dove's wing, a Christian symbol for the Holy Spirit. This wing "spoke to her [the soul] of the potential for flight." It is after the growth of the wing that Adán realizes that what is required is not only a moveable Lover, but also "an immobile Beloved."[34] But at the time the figure of the Beloved remained hidden from his soul. If we continue our national-allegorical reading, this necessity could be interpreted as a need to create a fixed construct out of what is the complex flux of Argentina.

In section 4 Adán describes a vision in which he finds himself "in an immense wasteland." He tries to advance through the "desolate place" but struggles greatly until a graceful Man (Christ) appears and speaks to him in a "fiery idiom." Adán follows him into the blackness, and the "wasteland, at the mere touch of his feet, turned into a most pleasant garden." This section contrasts what Marechal believes to be the current state of Argentine letters (a wasteland) with her potential glory (a luscious garden) that can only be achieved through Christ. The direction found by following Christ results in community: "amid the flowers, thronged bright and nimble beings who, seeking one another, joined to dance in a thousand rounds."[35] But this glorious vision is fleeting. When Adán loses sight of the man, a chill wind blows across the garden and he finds himself once again on the barren plain.

In section 5 the soul loses herself in her love for her surroundings and becomes divided on account of the multiplicity of her love:

> And I emphasize the nature of her [the soul's] movement so that my reader (should these pages of mine ever have one) may follow the soul on her path of love and surmount the obscurity, more apparent than real, of her story. I said she distanced herself from her centre in each revolution of the spiral; I say now that, from call to call and from love to love, she went so far away that she eventually lost and forgot herself. In forgetting her own essence, she was converted to the essence of what she loved; a singular being, she found herself divided into the multiplicity of her loves.[36]

Adán, like Dante, realizes the failure of his many earthly loves and repents: "she [his soul] came to suspect the failure was due not to the nature of her movement but to its direction." In other words, his soul realizes that there is failure in multiplicity and that direction is to be found in Christ. The soul, realizing she's "lost deep in a wood," tries to return to the first intimacy with Christ. From that point on the soul belongs to neither life nor death, but to a "frontier position" where life and death were both similar and different from one another.[37]

As in the *Vita nuova*, dreams are key to the interpretation of the narrative. In the seventh section, Adán describes a strange dream that begins in a barren landscape. He sees a star with an axis of the naked body of a woman, which commanded the four directions of the sphere: the head to the north, feet to the south, right arm to the east, the left to the west. Adán has trouble looking directly at this glorious vision: "I understood in my dream-state that as soon as my eyes looked up toward the prodigious vision, they wanted to lower again, as though they refused to contemplate it. Seeing this, the Lord of the night repeated his command: 'Look!'"[38] This is similar to Dante's difficulty in gazing at Beatrice in *Paradiso*. First in canto 1, Dante looks as Beatrice looks into the sun, but cannot sustain the vision:

> Molto è licito là, che qui non lece
> a le nostre virtù, mercé del loco
> fatto per proprio de l'umana spece.
> Io nol soffersi molto, né sì poco,
> ch'io nol vedessi sfavillar dintorno,
> com'ferro che bogliente esce del foco; (55–60).[39]

Again in canto 23, his eyes cannot sustain the brightness, and Beatrice commands him to look upon her again:

> e per la viva luce trasparea
> la lucente sustanza tanto chiara
> nel viso mio, che non la sostenea
> . . . .
> "Apri li occhi e riguarda qual son io;
> tu hai vedute cose, che possente
> se' fatto a sostener lo riso mio." (31–33; 46–48)

Adán, like Dante, stresses the difficulty of communicating his vision and feelings in language. He hears the sound of the spheres, "a deep sound, like a bow drawn across a string," which recalls the music of the spheres in the *Divine Comedy*.[40] When his eyes reach the image of the woman crucified on the sphere (she is clearly Christ-like), he surrenders utterly to her. He admits that she was not the same lady he had seen before, but rather "a sublimation of the other one." He realizes that the light emanating from her does not come directly from her, but he doesn't yet realize it comes from God:

"Afterward, the spell seemed to break when it occurred to me that the light shining from the woman of the sphere was not hers, but that it came from some sun, not yet visible to me, of which she would be the moon or mirror."[41] This vision of the woman on the cross is the vision of Argentina as seen through his soul's newfound spiritual lens. The emphasis on the cardinal directions enforces the idea that the interpretation of this vision should be linked to land.

With the end of the dream he closes the story of his soul in its abstract aspect. While sections 1–7 shared little similarity with the *Vita nuova*, sections 8 and onward mirror the plot closely. Section 8 begins, "It was springtime in Buenos Aires the day and the hour when she first appeared to me; her real name will not be written in these pages."[42] These lines reinforce the connection between Argentina and the beloved lady and will be repeated in section 9.[43] The fact that Solveig's name is not mentioned is in accordance with the conventions of courtly love which require that the beloved remained unnamed so as to protect her identity. In this section, Adán attends a gathering in a garden at Saavedra, where he talks to the women of the house, "all young and of gracious aspect."[44] The scene mirrors chapter 14 of *Vita nuova*, where Dante accompanies a friend to a gathering of gracious ladies where he knows Beatrice will be present:

> Appresso la battaglia de li diversi pensieri avvenne che questa gentilissima venne in parte ove molte donne gentili erano adunate; a la qual parte io fui condotto per amica persona, credendosi fare a me grande piacere, in quanto mi menava là ove tante donne mostravano le loro bellezze.[45]
>
> (After the war of divergent thoughts it chanced that this most graceful one came where many gentle ladies were gathered: to which place I was led by a friend, thinking to give me great delight, by showing me the place where so many ladies were displaying their beauty.)[46]

When Dante sees his beloved, he is assaulted by *spiritelli,* and fears giving his love away to the others present who start noticing his strange, lovesick behavior. Similarly, when Adán sees Solveig, he is overwhelmed by her presence, finds himself incapable of response, and is fearful that others might notice his confusion. While the only colors of clothing said to be worn by Beatrice are crimson and white (chapters 2 and 3), Solveig is dressed in azure (the color of the Argentine flag) both here in this section and later in section 11 when she meets Adán in a garden wearing a "sky-blue dress."[47] Adán, like Dante, is captivated by his lady's smile, which "went before her like an emissary."[48] She chastely lowers her eyes in greeting. Marechal describes her as being at the brink of her coming of age, much as he describes the Patria in "De la patria joven" and "Descubrimiento de la patria":

> Her youth was not yet in full flower, but rather the whole of her, in my eyes, hinted at a dawn comparable to the moment of first light hesitating at the brink of day.[49]

He also describes her as "fragile clay" and says that "her form seemed ready to sprout, painfully, like the bud of the leaf that swells and breaks and ventures a new lobe." This recalls Adán's speech on how the poet would sacrifice all for his vocation and stop at nothing: "Imagine a rosebush on the verge of producing a rose, and just then the angel's trumpet announces the end of the world. Would the rosebush stop?"[50]

Her grace makes Adán recall "the friend's" poem. While Dante mentions repeatedly in *Vita nuova* his "first friend" (generally believed to be Cavalcanti), here Marechal's "friend" is in this case himself, for the verses come from one of his own poems, "De la adolescente" (On the adolescent girl), first published in *Odas para el hombre y la mujer* (1929):

> Entre mujeres alta ya,
> la niña quiere llamarse Viento.[51]
>
> (Among women already tall,
> the girl wants to be called Wind.)

His response to witnessing her beauty is to leave the gathering and return to his room, "wishing to measure in solitude the proportions of that new conflict."[52] This is similar to Dante's reaction to encountering Beatrice in chapter 3: "ricorsi a lo solingo luogo d'una mia camera, e puosimi a pensare di questa cortesissima."[53] When Adán arrives home he begins to mentally reconstruct "The One," and his reconstruction is so perfect "that my soul again trembled in wonder before the image alone."[54] The verses that come to mind when he is in this state of contemplation are yet another indication that this reconstruction of Solveig should also be read as a metaphysical construct of Argentina. As Adán is gazing at the stars, a chorus of childish voices reaches his ears:

> Entre San Pedro y San Juan
> hicieron un barco nuevo:
> las velas eran de plata,
> los remos eran de acero . . . (489)
>
> (Between Saint Peter and Saint John
> they build a new boat:
> the sails were of silver,
> the oars were of steel.)

These quoted lines, the only ones in book 6 besides Marechal's own verses from "De la adolescente," are taken from a traditional Argentine children's song that continues: "Saint Peter was the pilot, / Saint John was a sailor, / and the captain-general / was Jesus of Nazareth."[55] The rather unexpected inclusion of these lines here once again links Solveig both to Argentina and to Catholicism.

Adán, having finally properly learned to love his lady, fears straying from the divine love back to the earthly love. "Will you again descend into the finitude and danger of earthly love, after having attained the notion of an infinite love?"[56] He fears that perhaps this too might be earthly love, but quickly discards this possibility due to the newfound rhythm of his soul. It is his love for Solveig that has given him a new life. Before loving her, his soul knew only "the sterile flight of my intelligence above its own ruin."[57] After finding Solveig, he has one divine purpose and direction: "I'll say now that, under the sole influence of the creature revealed in Saavedra, my whole being seemed to surrender to the rhythm of a nascent life and to a feeling of astonishment, a rising-up from the ashes."[58] He is like a phoenix, born again. He becomes a better person and is better able to love those around him: "a delicious intelligence of love was one with a desire to press the living sheaf of creatures tightly to my soul."[59] The phrase "intelligence of love" recalls Dante's famous canzone "Donne ch'avete intelletto d'amore."[60]

Like Beatrice, Solveig is associated with a "harmonious number."[61] In Dante it is the number nine, in order to associate Beatrice with the Holy Trinity. Once he learns to love properly, Adán cannot think of Solveig without thinking of God, her maker. His lady is not the object of his thoughts, but rather "a bridge of silver offered to I knew not what new pilgrimage of my mind."[62] These lines strengthen the connection between Solveig and Argentina (which takes its name from the Latin word for silver, *argentum*), while perhaps also referencing Dante the pilgrim.

When Adán urgently wants to see Solveig again, he knows not how to arrange a meeting. He does not want to go alone to Saavedra, for fear of revealing his secret. He instead tries to encounter her in the Barrancas de Belgrano park, where he knows she walks home from school with classmates. Awaiting her appearance on the horizon, Adán experiences all the typical symptoms of lovesickness, such as a rapidly beating heart, which plague Dante in the *Vita nuova:*

> I kept my eyes on the path's most distant point where she would rise like the dawn. My heart had begun to beat frantically, its drumbeats intensifying as the moment of truth approached.[63]

When Solveig doesn't appear, he experiences chills and self-pity, and wants to weep but finds no more tears. He looks into his being for the image of "The One," and the truth comes to him: "until that moment I'd believed that the woman of Saavedra, in all the empire of her truth, was within me; as it turned out, however, she did not reside within me, but I within her."[64]

In section 11 he does encounter Solveig again when he goes with the "friend" to the garden of their first encounter. Her arrival is heavenly. He hears her speak, and her voice is "warm, dry and golden as a spike of wheat."[65] This unusual use of synesthesia (a spike of wheat is related to her voice, i.e., the sense of sound) is a clear indication that we are to associate Solveig with Argentina, wheat being one of the country's main agricultural products. He also continues to associate her with memories of his childhood in Maipú.

In her presence he feels "the strange beatitude of living in poetry."[66] Everything is music, poetry, understanding of the divine: "she would say 'bird' and the essence of the bird appeared in the mind of her listener in a hitherto unknown light, as if The One somehow had the virtue of recreating the bird merely by saying its name."[67]

Then comes an interesting passage in which Adán reccounts how his "Friend" taught him about love. As aforementioned, the "friend" in Dante's

Vita nuova is generally believed to be Cavalcanti. In book 6, Adán's first mention of "Friend" refers to Marechal himself. Here the Friend gives him advice on loving:

> The first thing he pointed out was the loving virtue thanks to which the Lover, with eyes turned toward the Beloved, forgets himself, exchanges his form for the form of what is loved, dies by degrees to his own life, and comes to life again in the life of the Other; until finally the Lover transforms into the Beloved.[68]

Fernanda Bravo Herrera believes the friend in this case to be Dante himself, who has taught Marechal (Adán) all that he knows about love.[69] This is a viable possibility, as is the possibility that "Friend" is, as before, Marechal, who has in turn learned how to love from Dante. It could be that a more mature Marechal instructs Adán (the literary version of his younger self during the 1920s) what he has since learned.

Then it is Adán's turn to speak, and he relates the drama of the Lover converted to the Beloved who hides or flees or ignores the Lover. As he describes the anguish of the Lover, his lady looks at him with great compassion. He visits her many times, on glorious and light-filled days, but one afternoon, as they stroll through the perfumed garden, he comes to the painful realization that one day she will die:

> The grotto-like light, eroding shapes and forms, managed to exalt them miraculously; and the form of The One assumed for me a painful relief, a plenitude which, once glimpsed, made me shake with anguish, as if so much grace, so slightly supported, suddenly revealed to me how perilous her fragility was. And again the admonitory drums of the night began to beat in my soul, and before my terrified eyes I watched as The One withered and fell among the roses, she as mortal as they.[70]

He starts crying. She asks him why he is crying. Upon hearing her pronounce his name, it is as though he witnesses the complete revelation of his being. He cannot shake his fear that she will one day die. So distressed is he that he cannot return to the garden to visit her. But he recovers her in thought. After constant meditation on "The One" and her death, he reconstructs her in his soul. His resolution is to immortalize her in poetry. He says that he described the details of his love for his lady in an "obscure poem," the scope of which his friends did not understand. This corresponds to the end of the *Vita nuova*, when Dante declares his intention to say of Beatrice what has never been said of any woman: "Sì che, se piacere sarà di colui a cui tutte le cose vivono, che la mia vita duri per alquanti anni, io spero di dicer di lei quello che mai non fue detto d'alcuna."[71] Adán hopes that one day his friends will be able to discern the hidden meaning of his verses:

> My hope is that, should their eyes chance upon these lines some day, my
> friends will remember the poem and finally discern its obscure meaning;
> I hope they'll see why in the last phase I called the transmuted woman:
> *Niña-que-ya-no-puede-suceder*, "Girl-who-can-no-longer-happen."[72]

This mysterious line suggests that Adán's poetry has secret symbolic meaning, just as Luigi Valli believed Dante's poetry to contain secret meanings only apparent to the Fedeli d'Amore.

The notebook, allegedly written by Adán, is then abruptly interrupted by a note from its transcriber, L.M. (Leopoldo Marechal):

> (Note: The following chapters bring the Blue-Bound Notebook to a close. They were written, no doubt, by Adam Buenosayres after his definitive salon in Saavedra. The manuscript lies before me now, awaiting transcription. But before continuing, I contemplate its tormented lines, full of scratched-out phrases and corrected words, altogether different from the handwriting in the first part of the Notebook, whose exquisiteness speaks of an artist's slow, painstaking work. This last part begins with an extravagant fable or apologue. . . .)[73]

In the last part of the Notebook, he gives a detailed account of how he stores the virtues of Solveig in his soul, "where they might acquire the stability of things spiritual."[74] At this juncture he becomes aware of the opposition between the earthly woman and the celestial woman whom he is building in his soul. As the spiritual creature grows, the earthly creature diminishes, until the death of the earthly Solveig becomes inevitable. When "The One" dies, he is devastated, much like Dante upon losing Beatrice.

The final section of book 6, section 14, describes a strange vision. Adán dreams he is in a rickety boat, paddling ceaselessly over the waters of a lagoon. The corpse of The One lies across the bow of the boat. As he rows he stirs up chunks of dead meat. He takes her body in his arms up a set of stairs and deposits it inside a room. The door closes, and he is separated from her body. An old man appears and says, "Let death take its own." It is God: "I am he who has moved, moves, and will move your steps." God instructs him, "Pay no more mind to multitudinous images, and seek the single, true face of The One."[75] At that point, he suddenly awoke.

> Ever since then my life has had a well-defined direction, a well-placed hope in the vision of The One who, redeemed by the work of my loving mind, breathes in my mind and is nourished by my substance, rose that eludes death.[76]

The image of the Beloved being "nourished" by the "substance" of the poet recalls Dante's dream (chapter 3) in which the personification of Love feeds Dante's bleeding heart to Beatrice. However, Dante's vision at the beginning of the *Vita nuova* reflects a love that is yet physical and sexual; Adán's vision at the end of the soul's journey, on the other hand, is strictly spiritual. His lady exists in his mind only as a construct, and is nourished as the fruit of his thoughts. The Notebook ends with Adán saying that Solveig now triumphs in her immutable springtime and that she continues to transform and grow according to his soul's desire. He says that he will know her perfect form and unique form if "there is a day when man's thirst finds the right water and its true spring."[77]

In this chapter, I hope to have shown that Solveig, Adán's Beatrice, clad not in crimson but in the colors of the Argentine flag, is a clear allegory of Argentina. This reading of Solveig has several implications for our reading of book 7, "Journey to the Dark City of Cacodelphia," and also for the conclusions of this study. Let us recall that in the final chapter of the *Vita nuova*, Dante says that he will write no more of Beatrice until he can do so "più degnamente" (more worthily). To arrive at his goal, he will study as much as possible "com'ella sae veracemente" (how she really is). He vows that if, God willing, he lives long enough, he hopes to "dicer di lei quello che mai non fue detto d'alcuna" (to write of her what has not been written of any woman) (chap. 42). It is widely acknowledged that this promise alludes to Dante's future writing of the *Divine Comedy*, as do the final lines of the *Vita nuova*:

> E poi piaccia a colui che è sire de la cortesia, che la mia anima se ne possa gire a vedere la gloria de la sua donna, cioè di quella benedetta Beatrice, la quale gloriosamente mira ne la faccia di colui *qui est per omnia secula benedictus.*[78]

> (And then may it be pleasing to Him who is the Lord of courtesy, that my soul might go to see the glory of its lady, that is of that blessed Beatrice, who gloriously gazes on the face of Him *qui est per omnia secula benedictus*: who is blessed throughout all the ages.)[79]

This of course prefigures when Dante is finally able to gaze on Beatrice in *Paradiso*. Furthermore, the phrase "*qui est per omnia secula benedictus*" creates a deliberate ambiguity between Beatrice and Christ. Thus the writing of the *Vita nuova*, which is the story of Dante's journey of learning to love Beatrice properly (that is, by associating her with Christ), ultimately leads to his writing a much greater work, the *Divine Comedy*. Now, in terms of book 6 of *Adán Buenosayres*, if Solveig is Beatrice, and Solveig is Argentina, then it follows that by learning to love her properly (that is, with some spiritual direction), the poet will enable himself to write of her what has never been written of any other country. It is through a spiritually directed nationalism, Marechal suggests, that the authoring of Argentina's *Divine Comedy* will come about. What Marechal is *not* in any way suggesting is that *Adán Buenosayres* itself is this work. Rather, the sublimity of book 6 is followed by the inanity, absurdity, and vulgarity of book 7, "Journey to the Dark City of Cacodelphia," which is a parody of Dante's *Divine Comedy* and a reflection of the sorry state of Argentine letters.

EIGHT

The Journey to Cacodelphia: A Parody of *Inferno* and Modern-Day Argentina

Book 7, "Journey to the Dark City of Cacodelphia," is by far the longest section in *Adán Buenosayres*, spanning approximately a third of the entire novel. Marechal's inferno is a downward-spiraling helicoid track ordered loosely after Dante's *Inferno* and *Purgatory*, where each spiral corresponds to a different infernal barrio or *cacobarrio* (shit neighborhood).[1] As the astrologer Schultz, the creator of this infernal realm, explains to Adán, Cacodelphia (hell) and Calidelphia (paradise) are two aspects of the same city: "And that Urb, visible only to the eyes of the intellect, is the counterfigure of the visible Buenos Aires."[2] But Calidelphia has yet to be written, thus leaving only an inferno as the intelligible representation of Buenos Aires. The concept of the "visible" and "invisible" Buenos Aires alludes to Eduardo Mallea's 1937 essay "Historia de una pasión argentina." For Mallea, the visible Argentina was false and inauthentic, while the invisible Argentina was true and spiritual.[3] Marechal, seeking to highlight the spiritual depravity of the city, makes the invisible Buenos Aires an inferno that exaggerates elements of the visible Buenos Aires depicted in books 1–5.

The journey begins on Saturday, April 30, in the lowlands of Saavedra, at midnight. The astrologer Schultz is Adán's "strange Virgil" and is also the demiurge who created Cacodelphia. They depart on a night when the "calm, humid air creates a dense and static atmosphere, like a womb pulsing with the seeds of future upheavals."[4] The association of the city with a womb indicates that Buenos Aires is only in embryo, while "seeds of future upheavals" seems to prophecy a potentially tumultuous future.

When Schultz announces to Adán that he is destined to make the journey, Adán is plunged into doubt, for it is "a descent undertaken by precious few heroes even in antiquity, and by not a one, as far as I know, in the vulgar, prosaic age we live in now."[5] He is unsure whether he is worthy: "Even if we were crazy enough to follow in the footsteps of Ulysses, Aeneas, Alighieri, and other infernal tourists, what merit do we have that would make us worthy of such an adventure?" Schultz's response is that Adán has the merit of "penitence." Adán's reluctance mirrors Dante the pilgrim's humility and doubt when he learns of his predestined voyage. But given the national-allegorical significance of the novel, we might also read Adán's response as follows: Adán is the primary representative of Argentina, a new modern nation, and he doubts his position with regard to other world cultures, specifically with regard to European high culture. Schultz's response signifies that the country is in a state of penitence, having lost its spiritual path, and must regain this path before finding self-expression.

To enter hell, the two perform a ritual that involves tying a string to the trunk of an ombú tree and inscribing names in the sand: Santos Vega, Juan sin Ropa, and Martín Fierro.[6] Whereas previously Adán expressed his feeling of inferiority with respect to classical heroes, here he is forced to acknowledge Argentina's greatest literary heroes. As they enter hell through the ombú, Adán loses consciousness, thus echoing Dante's fall into unconsciousness in canto 3, 134–36. Adán warns readers at this point to think about whether they hadn't better flee the ombú and go back to the visible Buenos Aires instead of making the difficult descent.

Once in the suburbs of Cacodelphia, they find themselves in a dense fog that hinders their progress, and they stop to wait for it to pass. This mirrors the pause made by Virgil and Dante in canto 11 so that they might become accustomed to the stench of lower hell. In both instances, the hindrance, whether visual or olfactory, serves as a pause in the narrative action so that the structure of hell can be explained. Here Schultz sketches the basic outline of Cacodelphia's architectural plan and tells how he constructed the city:

> —When I decided to give a visible image to the intelligible Cacodelphia, the astrologer began, my first concern was to avoid crass imitations. Wary, then, of building a garden-variety Inferno, I conceived the form of the inverted-empty-cone, which I called *Divicone*, within which the Cacodelphians would be placed as though inside a gigantic glass, according to the greater or lesser burden of their souls. . . .
>
> —A poetic idea, I commented.
>
> —You're right, poetic, Schultz allowed. Merely poetic. I was obliged to discard it.
>
> —Why?
>
> —Because of its imprecision, typical of everything poetic. I needed to organize my infernal space mathematically so as to make it comprehensible and passable. So then I dreamed up a subterranean skyscraper. . . .
>
> —A prosaic idea.[7]

In the end, fearing that an inverted skyscraper with an elevator would look like "the Gath & Chaves department store during a liquidation sale," Schultz decides on a downward-spiraling helicoid track for his design: "It is made up of nine stages or turns of the spiral, each of them being the site of an infernal barrio or *cacobarrio*."[8]

The nine circles in question are:

Circle 1: The Neutrals
Circle 2: Lust
Circle 3: Gluttony
Circle 4: Avarice and Prodigality
Circle 5: Sloth
Circle 6: Envy
Circle 7: Wrath
Circle 8: Pride
Circle 9: The Great Pit

Dante's *Inferno*, on the other hand, proceeds in the following manner:

Circle 0: The Neutrals
Circle 1: Limbo
Circle 2: Lust
Circle 3: Gluttony
Circle 4: Avarice and Prodigality
Circle 5: Anger and Sullenness
Circle 6: Heresy
Circle 7: Violence
Circle 8: Simple Fraud
Circle 9: Treachery

The order of sins dealt with in Cacodelphia is actually closer to an inverted Mount Purgatory than it is to the Inferno, given that Marechal leaves both Limbo and Heresy out altogether and deals differently with the lowest circles. But if Schultz's Helicoid followed an inverted order of Mount Purgatory, the order of progression would be Lust; Gluttony; Avarice; Sloth; Wrath; Envy; Pride. We can see, then, that Marechal has inverted the order of Wrath and Envy, making wrath the more intellectual of these two sins.

Cacodelphia	Dante's Purgatory (inverted)
The Neutrals	Earthly Paradise
Lust	Lust
Gluttony	Gluttony
Avarice and Prodigality	Avarice and Prodigality
Sloth	Sloth
Envy	Wrath
Wrath	Envy
Pride	Pride
The Great Pit	

One aspect of Dante's scheme that Marechal adheres to closely in the construction of Cacodelphia is that the severity of the sin is linked to the degree of intellectualism with which the sinner committed it. While the circle of the neutrals and the sins of incontinence are associated with the Argentine masses, the lowest rings of the Helicoid are reserved for the intellectuals, and it is there that we will encounter most of Adán's friends. In fact, his best friend, the philosopher Samuel Tesler, will be our guide through the lowest circle, that of Pride. I will not treat of the various sections of Cacodelphia in the order they occur, but rather will save the most biting parodies of Argentine authors for last, and instead will start my discussion in the circle of Pride, with the worst sinner we encounter in Cacodelphia—Don Ecuménico.

Don Ecuménico is an uber-intellectual and failed poet. He has one of the longest speeches of any of the characters to explain his story of perdition, which at twenty pages comprises approximately 9 percent of the entire inferno.[9] His is the most intellectual of sins, and his punishment is to remain in the form of a gigantic Kafkaesque insect. His head is like that of a common butterfly, with a pair of protruding eyes, two fuzzy palpi, and a spiral-proboscis. His thorax has little legs and wings that are yellow, red, and blue. He is a talking bug who tells Adán and Schultz his whole life story, without, however, repenting: "when Don Ecuménico spoke of 'punishment' his tone was shamelessly cold and academic, with none of the contrition that would have been good to hear from a creature thrown by the gods into the eighth circle of an inferno."[10]

Don Ecuménico's sin is agnosticism. Already as a child, he claims, his "metaphysical distrust" grew to the point that he came to doubt "the regularity of natural phenomena."[11] He had a "curiously premature 'tragic sense of life'" and was prone to crying fits over the instability of existence.[12] His true perdition occurs following the death of his wife and child and is attributed to literature: "I had previously renounced the deceitful parade of images, passions, and sentiments that constitute a human existence—and what did literature do, if not multiply those images, stylize the passions, and fictionally prolong the colourful lie of worldly things?"[13] His perdition, or fall, occurs in three stages, which he refers to as "somersaults." In the first somersault he reads texts of orthodox theologians; in the second, stranger conceptions about the Divinity; and in the third, he devours oriental texts about a Non-Being anterior to God.

These readings bring about the metamorphosis of his soul. He starts out by fading and becoming ghost-like. He is increasingly lethargic and eventually undergoes a gradual process of metamorphosis into an insect. As a bug he ravenously devours more and more books, becoming larger and larger until a cocoon forms around his body. When he breaks free from the cocoon in the form of a butterfly, he flies out the opened skylight and descends directly into Cacodelphia.

Don Ecuménico's metamorphosis is what Marechal invents as punishment for intellectuals whose intellectualism and literary endeavors are not guided by a belief in God. For Marechal, agnosticism was a dangerous path. In the essay "Sobre la inteligencia argentina," he criticizes Romantic sentimentalism, which he describes as a rebellion against intelligence that leads to an inversion of order, causing the religious individual to turn against his spiritual authority. Philosophically speaking, "it will end in the most pure agnosticism by converting philosophy into a mere game of literary creation."[14] Interestingly, this is how the "Journey to the Dark City of Cacodelphia" and indeed the whole novel will end, in a mere game of empty literary play. The episode underscores Marechal's main point that what Argentina needs in order to avoid perdition, is a foundational text, like the *Divine Comedy*, that is spiritually driven.[15]

When Don Ecuménico, the epitome of pure agnosticism, flies away, Schultz and Adán enter the ninth and final circle of hell, which is a giant pit inhabited by a gelatinous mass known as the Paleogogue. When Schultz asks Adán his opinion on the beast, Adán, although speechless after the story of Don Ecuménico, now launches into a steady stream of absurd metaphors:

> Nastier than a fright at midnight. Got more gills than a dorado. Serious as a monk's codpiece. More ingratiating than a rich man's dog. Sharp-pointed, like an old man's knife. More puckered than an immigrant's tobacco pouch. Shit-smeared, like the boot of a Basque dairyman. More ornery than a draw-wheel nag. Uglier than a pig's somersault. Tougher than a vizcacha's paw. Skittish as a washerwoman's pony. Solemn as the fart of an Englishman.[16]

The text ends abruptly there, which seems to imply that Adán's mad string of metaphors will continue ad infinitum, or at least as long as it takes him to find spiritual direction. His metaphors are descriptions of the Paleogogue, which is the conglomeration of all the sins encountered in Cacodelphia's many barrios.

The Barrios of Cacodelphia

Each barrio or *cacobarrio* of Cacodelphia is equated to an area of Buenos Aires or its surroundings. Where the neutrals are punished, the landscape is said to be like that of the pampas:

> I looked and for an instant wondered whether what my eyes were seeing was in the realm of reality or fiction. Extending as far as the horizon, in a patchwork of salt flats and sand dunes, was a cheerless plain, arid and monotonous, cracked and furrowed by drought, shiny with saltpeter.[17]

Adán, who as we know from books 1–5 is used to conflating reality with flights of imagination, here also has difficulty distinguishing between the two. The "monotonous" plain is home to the neutrals, equated with the Argentine masses:

> Men and women, infinite in number, were swarming in throngs over the plain, running here and there, randomly, like autumn leaves swirling in unsettled winds: the multitude would pause suddenly, its thousands of heads swiveling round like so many indecisive weathervanes; then women and men would go back to running, knocking into each other, pausing, raising their revolving heads.[18]

After devouring the newsprint, magazines, and posters that rained down upon them like "grubby manna," they pulled down their pants, lifted up their skirts, and "solemnly defecated." Adán asks:

> What people are they, writhing in such agitation on the plain? All those faces look familiar to me, as if I'd seen them a thousand times on Florida Street, in Luna Park, or at the Boca Juniors' stadium.
>
> —It's poor old Demos, answered Schultz, our great *majority*, equally inclined to good and to evil, who go whichever way the wind blows. These days, it's clear from their actions and words that the majority is wooed by contemptible winds. But with this very clay, a Neogogue will work wonders.[19]

As explained earlier in chapter 6, this mention of a Neogogue who can work wonders is undoubtably a reference to Perón, who in Marechal's opinion had given direction to the otherwise directionless masses. Their place in Cacodelphia is this suburb of the irresponsible, those who cannot be held accountable. As Schultz explains to Adán, those who bear responsibility are to be found inside the Helicoid. They enter by sliding down a *holitoboggan*, Schultz's *neocriollo* word for a holy slide.[20] Schultz slides down first and is followed by a reluctant Adán, who hurls himself down after him, "cursing *in pectore* the infernal inventor who'd dreamed up that puerile transit system."[21] Thus the astrologer's *neocriollo* neologism (*holitoboggan*) is contrasted with Adán's Latinisms (*in pectore* and puerile); but in both cases their linguistic choices come across as excessive and unnatural. Adding to the humor of this parodic passage is the fact that Schultz (Virgil) heedlessly launches himself down the slide without Adán, which is contrary to what we expect him to do based on our recollection of canto 23, where Virgil slides down the slope to the sixth pouch of the Eighth Circle of Hell with Dante cradled safely in his arms.

As in the *Divine Comedy*, living souls who wish to enter the realm of the dead must first contend with Charon the ferryman. In Marechal's version Charon is an immigrant from Galicia wearing blue overalls. Adán recognizes him as the bus driver of Number 38. Charon refuses to give them crossing, stating, "I'm taking a grievance to the Union!" Both Schultz and Adán are hostile to him, and as in the *Comedy*, it is the guide who sees to it that he follows his duty, grudgingly or not. Schultz scolds him for having lost all the dignity he once had prior to his immigration:

> —You used to plough your land, prune your vineyard, slaughter your pig, sing the carols your mother taught you, and profess the wisdom of your grandparents. Admit it, bagpipe: you used to have wonderful dignity [in Galicia]. Do you admit it or not?
>
> —I admit it, stuttered the fellow in blue, intimidated.
>
> —And what did you do, as soon as you got to Buenos Aires? Schultz asked him in a pained tone.
>
> —Well, I . . .
>
> —You let your hair grow like a *compadrito*, you tied a silk scarf around your neck. You were seen in the neighborhood dance halls, strutting like a bully and making unheard-of efforts to imitate characters straight out of Vacarezza melodramas.
>
> —But . . .

> —There's a "but," I know, continued Schultz. No sooner did you open your mouth than you gave yourself away. So you started to swallow the "j"s and the "u"s that made you suspect, and you learned the local argot—*cathouse* and *broads* and *slammer* and *hey buster!* In a word, you forgot the dignity you surely once had, and crassly imitated your new environment.[22]

As we will learn a few pages later, this is the only time Schultz will get so angry at one of the inhabitants of Cacodelphia. Schultz's tirade against Charon brings up two key themes of book 7: loss of values and crass imitation. This passage reiterates the ideas articulated by Adán in book 2 at the salon at the Amundsen house, namely that the recently immigrated have lost touch with their roots and suffered a moral degeneration following the process of immigration.

Charon is only the first of the degenerate immigrants encountered in Cacodelphia. Once he boats them across the lagoon full of black monoliths, Adán and Schultz find themselves in an impoverished shantytown, reminiscent of a *conventillo*:

> At first I could see only a lustrous grey sky, a dense shower falling from it. But then, through the rain, I could make out a shantytown, a random scatter of shapeless shacks with battered zinc roofs. They were built right in the mud out of kerosene drums, bottomed-out barrels, and shells of old cars. A loud-mouthed multitude squelched around the muddy little streets: men and women, dressed in city clothes and covered in mud up to their eyeballs, plopped a foot down here, pulled the other out there, fell down, and got up again with no sign of distress.[23]

Marechal continually emphasizes the cacophony of the immigrant masses. Here they are said to be a "loud-mouthed multitude." Just lines later he mentions their shouts and "strident conversations filling the shacks."[24] Earlier the zone of the neutrals was compared to the tower of Babel, and the comingling of all the languages and voices creates a dull roar which was at first indistinguishable, "the diapason of a thousand human accents, a thousand interwoven voices, neither happy nor sad, reverberating as though inside a cavern."[25] The cacophony of Cacodelphia signifies linguistic, and therefore ethnic, diversity, but it also symbolizes lack of consensus, as throughout the novel myriad voices speak over one another.

Adán runs into people he knows from Monte Egmont Street, such as his neighbor Campanelli, who embodies all of the negative stereotypes about Italian immigrants at the turn of the century: namely, that they were materialistic and greedy. Everything boils down to a question of income for Campanelli, even the fact that Adán, who lived in the apartment just underneath him, could not tolerate all the noise he made. He imagines Adán to be disgruntled because he has a social inferiority complex due to his low salary as a teacher:

> Sir, I had my values: for me, one's monthly income was the foundation of the human hierarchy. And I knew that all you had was your measly teacher's salary, supplemented by the odd poorly remunerated poetic collaboration. Besides, I had an eight-cylinder automobile, whereas they said you had to get around by streetcar. So it's no surprise I took your complaint as a slap and an insult: it was a slap at my cheque book and an insult to each and every one of my eight cylinders. But what really exasperated me was the reverential way the Castillian concierge would talk about you—you, who probably wished him a good evening as your only tip![26]

Campanelli doesn't understand the actual human connection Adán has with the concierge. Only materialism makes sense to him, and he has lost the values of his homeland.

While Campanelli represents unbridled materialism, Doctor Scarpi Núñez, son of a Ligurian shoemaker, represents "not the learned ignorance that bore such good fruit in better days, but rather ignorant learning and titled illiteracy."[27] Núñez was corrupted by "a city where every single useful trade or virtue of the heart cowered before the pompous affectation of a university degree."[28] In order to overcome his feelings of social inferiority within Argentine society, he turned not to materialistic pursuits, but to higher education:

> Day and night he [the Ligurian shoemaker] hammered away at worn boots in Saavedra, taking bread from his own mouth and sacrificing sleep for daydreams, whilst this lump of coal reluctantly sat exams, pared his nails, wasted nights at the dance halls, and added the Castilian *Núñez* to his native Italian *Scarpi*, looking straight to his future and askance at his past.[29]

Núñez represents the second generation of immigrants who ascended the social ladder. They were able to attend school, and were also quick to forget their roots. Schultz accuses Doctor Scarpi Núñez of being ashamed of his origins, in response to which an indignant Núñez calls Schultz a "dime-store Virgil."[30] Schultz continues to criticize him:

> Sure, he probably did acquire the skills of pettifoggery, just as the chimney sweep acquires his, but in his core he remained uncultivated, coarse, grossly crude. Even worse, the pride of his new status made him forget every last vestige of his native virtues. If we were to compare them now, the Ligurian shoemaker would seem a paragon of refinement and sensibility alongside his son.[31]

The sons of immigrants are characterized by "vulgar opinions and fundamental ignorance."[32] Marechal exaggerates all the negative stereotypes of the impoverished immigrant population and attributes such behavior to lack of values, lack of identity, and loss of spiritual direction.

In the second circle of hell, that of the Lustful, Marechal takes on a major social issue of turn-of-the-century Argentina—the problem of prostitution. Because many male migrant workers came alone before sending for their wives and families, there was a predominantly male society, which resulted in prevalent prostitution. This circle of hell is enormous in scope and is divided into seven sections. At first their entrance is blocked by the gigantic figure of a naked woman, Dame Lust, who has two barking dog heads as breasts, a crab for her genitals, and a "gallinaceous wing" protruding from each of her buttocks:

> But Dame Lust was stirring; her two dogshead hooters stuck their muzzles out and began to bark furiously; her sexcrab extended menacing pincers; and the two ungainly gluteal wings started flapping vigorously in a futile attempt to take flight. Hopping like a chicken, the woman came closer and stared us in the face.
>
> —How 'bout it, boys! she cooed in a monotone. How 'bout it![33]

This monstrous Madame is an absurd and grotesque symbol of the promiscuity of the city. This circle is not a *barrio* but a "movie-production lot, where weird set-designers had seemingly mounted, one next to another, six heterogeneous sets unconnected by any passage."[34] These various sets are then referred to as "scenes." The first scene is decorated with pornographic plaster figurines, threadbare curtains, and fly-specked mirrors. Randy men fill the orchestra seats and galleries. Odors of "cigarette smoke, animal heat, old sweat, garlic soup, and cheap perfume" hang heavily in the air. In the crowd, Adán spots "the ornate jackets of milkmen, the blue coveralls of mechanics, the shiny suits of office workers, the wide-brimmed hats of students, the top hats of aristocrats, and the Perramus trenchcoats typical of burghers"—that is, all social strata.[35]

Here Adán encounters one of his friends, the pipsqueak Bernini, who stands up in front of the crowd and pontificates about the problem of prostitution not in moral and ethical terms, but in strictly economic terms of supply and demand. According to Bernini, the infamous Argentine melancholy[36] is attributable to the lack of women and is a serious national problem that may bring about the ruin of their country:

> I wouldn't be standing here before you if our cause were not also of concern to the nation, whose interest far surpasses the sum of our individual interests. For I wonder now: what will become of our homeland if this oppressive separation of the sexes continues? Ah, gentlemen, I seem to hear even now the bones of our forefathers turning in their graves! Toothless mouths open and cry out to us: "The Fatherland is in danger!"[37]

Within the separate sets or scenes (the Pornographic Theatre, the Pond of the Lustful, the Ravine of the Adulterers, the Wall of Dirty Old Men, the Meadow of the Ultras, the Canefield of the Sodomites, and the Labyrinth of Solitary Souls), Argentines suffer punishments unique to their specific sin. Marechal parodies the Dantean *contrapasso* by combining various aspects of different Dantean punishments, exaggerated to the point of absurdity. For example, the punishment of the sinners in the Pond of the Lustful is as follows:

> Standing in water up to their knees, thousands of naked men and women were vegetating. I say "vegetating" because such was the idea suggested by those torsos locked in motionless embraces, united to the point of agony in every form of love imaginable, encrusted in and clinging to one another like the myriad branches of a leafy glade. Artificial suns, strategically distributed, rained fire down upon the multitude, wringing from them dense goat-like odours and rivers of sweat which flowed over necks, gleaming backs, bellies pressed against one another, hairy tufts, and thighs. The pond water seemed dead beneath a scum of reddish mildew and vegetal putrefaction. Here and

> there, amid the welter of nude bodies, grew plants with fleshy flowers of frightful beauty, evil-coloured mushrooms, and reeds as sharp as awls covered in pink snails' eggs. Crazed by the human stench, swarms of glossy Spanish flies and horseflies furiously bombarded the multitude, stinging them repeatedly.[38]

Marechal's punishment is a hodgepodge of Dantean *contrapassi* pertaining to different sins. The nakedness and "torsos locked in motionless embraces" recalls Dante's second circle, where Francesca and Paolo are punished. Raining fire, however, is Dante's punishment for sodomites in circle seven, and the Spanish flies and horseflies recall the flies and wasps that sting the neutrals. Furthermore, the synesthesia, the "evil-coloured mushrooms" and "reeds as sharp as awls covered in pink snails' eggs," is not poetic, but ridiculous.

Other *contrapassi* are not conglomerations of Dantean punishments but are creative new punishments that nevertheless employ Dantean principles—that the sinner must suffer for all eternity a twisted version of what they did in life. The term *contrapasso* comes from the Latin *contra* and *patior*, to "suffer the opposite." Within the context of the *Inferno*, it refers to the punishment of souls "by a process either resembling or contrasting with the sin itself."[39] For example, the lustful are blown about by violent winds, which represents how they were controlled by passion during their lifetime (resemblance), while the diviners have their heads screwed on backward because during their lifetime they were constantly looking forward (contrast). Marechal devises a punishment for the winemakers of Mendoza that resembles their occupation but contrasts with their sin. In the text it is Schultz who describes the damnation of those who, in order to keep wine prices high, dumped perfectly good wine into the sewers:

> —I've put them in a winepress, said the astrologer, pushing his advantage, where they eternally stomp rotten grapes to the sound of a sour, screeching, diabolical fiddle being scratched by a one-eyed fiddler from the province of San Juan, Vargas by name; day and night, standing on a keg in a state of demonic possession, he plays his moronic Malambo de la Cabra Tetona.[40]

Here, their punishment of eternally making wine contrasts with their sin of throwing it away. The added musical accompaniment by the fiddler of San

Juan makes the punishment uniquely Argentine (the malambo being an Argentine folk dance), and hysterically absurd.

Although we might expect to find a female counterpart of Francesca in the Ravine of the Adulterers, the overwhelming majority of sinners punished here are male. The principal female figures in Marechal's circle of the Lustful are to be found in the Meadow of the Ultras. Here we encounter Lady Titania, a parody of Victoria Ocampo, which will be discussed at the end of this chapter. Adán also sees friends from the salon and his neighborhood, such as Marta Ruiz and Ruth of "The Golden Ant," who "hugged their lyres of gilded cardboard" or "belligerently brandished toy popguns." Only then does he notice "the excessive theatricality of both scenario and actors—a hyperbolic falseness that seemed intentional."[41]

The sixth scene of the circle of the Lustful is the Labyrinth of Solitary Souls, where Adán and Schultz encounter "the Grand Solitary." He expresses himself in confusing metaphors rather than plain language. He is looking for Valeria, who represents the new Argentine aristocracy:

> Valeria is the last, sublime descendant of a ranching family. "New aristocracy," you'll say. Bah! The alembics of Argentina distill rapidly. True, her grandfather was an old cowboy from the south, accustomed to spending nights on horseback out on the range—never got used to sleeping in a regular bed; still sleeps on a saddlery horse installed in his luxurious bedroom decorated with prairie landscapes. There the old man dozes on his wooden sorrel horse, his satin pyjama swathing him like a *chiripá*, while a simulated *pampero* blows over him from strategically placed fans, and the lowing of cattle comes from hidden phonographs to lull him.[42]

The episode of the Grand Solitary and his poetic creation, Valeria, makes fun of the image of the ideal Argentine (a cultured, Europeanized aristocrat) fostered by Mitre and Sarmiento's generation. Although her grandfather is a gaucho, completely unaccustomed to "civilization," Valeria has a bathroom of porcelain, "with illustrations from Ovid, Boccaccio, and other great masters of universal literature."[43] But she is only a product of the Grand Solitary's imagination. When Schultz and Adán tell him to forget about his "delirious metaphors," he insists that he no longer has to write because she is a reality:

> —Valeria exists! he declaimed fanatically. The wind that sways the lilies of her garden wears slippers of water and whistles the preludes of Debussy.
>
> Our pace became a frenzied trot.
>
> —Valeria's nightshirts, he insisted as he trotted at our side, were woven at the murmuring looms of aurora . . .[44]

The episode shows that the construction of the image of an ideal Argentine is no different than the construction of a poetic image, or ideal lady. The parody also evidences Marechal's level of contempt for the airs of the landowning elite.

Gluttony: Meat and Mixed Identity

Exiting the circle of the Lustful, Adán and Schultz come to two huge doors covered in bas-reliefs with Edenic garden scenes on the left and scenes of endless toil and strife on the right. Adán must decipher "their occult allegorical meaning" in order to gain entrance into the hell of Gluttony. Since Cacodelphia is said to be the counterfigure of the visible Buenos Aires, Marechal mentions many local eateries and traditional foods like the *parrillada criolla*. We also encounter Ciro Rossini, whose restaurant Ciro's Gazebo was the setting of book 4. Immediately upon entering the circle, Adán is bombarded by nauseating sights and smells. The circle of Gluttony is a monstrous banquet, consisting of kitchens, a dining area, and "vomitoria." The cooks are the Cyclops who tend the endless quantities of meat:

> Some chefs were turning monstrous spits on which whole animals were impaled and roasting golden brown: there were steers fat from winter pasture, greasy heifers with the skin on, and fillies that provide the juicy flank steak so dear to the Ranquel Indians, devourers of horsemeat. Other chefs were basting the suckling pigs and lambs roasting on vertical spits with copious brine, or pouring it over immense grills where thousands of chitterlings, large intestines, kidneys, udders, and testicles, as well as other internal and external mammalian organs were sizzling, alongside their brothers in fire, the sausages: *chorizos criollos*, Cantabrian blood sausage, Italian *cotechini*, long Andalusian sausages, and Teutonic frankfurters.[45]

As we can see from this playful passage, even the selection of meat varieties reflects the many ethnic influences present in Argentina. Perhaps the only common denominator among Argentines is their carnivorous habits.

Just as Dante varies his characters' speech patterns according to their social status and city of origin, Marechal's sinners speak in ways that mimic their cultural origin and occupation. Ciro Rossini's speech mixes Italian and Spanish: "¡Una fiestita *in familia*! ¡Bravo! *A tavola*!"[46] Such speech patterns were common among Italian immigrants who arrived with little or no schooling in Spanish, and therefore mixed Spanish with their native dialects. Their mixture of Spanish and Italian was dubbed *cocoliche* (a derogatory term) by the locals.

The speech of Don Celso, the priest, is laced with Latin and biblical terms and retains the rhythmic quality of the liturgy. He employs frequent metaphors from the Bible, for example that of Christ as shepherd:

> Gentle souls who listen to me, the Villa-Crespian flock of yesteryear was the one Our Lord entrusted to me, that I might watch over it, care for it, and lead it to the eternal meadows. To Him must I account for each and every one of my sheep when their hour arrives, as did He Himself to his Heavenly Father. "*Tui erant, et mihi eos dedisti, et sermonem tuum servaverunt.*" In the vernacular: "Thine they were, and thou gavest them to me; and they have kept thy word."[47]

The priest's speech patterns and quotations from the Bible (in this case John 17:6) contrast with the brutish utterances of the Cyclops, who use *lunfardo* terms and speak with a lisp. Marechal marks this orthographically by replacing all *s*'s with *z*'s:

> —¡Seleuco!—gruñó, dirigiéndose a su camarada—¿Qué hacen aquí estos dos tirifilos?[48]
>
> —Mironez, de juro—le respondióceceando el otro Cíclope—¡Dejámeloz a mí, Crizanto!"[49]
>
> (—Seleucus! he grunted to his companion. What's this pair of patsies doing here?
>
> —Rubberneckerth, for sure, lisped the other Cyclops in response. Leave'm to me, Chry*th*antu*th*!)[50]

Schultz claims to have rescued the Cyclops "from the junk bin of Mythology."[51] In the *Divine Comedy*, mythological figures serve as the gatekeepters of the circles of hell in fulfillment of God's will. Here, however, the unruly Cyclops deny Schultz's control. This prompts the theological question from Adán of how the created can rebel against its creator, just before the two narrowly escape with their lives.

Avarice: The Plutobarrio

While circle 3 took us through the myriad eateries of the "invisible" Buenos Aires, circle 4 is a tour of its downtown financial district. Here, where the sin punished is avarice, the focus is on corruption in banking and big business and on the uneven distribution of wealth. The landscape evokes the industrial areas of the city, with their "ruined factories, broken smokestacks, truncated skyscrapers, and crumbling mansions."[52] This section is populated by businessmen (capacious Perramus coats and fat cigars), heroes of the Stock Exchange (sporty suits and congested faces), merchants in stiff tuxedos or impeccable workcoats, directors of companies, and alchemists of speculation. They are all running, colliding with one another, and falling in yellow dust, "in the midst of a hurly-burly of bonds, banknotes, securities, and shares that a great, erratic wind swept and swirled over the ground according to no other law than its own caprice."[53]

The greedy business owners in Cacodelphia are responsible in part for the poor living conditions of the citizens of Buenos Aires. After witnessing the desolation of the sawmill, Adán and Schultz have to pass through factories, foundries, spinning mills, and washing plants. They pause in an urban housing development under construction. Here they meet Don Abel Sánchez de Aja Berija y Baraja, who has amassed a fortune by exploiting renters in the tenements he builds.[54] Marechal criticizes the squalid living conditions of *conventillos* and evidences the exploitation of the poor by the rich. Although various episodes in Cacodelphia such as this one have a moral message, morality is not the primary focus of Marechal's inferno. He clarifies this in "Las claves de *Adán Buenosayres*": "If I had wanted to whip, as a moralizer or a pervert, my happy fellow citizens, I would have imagined a solemn and angry inferno, à la Dante."[55] The majority of Marechal's inferno, rather than focusing on the moral depravity of Argentines, focuses on the inadequacies of their national literature. Marechal's Cacodelphia comprises myriad metafictional moments that highlight the challenges of creating meaningful, transcendent literature while avoiding crass imitation.

Metafictional Moments and Failures in Storytelling

Metafiction is a self-conscious literary style that draws attention to a work's fictional status by focusing on language, literary form, and storytelling. Patricia Waugh, in her book *Metafiction: The Theory and Practice of Self-Conscious Fiction*, defines metafiction as "fictional writing which self-consciously and systematically draws attention to its status as an artefact in order to pose questions about the relationship between fiction and reality."[56] This in turn challenges our understanding of "the world outside the literary fictional text" by provoking questions about representation and identity.[57] As Waugh explains, "If our knowledge of this world is now seen to be mediated through language, then literary fiction (worlds constructed entirely out of language) becomes a useful model for learning about the constructions of 'reality' itself."[58]

All of *Adán Buenosayres*, and the "Journey to the Dark City of Cacodelphia" in particular, is marked by metafictional moments. In most of the episodes, a writer's or storyteller's attempt to create fiction results in failure, a failure acknowledged either by other characters, or by the storyteller himself. The constant second-guessing of the storytelling process and the resultant bickering over stylistic choices creates a work which is so self-consciously fictional as to convey the Argentine sense of insecurity with regard to their national literature. In the following section, I will divide these metafictional moments into four main types: (1) Schultz, creator of Cacodelphia, must tell stories with a certain bravura to pass from one circle of hell to another; (2) Adán, our poet protagonist, must come to terms with failed experiences in storytelling; (3) secondary characters encountered in Cacodelphia share stories involving failed storytelling; and (4) comparisons are made between this story and its inadequacy with regard to other infernal journeys.

Let us begin with Schultz, whom the author portrays as ostensibly arrogant but inwardly insecure. At the beginning of the journey he explains to Adán that his priority in designing the Helicoid was to avoid the crass imitation of the classics: "When I decided to give a visible image to the intelligible Cacodelphia, . . . my first concern was to avoid crass imitations."[59] Schultz is constantly preoccupied with being original and becomes highly defensive when his originality is called into question. This happens, most notably, when Midas denies our heroes passage until Schultz can prove his identity through storytelling prowess.

Whereas in the *Divine Comedy* Midas is concerned with judging the morality of the sinners and assigning them to their due circle, Marechal's Midas is concerned only with judging the storytelling skills of his creator. When Schultz demands that as author of this inferno he should have the right of way through it, Midas calls him "a liar and a yellow-bellied coward" and forces him to undergo questioning to prove he is the demiurge. This identity-verifying, storytelling exam turns into an "exemplary display of pedantry on both sides."[60]

The question of the examination is: "Do you think . . . that the iniquities and depredations committed by the so-called bourgeois class, or third estate, warrant its being amputated from the social body?"[61] What ensues is a tour de force of argumentation. What matters most to Midas is that the content be expressed with "grace, concision, and brevity," and he finds many elements of Schultz's response unsatisfactory. His first reproach of Schultz's performance is directed at his use of stale metaphors. When Schultz speaks of how every organ must function for the good of the body, Midas scoffs, "A comparison as old as the hills!" When Schultz nevertheless continues with the metaphor, Midas shouts, "Enough of the organ, already!"[62]

Midas's second reproach is that Schultz is overly pedantic and exaggerated in his use of metaphor. He interjects, "Whoa there, mister! . . . Spare me the metaphorical ballistics!" But Schultz persists in his pedantry, citing both Seneca and verses from Psalms 2:10 in Latin. This causes Midas to draw the line: "I beg you! Midas reprimanded him again. State your case in straightforward language. Have you forgotten you are addressing the general public?"[63] This criticism causes Schultz to shift gears, but in doing so he overshoots his mark:

> —Decía—sentenció Schultze—que no hay bien que dure mil años. En lo mejor se da vuelta la taba, y, tras de suerte, culo; porque nunca falta un buey cornet, y el mundo es una bola que rodando y rodando . . . [64]
>
> (—I was saying, said Schultz sententiously, that all good things come to an end. Just when the going looks good, somebody's gotta upset the applecart, because there's always one bad egg, and that's just the way the cookie crumbles . . .)[65]

The contrast between extreme pedantry, abandoned for a ridiculous string of clichés intended to be intelligible to the "gran público," is a parody of two major tendencies of Argentine literature: the first of which Marechal portrays as Eurocentric and pedantic, and the other that he portrays as colloquial and uncouth.

As Schultz continues his response to Midas's question, Midas responds that it is "accurate in substance" although "vulgar in form." "Don't forget I'm addressing the general public," Schultz reminds him venomously.[66] Although nothing seems to please Midas, Schultz does not lose confidence, and instead starts to build momentum. This elicits a "not bad" from Midas, who then goes in for a major blow to Schultz's storytelling ego by pointing out that his ideas, far from being original, have been influenced by a "certain Gallic metaphysician."[67] This criticism in particular causes the previously composed Schultz to turn visibly red, which he later tells Adán is "not with embarrassment" but out of "righteous indignation." Not only does he later defend his originality in front of Adán, but he also becomes flustered on the spot:

> —Look here, sir, he stammered. If I used someone else's schema, and nothing more than a schema, I have on the other hand fleshed it out in quite an original fashion. Moreover, my own contribution is coming up.[68]

His defensiveness indicates insecurity. As an Argentine author trying to be original, he is particularly concerned about being viewed as an imitator. Since his inferno is based on Dante's schema, his first preoccupation with regard to its creation was to "avoid crass imitations." But yet even the neogogue will at times be guilty of the very imitation he claims to despise. For example, in circle 3, when telling the story of a former love, Nora, whom he abandoned prior to their wedding, he employs an artificial style typical of romance and melodrama:

¡oh primavera!, ¡oh juventud! ¡adiós, adiós! . . . ¿Quiénes andaban por el jardín? ¡Tristán e Isolda, Romeo y Julieta, Abelardo y Eloísa! Adiós, juventud! El romance ha muerto. ¡Una lápida! ¡Que pongan una lápida sobre la tumba del romance! Con un epitafio que diga: "Pasajero, aquí yace un amor."[69]

(Oh, springtime! O youth! Farewell, farewell! . . . Who was that couple walking in the garden? Tristan and Isolde, Romeo and Juliet, Abelard and Heloise! Romance has died. A tombstone! Place a tombstone on the grave of romance! With the epitaph: "Wayfarer, here lies a love affair.")[70]

On this occasion his storytelling is so bad that he is reprimanded by Adán, his pupil: "Take it easy! I said. And speak naturally! Can't you spare us that ghastly language of melodrama?"[71] At least on the occasion with Midas, Schultz is able to tone down his pedantry, rein in his colloquialisms, and produce a brilliant discourse on how the inferior class, the Vaishya, will usurp the true mysticism of the Brahmin and impose his gross mystic cult of materialism. Schultz concludes his story with descriptions of Vaishya's fundamental vulgarity, which actually get Midas to laugh. Schultz later recounts that "only after that moment did the crowned man put aside the stiff demeanor of the examiner." Schultz completely wins over his audience by imitating the thoughts and speech of the vulgar Vaishya. This causes Midas to proclaim, "I can just hear him!" At the conclusion of Schultz's examination, Mr. Midas "warmly congratulated him." His other audience member, Adán, however, is fast asleep. Still, Schultz interprets the event as a victory, and, his usual arrogance restored, assures Adán in his "infinite modesty" that his discourse "sums up the greatest wisdom ever uttered in the philosophy of history."[72] This also pokes fun at Dante the poet's feigned humility.

This is not the only occasion that Schultz will have to story-tell his way into the next circle. A similar rite of passage occurs prior to his encounter with Midas, when passing from the circle of Gluttony to the circle of Avarice. Here the heroes come face-to-face with a gaunt and menacing judge seated on a courtroom dais. When they approach him, he asks, "How were the poor devils?" and Schultz is required to tell three Argentine folktales before they are allowed to pass. They are part of a tradition of stories that begin with this formula, which is the equivalent of "How did the trouble start?" The first is the story of the fox and the sheep, the second of the woodtick and the roadrunner, and the third of the farmer, the tiger, and the fox. For each story correctly told, the judge advances a step down the dais.

Adán, perplexed, asks, "And what meaning is there in that mishmash of little fables you've just fed me?" Schultz responds that tomorrow's researchers "will bust their butts trying to dig out the admirable meaning hidden in those little fables."[73] According to Norman Cheadle, this is a pointed reference to Joyce's well-known explanation of *Ulysses:* "I've put in so many enigmas and puzzles that it will keep the professors busy for centuries arguing over what I meant, and that's the only way of ensuring one's immortality."[74] This is another example of Schultz's literary arrogance, and a reminder that storytelling can be reduced to literary enigmas.

The third time Schultz must resort to storytelling to gain passage to a deeper circle of Cacodelphia is to conquer Geryon. A far cry from Dante's great mythical beast, Marechal's Geryon is "a dwarf dragon."[75] It has eyes that sparkle mischievously and a toothless mouth: "this was a happy dragon, a decent sort. So, the animal was watching us and smiling at us; at the same time it was gently wagging its tail, not without jiggling a bunch of olive-green fecal marbles tinkling like glass beads as they bounced against one another."[76] Adán naively asks,

> —What are we supposed to do with this creature?
>
> —If you'd paid more attention to your classics, he answered, you'd know that in cases like this, facing a dragon, you've got to make it fall fast asleep.
>
> He looked around, suddenly anxious:
>
> —Son of a bitch! he groaned. Where did I put my aresenal of hypnotics?[77]

The so-called arsenal of hypnotics is not drugs as one might expect, but Argentine literature. They attempt to put the dragon to sleep with poetry: "Doing as I was told, I showered the dragon with a terrific flood of metaphors, and was lucky enough to see the monster's eyelids droop for a moment, as if an irresistible torpor had overcome it." Ultimately the poetry is not enough to defeat the dragon. It recovers and smiles at Adán "with the utmost tenderness and wag[s] its tail in a show of delight."[78] To get the resilient dragon to doze off, they have to read it the Code of Mining Regulations, the Telephone Directory, a Dissertation by the Council of History and Numismatics, and other such documents. Referring to Argentine literature as a "terrific flood of metaphors" also foreshadows how the book will end when Adán and Schultz come face-to-face with a more formidable monster, the Paleogogue.

The False Parnassus

The problem of bad Argentine poetry will be addressed head-on in the sector known as the False Parnassus. Schultz explains that it is the sector "where the *pseudogogues* metaphorically display their peacock tails, under the direction of the false muses or *Antimuses*, as I've named them."[79] Adán is reluctant to tour this sector because he does not want to converse with men of his métier, many of whom are his former friends encountered in books 1–5. Furthermore, he is uncomfortable here because he knows himself to be guilty: "Truth be told, my own tail of straw made me vulnerable."[80]

This episode is perhaps the most metafictional of them all. Those punished here are guilty of crass literary imitation. The new environment is said to be "decked out in all the poetic colours imaginable."[81] The setting for the false poets is a "cardboard Parnassus":

> No doubt it was, or aspired to be, a version of the Elysian Fields in the classical style. Verdant hills, blue brooks, glades generously laden with fruit and orchestral with birds, all befriended the eyes and caressed the ears. Men and women, crowned in laurel leaves and draped in majestic Greek robes, were conversing here and there, or joining in demure circles. Such was the intruder's first impression of those gardens. But, after the initial fascination, the interloper soon noticed that an absolute falseness ruled the entire scene: the streams and hillsides were of painted canvas, the trees of bristol board; the lights were neon, the nightingales trinkets. As for the denizens of that Eden, a similar disillusionment ended by reducing them to a troupe of actors wearing paper clothes and gilt-cardboard diadems.[82]

As they enter, Schultz takes on "a certain quizzical look typical of artists who, being not quite satisfied with a piece of work, hesitate to display it."[83] The first contingent of pseudogogues to appear is led by the False Euterpe (the muse of music in Greek mythology), who is an elderly and constipated spinster who hacks up greenish phlegm. Among her group of sinners Adán encounters Luis Pereda (Borges), whose presence here incites his outrage.

Although Adán and Pereda were often at each other's throats in the literary disputes in books 1–5, here Adán comes to his defense. Like Dante encountering Brunetto Latini, he shows affection for his literary friend, but unlike Dante (who comes to understand the decisions of a just God in condemning sinners), Adán protests with Schultz regarding Pereda's placement:

> This isn't right! I told Schultz. Sure, according to venerable tradition, the inventor of an Inferno enjoys the right to put his enemies in it; it's been common practice up to the present. But if the creator of an Inferno brought a friend in on the act, it was to give the friend a chance to look good in a smart role. So, what need was there to inflect upon our comrade Pereda the ignominy of showing up in this bordello?[84]

But the False Euturpe argues that Pereda has been justly placed in this inferno. She explains that he stands accused of "wandering around the barrios of Buenos Aires playing the *malevo*, his bully-boy glances slanting off left and right, spitting between his teeth, and muttering the poorly learned lyrics of some tango."[85] In other words, he is accused of imitating and glorifying an immoral figure. The *malevo* was a favorite character of a young Borges who sought to mythologize the space where the pampa and Buenos Aires meet. Beatriz Sarlo refers to his specific type of *criollismo* as "avant-garde urban criollismo."[86] The False Euturpe continues her accusation: "Don Luis wanted to give literary expression to his mystico-suburban fervour; he went so far as to invent a false Mythology in which the *malevos* of Buenos Aires acquire not only heroic proportions but even vaguely metaphysical dimensions."[87] Adán defends Pereda and says that for this very reason he deserves laurels:

> Has it not been said that a heavy cloud has been hanging over our literature, a tendency to imitate foreign models? It's been said, you can't deny it! And when a man like Pereda goes out and vindicates the right of the *criollo* spirit to ascend to the universal plane of art, he gets mocked and ridiculed and subjected to infernal indignities. Well, Madame, I bow before our champion; and I'd reverently take off my hat to him, if I hadn't lost it somewhere in this damned Helicoid.[88]

It's as if Marechal, who may not have agreed with Borges's poetics, and certainly not with the *criollismo* of his early years, is here acknowledging that whatever their differences, they both had the same mission at heart: to make Argentine literature universally influential and original. Marechal places him in the inferno but has Adán support him.

Pereda thanks Adán and promises that when he gets out of here, he'll buy Adán a gin at the pink general store on the corner (an allusion to one of Borges's favorite symbols for Buenos Aires).[89] But the False Euterpe insists that he is guilty and attacks his orthographic imitation of rural speech: "Does that circumstance give him the right to geld the words of our language and write *soledá* for "soledad" and *virtú* for "virtud," or *pesao* for "pesado" and *salao* for "salado"?"[90] This is making fun of Borges's imitation of gauchesque poetry which mimics the colloquial speech patterns of the rural Argentines. The next aspect of Borges's writing that is under attack is his neologisms: "This gentleman has had the cheek to coin terms like 'tile-floorishness' and 'cisternism' and 'bannisterdom' that scream bloody murder."[91]

The next group of writers on the chopping block are the *ultraists*, which Marechal had already belittled in the circle of the Lustful with his parody of Victoria Ocampo. The poetry read to the dragon ("the terrific flood of metaphors") and the grand finale paragraph of the book may also both be parodies of *ultraísmo*, which had given metaphor such a privileged place. As Cheadle points out in the notes to his translation, Borges had described the primary principle of the movement as "the reduction of lyric poetry to its primordial element: the metaphor."[92] Borges, along with Marechal, Eduardo González Lanuza, Francisco Luis Bernardez, and Oliverio Girondo, had all, at one time, practiced *ultraísmo*.

The pseudogogues of the ultraist contingent wear pompous purple tunics. The False Euterpe accuses one man in particular of "the reprehensible mania of stringing together comparison after comparison, with no restraint whatsoever, and against the fundamental dictates of prudence."[93] Her accusations against him involve a ridiculous set of arbitrary comparisons:

> This gentleman, for example, has hung on the hanger of his heart the grey overcoat of melancholy; and with alarming frequency he has donned and doffed the nightshirt of hope. He has compared his love, successively, to an automatic bar, a box of matches, and a pair of boots. Now he has muffled himself in the warm blanket of doubt, and no power in heaven could make him climb aboard the streetcar of mystery.[94]

Upon hearing this sorry string of metaphors, Adán looks at the Purple Tunic with a "fraternal gaze." He feels pity for this sinner because he himself is guilty of the same sin. This mirrors how the lustful Dante feels so much pity for Francesca's story that he faints. Adán identifies with the man in the Purple Tunic, but corrects him by saying that metaphors should not bring what is superior down to the level of the inferior; rather, they should raise the inferior to the level of the superior: "To compare the sky with a water-closet is to offend the sky and heap ridicule on the water-closet."[95] At this bit of criticism, things get heated. The man in the purple tunic strikes back at Adán: "look who's talking! A parrot of the new generation who has mortified us with the most absurd metaphors. Wasn't it you who wrote that line about 'love more joyous than a child's funeral'?" Next he attacks Adán's lines "your sky is round and blue like the eggs of a partridge" and "in the climbing vines of her voice, a bird of grace broods over three little eggs."[96] As Javier de Navascués and Cheadle point out in their notes, both verses are Marechal's. The first is from "Poema sin título" (*Días como flechas*, 1926), and the second is from "Elogio," published in the magazine *Caras y Caretas* (issue 1446, June 19, 1926).[97] This brings up an interesting point because it makes clear that Adán (Marechal) is as guilty as the rest of them, so much so that the False Euterpe wants to add Adán to her entourage. It is as if, then, Marechal is placing himself in hell rather than claiming, as Dante did, that he was the only one to enter hell who was saved. In "Las claves de *Adán Buenosayres*" Marechal emphasizes the fact that he was also making fun of himself throughout the novel. One of his goals in writing "Claves" was to calm some of his literary colleagues who had taken offense at his parody. He defends himself by affirming that there was no aggression in this endeavor and that after all, he too was among those parodied:

> What's certain is that I embarked, along with Adam in the symbolic "Ship of fools" (also in use in the Middle Ages) that crossed the city and the lowlands of Saavedra. But I didn't do it with the perverse intention of exposing or ridiculing their aesthetics (after all, Adam is another fool of the Ship); rather I did it with the objective of depicting the fervour, manias, and joys which we all exhibited in that literary movement.[98]

Marechal explains that he wrote the work in the intellectual climate of the literary revolution and in the spirit of the journal *Martín Fierro* that was a

"Parnaso Satírico." It was to his great surprise that his colleagues reacted with unexpected hostility, and Marechal's only explanation for this is that they had grown old, lost their sense of humor, and become defensive of their laurels. On the one hand, it's easy to understand their vexation, considering that Marechal is depicting their literary attempts as failures, but on the other hand, the main point of his work is not to ridicule his fellow authors, but to make light of how desperately and with great egoism, they all sought to produce poetry that was simultaneously universal, local, transcendent, and unique. Authors of Argentina felt a pressing need to prove themselves, and *Adán Buenosayres* is an expression of the collective lunacy of the literary sector in the early twentieth century as they fervently latched on to various trends. A metaphor for this frenzy, which Marechal very much considers a national problem, is to be found at the end of the episode of Don Moses Rosenbaum, who abruptly runs off the stage when his life story is being told. As he makes his escape, the orchestra starts playing with gusto:

> The curtain had just come down on the bacchanal, and the musicians were trying to cover up the glitch by playing *con brio* the same old tune, tricked out now as a River Plate folk dance, while the dancers, lashed into a sudden frenzy, went round and round, stamping their feet like madmen, laughing and shouting, waving white-and-blue kerchiefs.[99]

This is a metaphor for Argentine literature. Despite the nationalistic intent symbolized by the waving of the blue-and-white kerchiefs (the colors of the Argentine flag) and the great desire of her artists (symbolized by the frenzy of the dancers and the gusto of the musicians), the end result does not rise above crass imitation ("the same old tune, tricked out now as a River Plate folk dance").

The poets of the False Parnassus are all guilty of imitation within their respective genres. After the *criollistas* and the *ultraistas*, Marechal mocks the religious poets, libertarian poets, erotic poets, dramatic poets, and comic idyllic poets. Although in this sector he limits his parody to poetry, in other sections he addresses failed attempts in writing prose. I would like to look at one such episode which is of primary importance in the novel, the story of the "Personage," which spans twenty-one pages.

The story of the "Personage" is the story of a failed Argentine historical novelist. It is about loss of identity and the failure of the political system of a country. We meet the Personage in the sector of the *Homoglobes*, or balloon-men:

> In that portion of atmosphere, at just about six feet above the ground, floated a multitude of rubber men inflated to bursting point. They blew around in the wind in a grotesque contredanse, heads butting together and bellies bouncing off one another, all the while keeping up their ridiculously grave demeanour, their cold and solemn expressions.[100]

Adán runs into a deflated *homoglobe* lying on the ground, recalling how Dante bumps into Ugolino's head on the frozen pond of circle nine. Schultz and Adán reinflate the deflated balloon, and get him to tell them his story, which he titles "Invention and Death of a Personage."[101] As Cheadle explains in the note accompanying the episode, "*personaje*" (translated as "personage") has a dual meaning in Spanish: "(1) a public person of note; and (2) a character in a literary, theatrical, or cinematic work of fiction."

The Personage belongs to the Argentine landowning class. He is said to be from an "illustrious family"; his great-grandfather was Colonel X, who fought alongside General San Martín in his cavalry charge at San Lorenzo. He was one of the first-generation heroes, for whom "Patria was not a mother or even a bride; she was their newborn daughter, whose childhood would continue beyond their deaths."[102] His grandfather participated in the "desert" campaigns, the aim of which was to take possession of the land occupied by native peoples. He was a ranch owner and lover of the wilderness. When he died his sons divided up their ranch, La Rosada. The Personage's father "dreamed of establishing a 'patrician order' that might endow the wilderness with human forms and laws, and populate it with fervent multitudes who, by settling in our land, would add a new note to the universal chord."[103] His father's vision is that of Mitre's generation.

But his father's dream is not to be realized. With "infinite bitterness" his father watches as the patricians abandon their family and lands in order to give themselves over "to such dubious interests and pernicious ambitions as seethed in the abstract heart of the City."[104] His father witnesses the waves of immigration, and the people who came in search of a way of life to replace the one they'd left behind. They did not find what they were looking for on the prairie, "in its state of abandon and formlessness." Sadly, the father proclaims: "The era of the patricians is over; now comes the time of the lawyers."[105]

We learn early on in the tale that the Personage, like Adán, is prone to "literary inclinations."[106] He yearns to write the story of his family and of life on the pampas, but whenever he puts pen to paper, "all the talent I displayed so ardently at tertulias would peter out and vanish, like a ghost refusing incarnation." In irritable discontent, he tells himself, "as so many others have done," that his sterility "might be due to the lack of a 'propitious environment.'"[107] The Personage at this point attributes his failure as an author to a culturally barren Argentina. His solution is to go to the cultural center of Europe, Paris. While there, his father dies, and he and his brothers inherit the land. While his brothers sell their shares to finance electoral campaigns, he retains his land and returns from Paris, after realizing that his identity did not lie there. His purpose in going home is to reconstruct his identity, but upon arrival he is confronted with a bleak landscape void of the vivacity of Paris. The deserted countryside is "dotted with cow skeletons blanching under the sun," which represent Argentina as an inhospitable and desolate land in comparison to Europe.

He tries in vain to rekindle the memories from childhood: "I went out to the park, searched for traces, invoked ghosts, stroked the odd tree, and chewed blades of grass in my desire to reconstitute my childhood—if only for a moment! But sources of freshness and flavours had died, and they refused to come back to life for me."[108] He describes his generation as "a generation quite without grandeur or lyricism."[109] Having given up on himself, he places his hope in his nephew Germán, a fellow intellectual who sets out to write *Song in the Blood*, a novel covering five generations of Argentines.[110] When Germán and his father get into a fight and Germán calls him a *cipayo* (a popular term meaning those selling out the nation), he is kicked out of the house. The Personage sells his land to finance Germán's passage to Europe. Although Germán succeeds in his endeavor to write the story of their family, the Personage leads a dejected existence, hanging out in dance halls on Maipú street, "where vacant beings like me, females for rent, and tangos grubby with sadness attempted to construct an impossible architecture of jubilation."[111] Once again Argentina is depicted as "vacant," melancholy, and in need of meaning and identity.

The Personage gets himself into some trouble at these squalid hangouts, which merits the concern of his two brothers, who are involved in politics.

To keep him on a straight path, they offer him a job at "the General Directorate Z." In order to succeed in this position, the Personage sells out and becomes nothing but an empty mask. He tells Schultz and Adán that the job "methodically destroyed all that was human in me," and explains, "we were in a country where no man was allowed to exercise government who did not have one foot already in the grave."[112]

The story can be interpreted as three failures, all of which are linked: failure to find personal identity; failure of a political system to provide identity; and failure to write the story of Argentine identity. First, the Personage fails to find personal identity. His trip to Europe followed by his return home only complicates the matter so that he feels that he belongs neither to one nor to the other continent. Second, the story of the Personage is a story of national-political failure, as the country is unable to provide the Personage with a meaningful position in society. After failed attempts as a landowner, he becomes a sort of *malevo*, and then a corrupt politician. Although Argentina was once a promising country, it has not realized its potential:

> What's certain is that our country, after having flowered in the springtime of its military heroes and borne fruit in the summer of its civilian founding fathers, today languishes in the imbecilic autumn of its Personages or Poseurs.[113]

Argentina is a nation that produces Personages but fails to produce heroes: "The Hero was a chieftain, a leader; the Personage is a bureaucrat." Since heroes are the stuff of great literature, particularly of epic literature, the country is at a loss on the literary front. The Personages, unlike heroes, do not help to provide identity, because they themselves are void of it:

> (because . . . the Personage is not a "real entity" but rather an "entity of reason" invented by someone). But what constitutes the essence of the Personage is precisely his lack of essence, an absolute void, an internal desolation enabling him to assume all shapes and imitate all attitudes.[114]

The Personage is "'nothingness' in a plush top hat," which the old Oligarchy produces "by the truckload, in order to give at least some 'official' life to its otherwise lifeless, dessicated scions."[115]

Finally, the story of the Personage is the story of an unsuccessful literary endeavor. On every occasion, the Personage is unable to articulate the story of his family. The culturally vibrant environment he finds in Europe distracts him, and the culturally barren environment in Argentina sends him down a path of moral corruption. Although Germán's *Song in the Blood* is said to have been published to great acclaim, the Personage falls asleep on the second page. Furthermore, the oral tale that the Personage tells Adán and Schultz receives mixed reviews. Adán feels compassion at his sad story, so much so that he and Schultz untie the string around the *homoglobe*'s nozzle so that his divine *pneuma* can have freedom. But we must remember that Adán, like Dante, feels pity toward sinners who share the same sins. The Personage's story leaves the unbiased Schultz disgruntled:

> Let his divine *pneuma* have its freedom back! grumbled Schultz. He bored us long enough with his shaggy-dog story, going over the top, in my opinion, with his "freshness" and "flavours." But he defended his soul, and didn't go down without a fight. A real son of a gun! Why did he have to go all the way back to his great-grandfather?[116]

Schultz does not judge the morality of the character, but is critical of his over-the-top storytelling style and the length of his tale, proving that Marechal's inferno is more about failed storytelling than about morality, as is Dante's. On several occasions, Marechal directly addresses the reader to draw his consciousness toward the differences between his inferno and that of his literary predecessors. In the early circles of Cacodelphia he plays with our cultural knowledge of literary catabasis to inform us that his inferno will not be like Dante's in every respect:

> Those of my readers who have some knowledge of infernal excursions will be expecting here an invocation to the Muses or some other flourish of poetic rapture as has traditionally been the fashion in these situations. Well, such readers are just going to have to do without, because right from the get-go at the gates of Cacodelphia, Schultz clipped the wings of any possible lyrical whimsy I might have indulged in.[117]

He also informs us of the risk involved in undertaking a parody of the inferno:

> By putting on a false halo, brandishing feeble brassy thunderbolts, and parodying God's handling of the scales of justice, one risks falling into sacrilege and getting jeered at by the peanut gallery.[118]

These metafictional moments, along with the many instances of failed storytelling in the novel, make for a very self-conscious storytelling that takes into account the great potential for failure lurking at the turn of every page. It conveys the great insecurity felt by Argentine authors of the early twentieth century who had as their measuring sticks the great European classics. Marechal states the inadequacy of his own work with respect to Dante's. In a direct address to the reader, Adán points out the fundamental difference between his infernal journey and that of his ancestral predecessor:

> Reader, my friend, if I had to justify the drowsiness that came over me in the fourth circle of Schultz's inferno, I should remind you of a hundred illustrious precedents recorded in as many infernal excursions. Alighieri, being who he was, slept quite a bit in the descent he made. If the metaphysical character of his journey allows us to assign a symbolic value to that bard's siestas, we can say that Alighieri slept in the proper place at the proper time. Less fortunate than he, I made an infernal descent without theological projections. I didn't sleep when I should have, but rather when it was humanly possible to do so. How lucky are you, reader! For, having no metaphysical obligations or any cares whatsoever, you can cop a snooze on any page at all of this, my true story![119]

Here it makes little difference if the reader snoozes, because the story, without theological projections, is reduced to an empty literary game ending in a silly string of metaphors. The parody of the "Journey to the Dark City of Cacodelphia" is meant to contrast with book 6, which is written in a refined style with theological implications as the internal motor of the story.

While books 6 and 7 are based on Dante's *Vita nuova* and *Inferno*, respectively, books 1–5 are generally not associated with Dante. Albert de la Fuente, however, goes a step further, insisting that the internal structure of the entire novel is linked to that of the *Divine Comedy*. He associates books 1–5 with *Purgatory* in that they relate the purification process of Adán on earth, a process which culminates in the salvation of his soul in front of the Christ of the Broken Hand. Book 6 he relates to *Paradiso*, as it describes the abstract journey of the soul and its understanding of divine love. Book 7, of course, is the parallel of *Inferno*.[120] What is interesting, then, is that Adán's journey occurs out of order. While the progression from purgatory to paradise makes sense, it is noteworthy that the book should end in the middle of the lowest circle of hell. A likely answer is that Marechal wanted to emphasize that the city of Cacodelphia represents the Buenos Aires of the 1920s, in his opinion not yet emerged from a state of chaos, corruption, and crass imitation. Book 7 is the story of Argentines *in potentia*. Although Adán declares that he is "unable to endorse the reality our country's currently living," he describes himself as "an Argentine in hope."[121]

The problem, in Marechal's opinion (which is voiced by Adán in book 2), is that those who immigrated to Argentina "cut the thread of their tradition and destroyed their scale of values upon arrival." Adán's proposed solution is to "retie that thread and rebuild my identity according to the values of my race." The construction of identity is also seen as something that must be done collectively. When everyone does likewise, "the country will have a spiritual form."[122] Adán's voice corresponds to Marechal's opinion that the "doctrina justicialista" was the best solution for Argentina. He was attracted to the promise of spiritual betterment of the masses through culture. It makes sense that he would turn to Dante, a Catholic poet known for social justice, to advocate the necessity of spiritual direction for the creation of great art.

At the same time, however, Marechal's *Adán Buenosayres* is not meant to be a guide to protect against moral depravity like the *Divine Comedy*. As I hope to have shown, most of the "sins" of Marechal's Cacodelphia are not the Catholic sins of Dante's *Inferno*. Rather, the focus is on the division among the intellectual community, their snobbism, and what he perceived as the inadequacies of Argentina's national literature. The lowest circles of his hell are reserved for the anti-Peronist intellectuals from different ideologies. I would like to conclude by looking at one such parody. In the Meadow of the Ultras in the circle of the Lustful, we encounter Lady Titania, a parody of Victoria Ocampo. Ocampo was a famous female writer, intellectual, and editor of the literary magazine *Sur* (1931–32).

Lady Titania (Ocampo) is punished along with other Ultras: "ultra-courtesans, ultra-poetesses, ultra-intellectuals: super-females, as finely tuned as lutes."[123] Although Jorge Luis Borges referred to her as "la mujer más argentina," Marechal depicts her as a total phony. The focus of the episode, in fact, is not promiscuity, but imitation of foreign culture:

> —Alas! sighed Schultz. There you see them, trying to look like Sappho and imitating the pose of Lysistrata. If you draw near, you'll hear them debating arduous problems in philosophy, art, or economics. But it's easy to see they speak only through their sex.[124]

Lady Titania holds a balance-scale made of gold, and on each of its plates a human brain. She speaks out against the condition of inferiority imposed upon women by patriarchal society. The interaction gets heated when she accuses Schultz, and all men, of being patronizing. Schultz in turn accuses her of being a pseudo-intellectual:

> Victim of a fervour not at all intellectual, did you or did you not outrageously troll the American continent?
>
> —So what? rejoined the Ultra defiantly.
>
> —Is it true that local production wasn't enough for you, so you went fishing in other continents and managed to attract numerous male specimens, all of them refined in the use and abuse of intelligence?
>
> —I had to do my research, objected the Ultra.
>
> —And something else, insisted Schultz. Let the accused declare whether or not she persisted, on her return to Argentina, in the ridiculous, dangerous, and fortunately useless task of trying to refine the peons of her *estancia*, forcing upon them Honneger's concertos, novels by D.H. Lawrence and André Gide, as well as Freudian doctrine.[125]

Marechal depicts Ocampo as a pretentious, Eurocentric author, guilty of forcing European high culture down people's throats. She is condescending toward the average Argentine: "Brutish peasants! muttered the Ultra. They used to fall asleep at the first chord or sentence. Impossible to get a single line of Mallarmé into their thick skulls."[126] Here and in his nonfiction, Marechal was critical of the elitism of the producers of culture in Argentina. In "Proyecciones culturales del momento argentino" he warns against their intellectual isolation:

> Within the whole of society, however, the creators make up a minority, an elite which can be fertile if their creative activity reaches others, or it can be wasted in the sterile isolation of an "ivory tower."[127]

Marechal uses Dante to create a caustic parody of Ocampo, depicting her as a patronizing elitist. This is particularly ironic because Ocampo herself had written a book about the *Divine Comedy* which is nothing of the sort. In her 1924 book titled *De Francesca a Beatrice: A través de la Divina Comedia*, she tries to make Dante accessible and relatable.[128] Writing for a nonacademic audience, she explains that she will not create a commentary plagued with erudition and taking an aggressive stance on every canto. For Ocampo, the power of Dante's poem has no need of explanation of this kind in order to traverse centuries and touch present-day readers:

> I do not believe that a great erudition—which is, of course, indispensable if we intend to follow the Poem line by line—is a *sine qua non* for the instruction and pleasure that any given reader can derive from [the *Comedy*], which succeeds in moving even the least informed.[129]

What Ocampo is saying here is the opposite of Lady Titania's claim that high culture cannot be forced into the "thick skulls" of the masses; rather, she is arguing that poems like Dante's can touch everyone, regardless of their background. Hers is an anti-pedantic approach. What she seeks to do is to make the three *cantiche* more accessible by elaborating upon what she considers the most personally poignant episodes. In her opinion, "it's easier to remain at the door of the *Divine Comedy* on account of a certain lack of feeling than because of a deficiency of erudition or cerebral ineptitude."[130]

Marechal, however, spitefully depicts Ocampo as condescending toward the "peons of her *estancia*." The passage is also critical of Ocampo's "sensibility." Schultz says to Adán:

> What I find hardest to take about Titania is her detestable mania for subordinating things of the spirit to the vague, exquisite, ineffable titillations of her "sensibility." There isn't a single piece of music, not a metaphysical idea or psychological observation, that she doesn't immediately refer to her all-embracing sympathetic nervous system.[131]

If Marechal had read Ocampo's commentary on the *Divine Comedy*, it would have annoyed him to the quick, for it is filled with personal and hypersentimental reflections. In the following passage from the book, she relates how she felt the first time her professor of Italian read her certain passages from *Inferno*:

> The impression that this reading had on me is comparable only to what I felt as a small child the first time that I went for a swim in the ocean and was enveloped and knocked flat onto the sand by the magnificent impact of a wave. In all of my being, I received the baptism of those *words of obscure color*, so perfectly said by the author, and I arose from the emersion staggering, my lips saturated with bitterness.[132]

Her "all-embracing sympathetic nervous system" here seems to be turned upside-down by this reading of the *Comedy*. Her reason for writing about the *Comedy* is that it moved her. In the place of a lengthy preface, she transcribes a single verse: "*Amor mi mosse, che mi fa parlare.*"[133]

Marechal's original parody of Ocampo was apparently too over-the-top for his times. Jorge Lafforgue and Héctor Fernando Colla found a longer and more detailed version of this section in Marechal's original proofs (reproduced by Navascués in his critical edition),[134] but the editor of *Sudamericana* told him to tone it down, which resulted in the version we have today. Given such unkind treatment of fellow Argentine authors, it's not surprising that *Adán Buenosayres* garnered harsh literary criticism. González Lanuza's review published in *Sur* in 1948 announced that "*Adán Buenosayres* will corrode for centuries in the dust of the libraries."[135] During the fifties and part of the sixties, the novel and its author would largely remain in oblivion until the storm of anti-Peronist sentiments subsided and a new group of literary critics less affected by the political divide could reevaluate his work and renew interest in it.[136]

Of the authors discussed in this book, Leopoldo Marechal is the one who most thoroughly engages with Dante's texts. His sprawling parody is the culmination of the trend to rewrite Dante in order to (1) cleverly critique or refute the ideas of rival writers, (2) shed light on the almost embarrassing lack of consensus between Argentine authors regarding the direction Argentine literature should take, and (3) underscore that Argentina failed to produce a *Divine Comedy* of its own.

CONCLUSION

Argentina's Failure to Produce a *Divine Comedy*

What all the authors herein discussed have in common is that they desired for their country a great and unique work of literature that would fulfill for Argentina the role that the *Divine Comedy* had in Italy. Dante was not only the "father of the Italian language"; he created a text that would serve as an ethical and spiritual guide for centuries of Italians. During the Risorgimento period, the work played a key role in the emergence of Italian national consciousness. Intellectuals such as Giuseppe Mazzini promoted the idea of Dante as the *pater patriae* and associated him with moral integrity and political unity.

In Argentina, on the other hand, the work most widely acknowledged to be the nation's epic was and is José Hernández's *Martín Fierro*. Although of great literary merit and linguistically innovative, with its outlaw gaucho protagonist, the work cannot be said to promote any sort of national unity or moral behavior. Rather, it suggests a lack of patriotism among minority groups who experience rampant injustice. The protagonist is exploited and persecuted by both the Argentine military and the government, and with no possibilities for integration into society, is forced to remain an outlaw. It is not surprising, then, that the work produced such polarized responses from Bartolomé Mitre, Leopoldo Lugones, Jorge Luis Borges, and Leopoldo Marechal, depending on the political orientation of each author. As Nicolas Shumway argues in *The Invention of Argentina*, the "guiding fictions" of postindependence Argentina failed because they fostered a mythology of exclusion rather than inclusion.[1] Either they are elitist, liberal, pro-European, and *porteño*,[2] or populist, nationalist, nativist, and federalist—*Martín Fierro* being an obvious example of the latter.

Indeed, *Martín Fierro* could not be embraced by an elitist, liberal, pro-European, and *porteño* intellectual such as Mitre, who perfectly represents the other side of the ideological divide. For Mitre, *Martín Fierro* was a work that would foster friction and rebellion among the rural population. It could certainly not fulfill the role of the *Divine Comedy* within Argentina. Mitre's strategy was simply to adopt the *Divine Comedy* itself in translation, until the country was mature enough to produce its own epic.

As I have shown in the first two chapters, during the nation-building period of the nineteenth century, Mitre and many of his generation associated Dante with political unity, morality, and high culture. Mitre's 1897 translation of the *Divine Comedy* was marketed to an elite readership of Argentine men of letters who considered themselves the inheritors of European civilization. Linguistically and aesthetically, the translation contrasted with Hernández's *Martín Fierro* (1872), while offering a divergent social message. As a liberal leader, Mitre had an inclusive vision of the nation that welcomed Italian immigration as well as Italian culture. His familiarity with the doctrine of Young Italy and Giuseppe Mazzini's reading of Dante indicates that Mitre associated Dante primarily with political unity.

By the turn of the century, the influx of immigration promoted by Mitre's generation had resulted in a rapidly changing Argentina and ever-increasing concerns among Argentines regarding their cultural identity. Xenophobic sentiments developed among the creole elite. One author and literary critic who was particularly influential in articulating Argentine national identity was Leopoldo Lugones. Early in his career, as one of the leaders of the modernist movement in Argentina, he had embraced European high culture and Dante as a source of inspiration for poetic innovation. The fifth canto of the *Inferno* also inspired his Eurocentric short story "Francesca." Subsequently, however, his vision of culture began to take on fascistic elements, and he advanced a cultural nationalism that glorified the by-then-almost-obsolete gaucho and rural creole culture.

Jorge Luis Borges took a contrasting approach. Although he had experimented with literary nationalism in his younger years, he later came to be ashamed of such an outlook and instead adopted an antinationalistic, universalist approach in his writing. He did not approve of the nationalistic arguments advanced by Lugones in *El payador*, and he was critical at times of Lugones's poetics, which he interpreted as pedantic verbal play lacking true emotion. On two separate occasions, Borges rewrote Dante to create cleverly veiled criticisms of his distinguished antecedent. In "The Aleph," with its many parallels to the *Divine Comedy*, Borges parodies Lugones's poetics in the character of Carlos Argentino Daneri, while Borges as protagonist is the Dante figure in love with Beatriz. In "The Intruder," he subverts the fifth canto of the *Inferno*, while rewriting a Francesca story that takes place on the pampas and parodies the nativist theories Lugones advanced in *El payador*.

Leopoldo Marechal too would employ Dante to parody not one, but many Argentine authors in *Adán Buenosayres*. In this expansive novel he depicts the diverse demographic of Buenos Aires in the 1920s and the lack of consensus among Argentina's intellectual elite as regards cultural production. His rewriting of Dante conveys the great anxiety over lack of national expression felt by Argentine authors who had as their model the great European classics. Frustrated by seeing European high culture as something reserved for the elite, in *Adán Buenosayres* Marechal uses Dante to mock the anti-Peronist intellectuals who he believed conserved a cultural hegemony that excluded the masses and lacked a spiritual order. He likewise ridicules *criollismo* and the mythologization of figures such as the *gaucho* and *compadrito*. Through the voice of Adán, who is both a Dante-the-pilgrim figure and Marechal's literary alter ego, he advocates for the necessity of spiritual direction for the creation of great art. Yet Marechal does not suggest that *Adán Buenosayres* itself is the great work of literature that all the Argentine authors have been hoping for. Rather, he parodies Dante precisely to illustrate how much his text and works of other Argentine authors fall short. *Adán Buenosayres* ends abruptly in an absurd string of vulgar metaphors:

> Uglier than a pig's somersault. Tougher than a vizcacha's paw. Skittish as a washerwoman's pony. Solemn as the fart of an Englishman.
>
> THE END

Ultimately, Argentina failed to produce a *Divine Comedy*.

NOTES

INTRODUCTION

1. Leopoldo Marechal, *Adam Buenosayres*, trans. and ed. Norman Cheadle (Montreal: McGill-Queen's University Press, 2014), 353. All English translations of quotations from *Adán Buenosayres* are from that edition.

2. Andrea Ciccarelli, "Dante and Italian Culture from the Risorgimento to World War I," *Dante Studies, with the Annual Report of the Dante Society*, no. 119 (2001): 125.

3. Ciccarelli, 126.

4. Reprinted as a preface to the 1914 edition of the *Comedy*. Giuseppe Mazzini, "Dante" in *La commedia* (Milan: Istituto Editoriale Italiano, 1914), 11–12.

5. Mazzini, 12.

6. Mazzini, 12.

7. Mazzini, 13.

8. See *Paradiso*, 17.67–69, Cacciaguida's prophetic speech to Dante: "Di sua bestialitate il suo processo / farà la prova; sì ch'a te fia bello / averti fatta parte per te stesso."

9. Mazzini, "Dante," 15.

10. Mazzini refers to a Latin letter in which Dante honorably declines to return to Florence following the amnesty offered him in 1315, the terms of which would have required him to pay fines. Dante insists that he will only return to Florence if on honorable conditions. See *Epistola* 9 in *Dantis Alagherii Epistolae: The Letters of Dante*, with introduction, translation, and notes by Paget Toynbee (Oxford: Clarendon, 1966), 148–59.

11. Mazzini, "Dante," 11.

12. Mazzini, 15.

13. Mazzini, 20.

14. Mazzini, xi.

15. Edmund S. Morgan, *Inventing the People: The Rise of Popular Sovereignty in England and America* (New York: Norton, 1988), 13; partially quoted in Nicolas Shumway, *The Invention of Argentina* (Los Angeles: University of California Press, 1991), xi.

16. Morgan, *Inventing the People,*14.

17. Eric Hobsbawm and Terence Ranger, eds., *The Invention of Tradition* (Cambridge: Cambridge University Press, 1983), 8.

18. Benedict Anderson, *Imagined Communities: Reflections on the Origin and Spread of Nationalism* (London: Verso, 1991).

19. Shumway, *Invention of Argentina*, 9.

20. Shumway, 12.

21. Shumway, x.

22. The term *porteño* pertains to the port city of Buenos Aires.

23. Shumway, *Invention of Argentina*, xii.

24. The majority of European immigrants to the United States, 425,693 in the latter half of the nineteenth century, came from Ireland, Britain, and Germany.

25. John W. White, *Argentina: The Life Story of a Nation* (New York: Viking), 135.

26. In Samuel L. Baily's article, "The Adjustment of Italian Immigrants in Buenos Aires and New York, 1870–1914," *American Historical Review* 88, no. 2 (April 1983): 303. Sources: República Argentina, Dirección de Inmigración, *Resumen estadística del movimiento migratorio en la República Argentina, 1857–1924* (Buenos Aires, 1925) and the U.S. Bureau of the Census, *Historical Statistics of the United States, Colonial Times to 1972* (Washington, DC, 1975).

27. Herbert S. Klein, "The Integration of Italian Immigrants into the United States and Argentina: A Comparative Analysis," *American Historical Review* 88, no. 2 (April 1983): 321.

28. Klein, 320.

29. This table is a modification of table 9 on p. 323 of Klein, "Integration of Italian Immigrants." The source for the information in the table is República Argentina, *Tercere censo national de . . . 1914*, 2:395–96, 3:295–309, 4:68, 5:837, and 6:679.

30. Tulio Halperín Donghi, *José Hernández y sus mundos* (Buenos Aires: Editorial Sudamericana, Instituto Torcuato di Tella, 1985), 340.

31. These figures, given by Samuel L. Baily in his comparative study on Italian immigrants in Buenos Aires and New York, are estimates based on the 1887 census of Buenos Aires. See *Censo general de la Ciudad de Buenos Aires, 1887*, 2 (Buenos Aires, 1889): 36, 306, 379.

32. Baily, "Adjustment of Italian Immigrants," 284–85.

33. The return rate for those who immigrated to the United States was 54 percent, versus a 51 percent return rate for those who came to Argentina. Jorge Balán, "Comments to 'The Integration of Italian Immigrants into the United States and Argentina: Comparative Analysis,'" *American Historical Review* 88, no. 2 (April 1983): 333.

34. Among Italian migrants to the United States, 12 percent of the northerners were illiterate, while a substantially higher 54 percent of the southerners were illiterate. See Balán, "Comments to 'The Integration of Italian Immigrants,'" 332.

35. Baily, "Adjustment of Italian Immigrants," 286–87.

36. For a comparison of Italian adjustment in the urban centers of Buenos Aires and New York, see Baily, "Adjustment of Italian Immigrants," 281–305. For a broader comparative analysis that includes rural areas, see Klein, "Integration of Italian Immigrants," 306–29.

37. Balán, "Comments to 'The Integration of Italian Immigrants,'" 333.

38. Klein, "Integration of Italian Immigrants," 318.

39. Klein, 323.

40. Adolfo Mitre, *Italia en el sentir y pensar de Mitre*, Cuadernos de la Dante Número 15 (Buenos Aires: Asociación Dante Alighieri, 1960), 35.

41. In Argentina the word *criollo* (creole) refers to people whose ancestors were already present during the colonial period, as opposed to the newly immigrated.

42. Leopoldo Lugones, *Lunario sentimental* (Buenos Aires: M. Gleizer, 1926), 20.

43. Leopoldo Lugones, *El payador* (Buenos Aires: Editorial Huemel S.A., 1972), 27.

44. Borges selected this story to be included in the collection *La estatua de sal* (published posthumously), for which he wrote a prologue.

45. In Argentina, a *payador* is a folksinger, traditionally part of gaucho culture, who performs improvised verses to the accompaniment of a guitar.

46. The Fedeli d'Amore (Faithful of Love) were a group of poets in thirteenth-century Italy who wrote love poetry focused on the philosophical and spiritual aspects of love.

1. BARTOLOMÉ MITRE ON IMMIGRATION AND ARGENTINE IDENTITY

1. Bartolomé Mitre, "Discurso en el Senado de la Nación (septiembre de 1870)," in *Arengas de Bartolomé Mitre: Colección de discursos parlamentarios, políticos, económicos y literarios, oraciones fúnebres, alocuciones conmemorativas, proclamas y alegatos in voce pronunciados desde 1848 hasta 1902*, vol. 2 (Buenos Aires: Biblioteca de la Nación, 1902); quoted in Adolfo Mitre, *Italia en el*

sentir y pensar de Mitre, Cuadernos de la "Dante" 15 (Buenos Aires: Asociación Dante Alighieri, 1960), 5.

2. A version of this chapter was previously published in *California Italian Studies* 9 (2019): 1–22.

3. The two later amended editions were *Fe crítica de erratas y de correcciones dantescas: Correcciones á la traducción del Infierno del Dante. Con notas complementarias*; and *Segundo apéndice: Correcciones á la traducción del Dante.*

4. Anecdote as recounted by Martin Paz in "El Infierno de los traductores: El noveno círculo," *Página 12*, *Radar Libros*, June 15, 2003, http://www.pagina12.com.ar/diario/suplementos/libros/10-615-2003-06-15.html.

5. In some versions Mitre's interlocutor is Lucio V. Mansilla, a fellow diplomat and statesman. Versions of this anecdote can be found in Sergio Waisman, "Foundational Scenes of Translation," *Estudios interdisciplinarios de America Latina y el Caribe* 21, no. 1 (2010): 60; Giuseppe Bellini, "Dante nella versione di Mitre," in *Del Tradurre*, 2, ed. Teresa M. Rossi (Rome: Bulzoni, 1995), 73–84; and Paz, "El Infierno de los traductores."

6. See Ángel J Battistessa, "Dante y las generaciones argentinas," *Boletin de la Academia Argentina de Letras* 30, no. 115–16 (June 1965): 17, 22. Battistessa's translation of the *Comedy* was published in 1972: Dante Alighieri, *La divina comedia*, trans. Ángel J Battistessa (Buenos Aires: Ediciones Carlos Lohlé, 1972).

7. Pertaining to the port city of Buenos Aires.

8. Nicolas Shumway, *The Invention of Argentina* (Los Angeles: University of California Press, 1991), xii.

9. Bartolomé Mitre, letter to Señor don Miguel M. Ruíz, Buenos Aires, March 26, 1887, in *Correspondencia literaria, histórica y política*, vol. 3 (Buenos Aires: Imprenta de Coni Hermanos, 1912), 169.

10. Mitre, 170.

11. Mitre, 170.

12. Mitre, 170.

13. For further details on the history of Pero Grullo, see José Godoy Alcántara, *Ensayo histórico etimológico filológico sobre los apellidos castellanos desde el siglo X hasta nuestra edad* (Madrid: Rivadeneyra, M., 1871).

14. Francisco de Quevedo, *Sueños y discursos* (Madrid: Clásicos Castalia, 1972).

15. Mitre, *Correspondencia literaria*, 173. My emphasis.

16. Mitre, 170–71.

17. Pierre Bourdieu, "À propos de la famille comme catégorie réalisée," *Actes de la recherche en science sociales* 100 (1993): 32–36.

18. Mitre, *Correspondencia literaria*, 171.

19. Dante Alighieri, *De vulgari eloquentia*, ed. and trans. Stephen Botterill (Cambridge: Cambridge University Press, 1996), bk. 1, chap. 6, 13.

20. Mitre, *Correspondencia literaria*, 172.
21. Mitre, 172.
22. Mitre, 173. My emphasis.
23. Mitre, 173.
24. Mitre, 173.
25. Mitre, 1902; quoted in Adolfo Mitre, *Italia en el sentir y pensar de Mitre*, 5.
26. Waisman, "Foundation Scenes of Translation," 55.
27. Waisman, 55.
28. Itamar Even-Zohar, "The Position of Translated Literature within the Literary Polysystem," in *Papers on Poetics and Semiotics 8: Papers in Historical Poetics* (Tel Aviv: Porter Institute for Poetics and Semiotics, 1978), 24.
29. Ofelia I. Stahringer de Caramuti, *La política migratoria argentina* (Buenos Aires: Depalma, 1975), 14.
30. Some notable members of this group include Esteban Echeverría, Juan Bautista Alberdi, Juan María Gutiérrez, Domingo Faustino Sarmiento, and Bartolomé Mitre.
31. *Bases y puntos de partida para la organización política de la República Argentina*, in *Obras completas de Juan Bautista Alberdi*, vol. 3 (Buenos Aires: La Tribuna nacional, 1886–87). All Alberdi quotations here cited in English are from the translation by Ian Barnett as "Bases and Starting Points for the Political Organization of the Argentine Republic (1852) (Excerpts)," in *Liberal Thought in Argentina, 1837–1940*, ed. Natalio R. Botana and Ezequiel Gallo (Indianapolis: Liberty Fund, 2013), 115–76.
32. Alberdi, "Bases," 169.
33. Alberdi, 132.
34. Alberdi, 136.
35. Alberdi, 132.
36. Alberdi, 134. My emphasis.
37. Alberdi, 124.
38. Article 25 of the Constitution states that "The Federal Government shall encourage European immigration; and it shall not restrict, limit or impose taxation of any kind upon the entry into Argentine territory of aliens coming to it for the purposes of tilling the soil, improving industries, or introducing and teaching sciences and arts."
39. Julia Albarracin, "Selecting Immigration in Modern Argentina Economic, Cultural, International and Institutional Factors" (PhD diss., University of Florida, 2004), 2, http://purl.fcla.edu/fcla/etd/UFE0008385.
40. Albarracin, 35.
41. Alberdi, "Bases," 138.
42. Alberdi, 137.
43. Alberdi, 137.

44. Alberdi, 138.

45. In Article 21, he declares that "No foreigner is more privileged than another." In Article 33, "Immigration cannot be restrained, nor can it be limited in any way, under any circumstance, or under any pretext."

46. Sarmiento relates his experiences in the United States in a lengthy letter to Don Valentín Alsina in 1847. See "Estados Unidos," *Viajes por Europa, África y América: 1845–1847*, in *Obras completas de Domingo Faustino Sarmiento*, vol. 5 (Buenos Aires: Luz del Día, 1949).

47. "In the Argentine Republic, it makes one feel pity and shame to compare the German or Scottish colonies to the south of Buenos Aires with the towns existing in the interior. In the first, the little houses are painted, always clean in front, adorned with flowers and nice little shrubs; the furnishings simple but complete . . . ; and the inhabitants in constant motion and action. . . . The native town is the disgraceful reverse side of this coin; dirty children covered in rags, living amid packs of dogs; men stretched out on the ground, in utter inactivity; filth and poverty everywhere; a little table and leather chests, the only furnishings; miserable huts for habitation, notable for their generally barbaric and neglected appearance." Domingo Faustino Sarmiento, *Facundo* (Madrid: Editorial-América, 1922), 28–29. English trans. by Kathleen Ross (Berkeley: University of California Press, 2003), 58.

48. John W. White, *Argentina: The Life Story of a Nation* (New York: Viking, 1942), 135.

49. Ironically, while both Alberdi and Sarmiento had traveled to Italy, Mitre had not.

50. The discourses were first published as installments in 1870 and are included in their entirety in the second volume of the definitive edition of *Arengas* published by the Biblioteca de la Nación. Bartolomé Mitre, "Discurso en el Senado de la Nación (septiembre de 1870)," in *Arengas de Bartolomé Mitre: Colección de discursos parlamentarios, políticos, económicos y literarios, oraciones fúnebres, alocuciones conmemorativas, proclamas y alegatos in voce pronunciados desde 1848 hasta 1902*, vol. 2 (Buenos Aires: Biblioteca de la Nación, 1902).

51. Mitre, *Arengas*, 108.

52. Mitre, 107.

53. Mitre, 95. My translation.

54. English translation by Ian Barnett in *Liberal Thought in Argentina 1837–1940*, ed. Natalio R. Botana and Ezequel Gallo (Indianapolis: Liberty Fund, 2013), 254. My emphasis.

55. Mitre, *Arengas*, 112.

56. Mitre, 112–13: "que nos dan este ejemplo del capital acumulado por la economía."

57. Mitre, 113.

58. Adolfo Mitre, "Italia en el sentir y pensar de Mitre," in *Cuadernos de la Dante Número 15* (Buenos Aires: Asociación Dante Alighieri, 1960), 35.

59. Cantos 1, 3, 5, 32, and 33 were the first to be published.

60. Mitre, *Correspondencia literaria*, 174.

61. Mitre, 174.

62. Mitre, 176.

63. Mitre mentions the lyric poets Heredia (Cuban) and Olmedo (born in Guayaquil); the dramatic poets Alarcón (Mexican), Goristiza (Mexican), and Ventura de la Vega (who was born in Argentina but gained fame in Spain); the epic poets Pedro de Oña (Chile) and Ruíz de León (Mexican).

64. Mitre, *Correspondencia literaria*, 178.

65. Mitre, 177.

66. Although Lugones insists that *Martín Fierro* is an epic, the work's genre is debatable. Borges described the work as more of a "verse novel" than an "epic."

67. Mitre, "Teoría del Traductor."

68. *Mazorca* means "ear of corn" in Spanish; an ear of corn was their symbol and stood for their unity. Opponents to the group, however, said that the name should be spelled *más horca* or "more hangings," on account of their brutal tactics.

69. In 1846 they changed their name to *Asociación de Mayo*, after the May Revolution that began Argentina's independence movement.

70. Juan Antonio Solari, *A un siglo del "Dogma Socialista"* (Buenos Aires, 1937), 18.

71. Solari, 19.

72. First published in Montevideo in 1846. There is some discrepancy regarding the exact date of foundation of the Asociación de Mayo. Most sources list 1847 as the date, but others a year later in mid-1848.

73. Esteban Echeverría, *El Dogma Socialista a la juventud argentina (1837)* (Biblioteca Virtual Universal, 2003), 6.

74. Other contributors include Juan Bautista Alberdi, Juan María Gutiérrez, Florencio Varela, Esteban Echeverría, and Juan Cruz Varela.

75. Bartolomé Mitre, *El Nacional* (Montevideo), November 30, 1838. Museo Mitre.

76. See Jorge Myers, "Giuseppe Mazzini and the Emergence of Liberal Nationalism in the River Plate and Latin America," in *Giuseppe Mazzini and the Globalisation of Democratic Nationalism, 1830–1920*, ed. C. A. Bayly and Eugenio F. Biagini (Oxford: Oxford University Press, 2008).

77. Letter from Miguel Cané to Mitre regarding his translation of the *Divina Comedia*, August 29, 1894, in *Correspondencia literaria, histórica y política*

del General Mitre, vol. 3 (Buenos Aires: Imprenta de Coni Hermanos, 1912), 318.

78. Cané, 318–19.

79. Cané, 323.

80. Cané, 323.

81. Cané, 320.

82. Miguel Cané (the elder) was one of the founders of the journal *El Iniciador*.

83. Letter from Mitre to Miguel Cané (the younger), Museo Mitre: "la época lejana en que lo [la *Divina Commedia*] deletreaba . . . aleccionado por los proscritos italianos que soñaban con la Italia Unida presentida por el Poeta, a la vez que los emigrados argentinos esperaban la libertad de su patria."

84. Albert Russell Ascoli and Krystyna von Henneberg, "Introduction," in *Making and Remaking Italy: The Cultivation of National Identity around the Risorgimento*, ed. Albert Russell Ascoli and Krystyna von Henneberg (Oxford: Berg, 2001), 11.

85. Ascoli and von Henneberg, 5.

86. Quoted in Marziano Guglielminetti, "'Decadenza' e 'progresso' dell'Italia nel dibattito fra classicisti e romantici," in *La restaurazione in Italia: Strutture e ideologie, Atti del XLVII Congresso di storia del Risorgimento italiano* (1974) (Rome: Istituto per la storia del Risorgimento italiano, 1976), 253, and in Adrian Lyttelton, "Creating a National Past: History, Myth and Image in the Risorgimento," in Ascoli and von Henneberg, *Making and Remaking Italy*, 42.

87. For European views on Italy and Italians in travel literature and historical accounts, see Franco Venturi, "L'Italia fuori d'Italia," in *Storia d'Italia*, vol. 3, *Dal primo Settecento al'Unità*, ed. Ruggiero Romano and Corrado Vivanti (Turin: Einaudi, 1973); Carlo Bernari et al., *L'Italia dei grandi viaggiatori*, ed. Franco Paloscia (Rome: Abete, 1986); and Jeremy Black, *Italy and the Grand Tour* (New Haven, CT: Yale University Press, 2003). Some salient examples of nineteenth-century literary works (written by foreigners) that feature such descriptions of Italy include Nathaniel Hawthorne's *The Marble Faun* and Henry James's *Roderick Hudson*, *Daisy Miller*, and *The Portrait of a Lady*.

88. Alphonse de Lamartine in the mid-1820s, for example, had described Italy as a land where everything is asleep. Silvana Patriarca, "Indolence and Regeneration: Tropes and Tensions of Risorgimento Patriotism," *American Historical Review* 110, no. 2 (April 2005): 382.

89. We can also see this idea in the opening of Mitre's aforementioned poem: "Italy, Italy, land of a thousand heroes, / Raise from the ruins your downcast head, / A century of existence in decay / Is erased in one day of equality."

90. Cesare De Seta, "L'Italia nello specchio del 'Grand Tour,'" in *Storia d'Italia*, Annali 5, *Il paesaggio*, ed. Cesare De Seta (Turin, 1982), 135. Quoted in Patriarca, "Indolence and Regeneration," 387.

91. Giulio Bollati, *L'italiano: Il carattere nazionale come storia e come invenzione*, 2nd ed. (Turin: Einaudi, 1983), 41; quoted in Patriarca, "Indolence and Regeneration," 381.

92. Vincenzo Gioberti, *Del primato morale e civile degli Italiani*, ed. Giuseppe Balsamo-Crivelli, 3 vols. (Torino: Unione tip.-editrice torinese, 1920), 2:147.

93. Mitre, "Discurso"; quoted in Adolfo Mitre, *Italia en el sentir y pensar de Mitre*, 5.

94. See Venturi, "L'Italia fuori d'Italia," 985–1481; Bernari, *L'Italia dei grandi viaggiatori*; Black, *Italy and the Grand Tour.*

95. Cesare Balbo, *Delle speranze d'Italia*, ed. Achille Corbelli (Paris, 1844; Turin, 1925), 196.

96. Ascoli and von Henneberg, *Making and Remaking Italy*, 7.

2. BARTOLOMÉ MITRE'S TRANSLATION OF THE *DIVINE COMEDY*: AN ANTI–*MARTÍN FIERRO*

1. A version of this chapter was previously published in *Annali d'italianistica* 38 *Nation(s) and Translations* (2020): 325–42.

2. *Concise Encyclopedia of Latin American Literature*, 304.

3. Although Lugones insists that *Martín Fierro* is an epic (as cited in Walter Sava, "Literary Criticism of *Martín Fierro* from 1873 to 1915," *Hispanófila* 75 [May 1982]: 52), the work's genre is debatable. For example, Jorge Luís Borges, among others, throughout his own *El "Martín Fierro"* (Buenos Aires: Editorial Columba, 1953), described it as a verse novel more than an epic.

4. Bartolomé Mitre, letter to Señor don Miguel M. Ruíz, Buenos Aires, March 26, 1887, in *Correspondencia literaria, histórica y política del general Bartolomé Mitre*, vol. 3, Museo Mitre (Buenos Aires: Imprenta de Coni Hermanos, 1912), 170.

5. Mitre, 173.

6. Tulio Halperín Donghi, *José Hernández y sus mundos* (Buenos Aires: Editorial Sudamericana, Instituto Torcuato di Tella, 1985), 275.

7. José Hernández, quoted in Rodolfo Borello, *Hernández: Poesía y política* (Buenos Aires: Plus Ultra, 1973), 73.

8. Hernández, cited in Halperín Donghi, *José Hernández*, 275.

9. During his presidency, Avellaneda allowed thousands of emigrants, persecuted politicians, fugitives, and outlawed guerrillas to be reintegrated into the political life of the country. This policy is reflected in *La vuelta.*

10. Letter from José Hernández to Bartolomé Mitre, written on the flyleaf of Mitre's personal copy of *Martín Fierro*, Museo Mitre. My translation.

11. Mitre, *Correspondencia literaria*, 3:173.

12. Bartolomé Mitre, letter to José Hernández, April 14, 1879, Museo Mitre.

13. On the development of gauchesque literature, see Horacio J. Becco et al., *Trayectoria de la poesía gauchesca* (Buenos Aires: Plus Ultra, 1977); and Ángel Rama, "El sistema literario de la poesía gauchesca," prologue to *Poesía gauchesca* (Caracas: Biblioteca Ayacucho, 1977), ix–xlvii.

14. Mitre, letter to José Hernández.

15. For more on Mitre and Garibaldi, see my article "'The Hero of Two Worlds': The Equestrian Monument to Giuseppe Garibaldi in Buenos Aires, Argentina," *Italian American Review: Monuments, Memorials, and Italian Migrations* 12, no. 1 (2022): 36–60.

16. Letter from Mitre to Miguel Cané (the younger), 1894, Museo Mitre.

17. On Italian immigration to Argentina during the second half of the nineteenth century, see Ofelia I. Stahringer de Caramuti, *La política migratoria argentina* (Buenos Aires: Depalma, 1975) and John W. White, *Argentina: The Life Story of a Nation* (New York: Viking, 1942).

18. For more on this topic, see my article "Dante's Afterlife in Argentina," *California Italian Studies* 9 (2019): 1–22, https://escholarship.org/uc/item/2qq1510s.

19. ("I am not a learned singer," *Martín Fierro*, line 49, 21). All English translations of *Martín Fierro* are by Emily Stewart from the bilingual edition (Buenos Aires: Ediciones Lea S.A., 2016).

20. Hernández, 70.

21. Hernández, 56.

22. Mitre, letter to José Hernández.

23. Bartolomé Mitre, "Teoría del Traductor: Introducción a la *Divina Comedia*" (Buenos Aires: Peuser, 1897), xi–xii.

24. Mitre, ix.

25. Claudia Fernández Speier, "Las traducciones argentinas de la Divina Commedia" (PhD diss., Universidad de Buenos Aires, 2013), 142.

26. On the same page (142), Speier notes the following examples: amparanza for "amparo" (*Par.* 31); esparramar for "desparramar" (*Inf.* 14); cambiante for "variación" (*Inf.* 20); demudar for "variar," "mudar" (*Inf.* 20); conjurar for "jurar siniestramente" (*Inf.* 32); enguirlandar for "enguirnaldar" (*Purg.* 13); licencia for "claridad" or "esplendor" (*Purg.* 13); leticias for "felicidades" (*Purg.* 29); humildosamente for "humildemente" (*Purg.* 29); allegar for "unir" or "juntar" (Par II); conforto for "confortacion" (*Par.* 11); vosco for

"vos" (*Purg.*16, *Par.* 22); enarcar for "arquear" (*Par.* 23); delectar for "deleitar" (*Par.* 23); comenzamento for "comienzo" (*Par.* 22); dolorio for "dolor" (*Par.* 27); arredonar for "redondear" (*Par.* 28); perdonanzas for "perdones" (*Par.* 29); celar for "encubrir" or "ocultar" (*Par.* 29); and nodriz for "nodriza" or "madre" (*Par.* 30).

27. Zygmunt G. Barański, "Inferno XVIII," in *Lectura Dantis Bononiensis*, vol. 3, ed. Emilio Pasquini and Carlo Galli (Bologna: Bononia University Press, 2014), 84.

28. Barański, 84–85.

29. Teodolinda Barolini, "Inferno 18: Fraud and Sex in a Post-Geryon World," *Commento Baroliniano, Digital Dante* (New York: Columbia University Libraries, 2018).

30. José Hernández, Prologue to *La vuelta de Martín Fierro*, in *Martín Fierro* (Buenos Aires: Editorial Huemul S.A., 1967), 136.

31. Reprinted in Leopoldo Longhi de Bracaglia, *Mitre traductor de Dante*, ed. Nicolás Besjo Moreno (Buenos Aires: Centro Cultural "Latium," 1922), 83–84.

32. Reprinted in Longhi de Bracaglia, 83–84.

33. The six hundred copies were subdivided according to the quality of paper and the art. Nos. 1–15 were printed on imperial paper of Japan with two series of engravings and watercolor illustrations: "Encuadernacion de lujo de Marroquin del Levante." The fifteen copies in this edition were priced at 20 $ORO and had to be reserved in advance. Nos. 26–35 were printed on paper from China with watercolor illustrations (20 $ORO). The following nos. 36–100 were printed on imperial paper of Japan with one series of illustrations and "Encuadernacion de *amateur*" (15 $ORO). Finally, nos. 101–600 were printed on the paper made especially for this edition (8–10 $ORO, depending on binding). It is interesting to compare the price of these editions with the price of *Martín Fierro* when it was first published. *El gaucho Martín Fierro* was 0.40 $ORO and *La vuelta de Martín Fierro* 0.80 $ORO. The average monthly wage of a rural worker was 12 $ORO, making a copy of *Martín Fierro* accessible, which was not the case of an edition of the *Divine Comedy*. Longhi de Bracaglia, 84.

34. Longhi de Bracaglia, 84.

35. Longhi de Bracaglia, 84.

36. Letter from Osvaldo Magnasco to Mitre, Museo Mitre.

37. Letter from the Academy of the Arcadia to Mitre, August 25, 1897, Museo Mitre #13219.

38. Hernández, *La vuelta de Martín Fierro*, lines 55–56, 7.

39. Hernández, Prologue to *La vuelta de Martín Fierro*, 5.

40. Mitre, letter to José Hernández, April 14, 1879, Museo Mitre.

3. LEOPOLDO LUGONES ON IMMIGRATION AND ARGENTINE IDENTITY

1. Domingo Faustino Sarmiento, *Facundo* (1845) (Buenos Aires: Editorial Losada, S.A., 1981), 240.

2. Letter from Bernardino Rivadavia to J. M. Pueyrredón, cited in Tulio Halperín Donghi, "Para que la inmigración? Ideología y política inmigratoria y aceleración del proceso modernizador: El caso argentino," *Jahrbuch für Geschichte von Staat, Wirtschaft und Gesellschaft Lateinamerikas* (JBLA) 13 (Köln: Bohlau Verlag, 1976), 443; and Jeane Delaney, "Making Sense of Modernity: Changing Attitudes toward the Immigrant and the Gaucho in Turn-of-the-Century Argentina," *Comparative Studies in Society and History* 38, no. 3 (July 1996): 442.

3. Between 1850 and 1930 fewer than 5 percent of immigrants took Argentine citizenship. David Rock, *Argentina, 1516–1982* (Los Angeles: University of California Press, 1985), 143.

4. David Rock, *Argentina 1516–1982* (Los Angeles: University of California Press, 1985), 165.

5. Rock, 141.

6. For Argentina's economic growth during the early twentieth century see the chapter "Four Seasons of Democracy, 1890–1930" in Rock, *Argentina, 1516–1982*, 162–213.

7. In 1895 only 8 percent of the immigrant population were landowners. Rock, 140.

8. Delaney, "Making Sense of Modernity," 435.

9. Delaney, 440.

10. In 1895 only 8 percent of the immigrant population owned land. Rock, *Argentina, 1516–1982*, 140.

11. Rock, 143.

12. Julia Albaraccin, "Selecting Immigration in Modern Argentina: Economic, Cultural, International and Institutional Factors" (PhD diss., University of Florida, 2004), http://purl.fcla.edu/fcla/etd/UFE0008385, 46.

13. Carl Solberg, *Immigration and Nationalism: Argentina and Chile, 1890–1914* (Austin: University of Texas Press, 1970), 108.

14. Errico Malatesta (in Argentina from 1885 to 1889) drew up the charter for the bakers' union, which established the norm for other similar activist working-class organizations. Pietro Gori (in Argentina from 1898 to 1902) was fundamental in the founding of the Federación Obrera Argentina (FOA), the first national labor union. Of the forty-seven delegates present at the inaugural congress in 1901, twenty-six of them had Italian last names. See Osvaldo Bayer's essay "L'influenza dell'immigrazione italiana nel movimento anarchico argentino," in *Gli italiani fuori d'Italia*, ed. Bruno Bezza (Milan:

Franco Angelo, 1983), 145–62; translated as "The Influence of Italian Immigration on the Argentine Anarchist Movement," on libcom.org, submitted by Quinlan Vos, January 24, 2010, https://libcom.org/library/influence-italian-immigration-argentine-anarchist-movement-osvaldo-bayer.

15. Argentina Superintendente del Censo, *Primer censo de la República Argentina: Verificado en los días 15, 16, 17 de septiembre de 1869*, bajo la dirección de Diego G. de la Fuente (Buenos Aires: Imprenta del porvenir, 1872), 44–45; David Rock, *State Building and Political Movements in Argentina, 1860–1916* (Stanford, CA: Stanford University Press, 2002), 72.

16. Luis Pascarella, *El conventillo* [1918], cited in *Testimonios culturales Argentinos: La década del 10*, ed. Osvaldo Pellettieri (Buenos Aires: Editorial Belgrano, 1980), 43; and cited in Delaney, "Making Sense of Modernity," 447–48.

17. Delaney, 447.

18. See for example Carlos Altamirano and Beatriz Sarlo, "La Argentina del Centenario: Campo intelectual, vida literaria y temas ideológicos," in *Ensayos argentinos: De Sarmiento a la vanguardia* (Buenos Aires: Centro Editor de América Latina, 1983), 72; Rafael Olea Franco, "Lugones y el mito gauchesco: Un capítulo de historia cultural argentina," *Nueva revista de filología hispánica* 38, no. 1 (1990): 308–9.

19. Solberg, *Immigration and Nationalism*, 132; quoted in Olea Franco, 309.

20. Critics who have written on the quest for national identity include Beatriz Sarlo, Ivonne Bordelois, Alejandro Cattaruzza, Silvia Saytta, Rafael Olea Franco, and Juan José Sebreli.

21. The poem was originally published in two parts, *El gaucho Martín Fierro* (1872) and *La vuelta de Martín Fierro* (1879).

22. http://www.ale.uji.es/lugones.htm. Website created by Patricia Claros, Sandra Tena, Nadia Santo, and Inma Viedma, Universitat Jaume I. Accessed March 30, 2015.

23. Although *modernismo* does share some characteristics with modernism, which took place in Europe, it is a distinct Latin American literary movement, and the two should not be confused. Beginning with the publication of Rubén Darío's *Azul* in 1888, *modernismo* is characterized by exotic imagery, innovative meters, concern with "art for art's sake," and proud expressions of cultural identity.

24. Lugones, who had joined the fascist cause in 1924 by giving a famous speech entitled "The Hour of the Sword," was appointed as the writer of the fascist government's first proclamation.

25. Leopoldo Lugones, "Oda a los ganados y a las mieses," in *Obras poéticas completas* (Madrid: Aguilar, 1959), 468.

26. Leopoldo Lugones, "On Immigration," from *The Great Argentina* (1930), in *Leopoldo Lugones: Selected Writings*, trans. Sergio Waisman (Oxford: Oxford University Press, 2008), 86.

27. Lugones, "On Immigration," 86.

28. Lugones, 86–87.

29. For example, German laws of 1914 and the Spanish Constitution of 1931 allowed for dual citizenship.

30. Lugones, "On Immigration," 87.

31. Lugones, 87.

32. Lugones, 89.

33. Lugones, 88.

34. Lugones, 88.

35. Lugones, 88.

36. Lugones, 89.

37. Lugones, 89.

38. This system was in effect until 1965.

39. Lugones, "On Immigration," 86.

40. James R. Scobie, *Buenos Aires: Del centro a los barrios, 1870–1910* (Buenos Aires: Solar/Hachette, 1977), 281; quoted in Altamirano and Sarlo, *Ensayos argentinos*, 94n36.

41. Altamirano and Sarlo, *Ensayos argentinos*, 95.

42. *Encyclopedia of Latin American and Caribbean Literature, 1900–2003*, ed. Daniel Balderston and Mike Gonzalez (New York: Routledge, 2004), 160.

43. Borges makes this argument in "La poesía gauchesca," in *Obras completas* (Buenos Aires: Emecé Editores, 1974), 179–97.

44. An important study on the myth of the gaucho and immigration is Gladys Onega, *La inmigración en la literatura argentina (1880–1910)* (Rosario: Facultad de Filosofia y Letras, Universidad Nacional del Litoral, Cuadernos del Instituto de Letras, 1965).

45. Manuel Gálvez, "¿Cuál es el valor del *Martín Fierro*?," in *Nosotros*, no. 50 (June 1913); quoted in Altamirano and Sarlo, *Ensayos argentinos*, 98.

46. Domingo di Núbila, *La época de oro: Historia del cine argentino* (Buenos Aires: Ediciones del Jilguero, 1998), 392; Claudio España, "El cine sonoro y su expansión," in *Historia del cine argentino*, ed. Jorge Miguel Couselo (Buenos Aires: Centro Editor de América Latina, 1984), 80.

47. The sections of *El payador* are as follows: I. La vida épica, II. El hijo de la pampa, III. A campo y cielo . . . , IV. La poesía gaucha, V. La música gaucha, VI. El lenguaje del poema, VII. Martín Fierro es un poema épico, VIII. El telar de sus desdichas, IX. La vuelta de Martín Fierro, X. El linaje de Hércules. Leopoldo Lugones, *El payador* (1916; Buenos Aires: Editorial Huemul S.A., 1972).

48. Quoted in Altamirano and Sarlo, *Ensayos argentinos*, 73.

49. Altamirano and Sarlo, "La Argentina del Centenario," in *Ensayos argentinos*, 95.

50. Ángel Rama, *Los gauchipolíticos rioplatenses* (Buenos Aires: Centro Editor de América Latina, 1982), 236.

51. Lugones, *El payador*, 126, 50, 51.

52. Lugones, 21.

53. Lugones, 29.

54. Lugones, 22.

55. As Rafael Olea Franco argues, "By locating the essence of "*argentinidad*" in a pre-immigration past, and by not adding any of the characteristics of the immigrants to the national heritage, Lugones was in fact expressing a strong rejection of the masses." Olea Franco, "Lugones y el mito gauchesco," 324.

56. "Cronica de *La Nación*," which includes the closing remarks of his lectures, later included in *El payador*, 361; quoted by Altamirano and Sarlo, *Ensayos argentinos*, 101.

57. Altamirano and Sarlo, 100.

58. Olea Franco, "Lugones y el mito gauchesco," 323.

4. HYPERMEDIEVALIZING AND DEMEDIEVALIZING DANTE: LEOPOLDO LUGONES'S AND JORGE LUIS BORGES'S REWRITINGS OF *INFERNO* V

1. A version of this chapter was previously published in *Iberoamerican Neomedievalisms: "The Middle Ages" and Its Uses in Latin America*, ed. Nadia R. Altschul and Maria Ruhlmann (Leeds: ARC Humanities, 2023), 121–38.

2. "Siede la terra dove nata fui / su la marina dove 'l Po discende / per aver pace co' seguaci sui" (Dante Alighieri, *Inferno*, trans. Robert Hollander and Jean Hollander [New York: Anchor Books, 2002], 5.97–99); "i due cognati" (*Inf.* 6.2); "Caina attende chi a vita ci spense" (*Inf.* 5.107).

3. "Galeotto fu 'l libro e chi lo scrisse / quel giorno più non vi leggemmo avante" (A Galeotto was the book and he that wrote it. / That day we read in it no further) (Dante, *Inf.* 5.137–38; trans. Hollander, 99).

4. It was later included in a posthumous collection of his short stories entitled *La estatua de sal* (1985) as part of the series La Biblioteca de Babel.

5. "Abuelo arduo y conciso, / Por cuyo Paraíso / Jamás pasó un pedante" (Leopoldo Lugones, *Lunario sentimental* [Buenos Aires: M. Gleizer, 1926], 20).

6. "pues en mi programa de joven viajero, entraba, naturalmente, una visita a la patria de Francesca" (Leopoldo Lugones, "Francesca," in *Lunario sentimental* [Buenos Aires: M. Gleizer, 1926], 343).

7. "La *o* atravesada por una línea oblicua que baja de derecha a izquierda, significando *cum*, signo peculiar de los últimos años del siglo XIII, al

comienzo del cual, así como en los anteriores y en los sucesivos, tuvo otras formas; el 2, coronado por una *b* a manera de exponente algebraico (2b) significando *duabus*, y agregando con su presencia un dato más, puesto que las cifras arábigas no se generalizaron en Europa hasta el siglo XIII; el 7, representado por una A sin travesaño, como para marcar dicha transición; la palabra *corpus* abreviada en su primera sílaba y coronada por un 9 (cor9) y el vocablo *fratibus* abreviado en *ftbz* con una *a* superpuesta a la *f* y una *i* a la *t*; amén de diversos signos que omito. No quiero olvidar, sin embargo, las iniciales de la heroína, aquella F y aquella R tan características también en su parecido con las PP manuscritas de nuestra caligrafía, salvo el travesaño que las corta" (Lugones, "Francesca," 344–45).

8. See Teodolinda Barolini, "Dante and Francesca da Rimini: Realpolitik, Romance, Gender," *Speculum* 75, no. 1 (January 2000): 1–28.

9. "Existen, además, en la margen del texto, a manera de apostilla, dos escudos: uno en forma de ancha almendra, característico también del siglo XIII, y el otro romboidal, es decir, blasón de dama, salvo excepciones rarísimas como las de algunos Visconti; pero los Visconti eran lombardos, y en la época de mi documento, recién conquistaban la soberanía milanesa. Además, los blasones en cuestión, se hallan acolados, lo que indica unión conyugal. Desgraciadamente, su campo no conserva sino partículas informes de las piezas y colores heráldicos" (Lugones, "Francesca," 345).

10. "tan libre come me plazca" (Lugones, "Francesca," 346).

11. "Jamás hubo otra relación que una *exaltada amistad* entre Paolo y Francesca. Aun sus manos estuvieron exentas de culpa; y sus labios no tuvieron otra que la de estremecerse y palidecer en la dulce angustia de la pasión inconfesa" (Lugones, "Francesca," 346).

12. "Paolo se ingeniaba de todos modos para hacer a aquella juventud más llevadera su clausura en castillo tan lóbrego; y su exquisita cortesía, tanto como su grave ternura, derretían hasta las heces el corazón de aquella mujer, en quien los refinamientos todavía bizantinos de su ciudad natal habían profundizado sensibilidades" (Lugones, "Francesca," 349).

13. "Paolo era diestro en componer enigmas, que el gusto de la época había elevado a un puesto superior de literatura" (Lugones, "Francesca," 350).

14. Lugones, "Francesca," 350–51.

15. "*Galeoto* fue el libro . . . -dice el poeta-. ¡Oh, no, Dios mío! Fue el astro" (Lugones, "Francesca," 352).

16. "Materialmente, no habían pecado, pues ni a tocarse llegaron, ni a hablarse siquiera; pero el esposo *vió* en sus ojos el adulterio con tan vertiginosa claridad, con tal consentimiento de rebelión y de delito, que les partió el corazón sin vacilar un ápice. Y el pergamino le halla razón, a fe mía" (Lugones, "Francesca," 354).

17. "aquellos ojos negros como dos golondrinas de la Pasión, qué sacrificio de ternura abismaban en el heroísmo de su silencio!" (Lugones, "Francesca," 352).

18. As Rafael Olea Franco argues, "By locating the essence of "*argentinidad*" in a pre-immigration past, and by not adding any of the characteristics of the immigrants to the national heritage, Lugones was in fact expressing a strong rejection of the masses" (Olea Franco, "Lugones y el mito gauchesco: Un capítulo de historia cultural argentina," *Nueva revista de filología hispánica* 38, no. 1 [1990]: 324). Also see Altamirano and Sarlo, who share this opinion. They point out that Lugones's advocacy of *Martín Fierro* affirms, "through the myth of origin, the guiding right of the elite "*criollos viejos*" over the country. A right that the recently immigrated seemed to challenge" (Altamirano and Sarlo, *Ensayos argentinos*, 100).

19. "las diversas sinceridades de un hombre a quien le interesa un mismo problema y que da, a lo largo del tiempo, con soluciones contradictorias" (Jorge Luis Borges, Prologue to Leopoldo Lugones, *La estatua de sal* [Madrid: Ediciones Siruela, 1985], 11).

20. "A *Los criollos* les quiero hablar: a los hombres que en esta tierra se sienten vivir y morir, no a los que creen que el sol y la luna están en Europa. Tierra de desterrados natos de ésta, de nostalgiosos de lo lejano y lo ajeno; ellos son los gringos de veras, autorícelo o no su sangre, y con ellos no habla mi pluma. // Quiero conversar con los otros, con los muchachos querencieros y nuestros que no le achican la realidá a este país. Mi argumento de hoy es la patria: lo que hay en ella de presente, de pasado y de venidero" (Borges, "El tamaño de mi esperanza," in *El tamaño de mi esperanza* [Buenos Aires: Espasa Calpe/Seix Barral, 1993], 11).

21. "Quiero formular y justificar algunas proposiciones escépticas sobre el problema del escritor argentino y la tradición. Mi escepticismo no se refiere a la dificultad o imposibilidad de resolverlo, sino a la existencia misma del problema. Creo que nos enfrenta un tema retórico, apto para desarrollos patéticos; más que de una verdadera dificultad mental entiendo que se trata de una apariencia, de un simulacro, de un seudoproblema" (Borges, "El escritor argentino y la tradición," in *Obras completas* [Buenos Aires: Emecé Editores, 1974], 267). Presented in 1951, the work was first published in 1953 in *Cursos y conferencias.*

22. Borges, "El escritor argentino y la tradición," 267.

23. Nicolas Shumway, *The Invention of Argentina* (Los Angeles: University of California Press, 1991), 71.

24. Shumway, 70.

25. Shumway, 70.

26. Borges, "El escritor argentino y la tradición," 268.

27. Borges, 268. Estanislao del Campo (1834–1880) was an Argentine poet whose *Fausto* is one of the major works of gaucho poetry. Hilario Ascasubi (1807–1875) was an Argentine poet and opponent of Juan Manuel de Rosas.

28. "los nacionalistas simulan venerar las capacidades de la mente argentina pero quieren limitar el ejercicio poético de esa mente a algunos pobres temas locales, como si los argentinos sólo pudiéramos hablar de orillas y estancias y no del universo" (Borges, "El escritor argentino y la tradición," 271).

29. "En *Francesca* se atreve a competir con el canto V del Infierno y el hallazgo de esa aventura está en el tono íntimo" (Borges, *La estatua de sal*, 13).

30. Dejan caer el libro, porque ya saben

> que son las personas del libro.
> (Lo serán de otro, el máximo,
> pero eso qué puede importarles.)
> Ahora son Paolo y Francesca,
> no dos amigos que comparten
> el sabor de una fábula.
> Se miran con incrédula maravilla.
> Las manos no se tocan.
>
> (Borges, "Infierno, V, 129," 559)

31. 1) "Ya no leían; y así pasaron muchas horas, con las manos tan heladas sobre el libro," 2) "el llanto desbordó en gotas vivas—lo único que vivía en ellos—sobre sus manos," and finally, 3) "materialmente, no habían pecado, pues ni a tocarse llegaron." [1) "They had already stopped reading; and thus they passed many hours, with their hands frozen on the book," 2) "The weeping overflowed in living drops—the only thing that lived in them—on their hands," and finally, 3) "materially, they had not sinned, for they did not touch each other."] (Lugones, "Francesca," 352–53).

32. Sylvie Davidson, "Borges and Italian Literature," *Italian Quarterly* 27, no. 105 (Summer 1986): 46–47. The connection between the fifth canto of *Inferno* and Borges's "La Intrusa" has also been acknowledged by Julio Chiappini, *Borges y Dante* (Rosario: Editorial Zeus, 1993; Patricia Novillo-Corvalán, *Borges and Joyce* (London: Legenda/MHRA and Maney, 2011), 126; and Humberto Nuñez-Faraco, *Borges and Dante: Echoes of a Literary Friendship.* (Berlin: Peter Lang, 2006), 20.

33. Jorge Luis Borges, "The Intruder," in *Doctor Brodie's Report*, trans. Norman Thomas di Giovanni (New York: E. P. Dutton, 1972), 72.

34. Borges, 72.

35. Jorge Luis Borges, "Commentaries," in *The Aleph and Other Stories, 1933–1969: Together with Commentaries and an Autobiographical Essay*, ed. and

trans. Norman Thomas di Giovanni in collaboration with the author (New York: E. P. Dutton, 1978), 278.

36. Borges, "The Intruder," 68.
37. Borges, 67.
38. "tan libre come me plazca" (Lugones, "Francesca," 346).
39. Borges, "The Intruder," 68.
40. Borges, 68.
41. Borges, 68.
42. Borges, 69.
43. Borges, 70.
44. Borges, 70.
45. Borges, 71.
46. Borges, "The Intruder," 71; "En el duro suburbio, un hombre no decía, ni se decía, que una mujer pudiera importarle, más allá del deseo y la posesión, pero los dos estaban enamorados. Esto, de algún modo, los humillaba." Jorge Luis Borges, "La intrusa," in *Obras completas* (Buenos Aires: Emecé Editores, 1974), 1026–27.
47. Borges, "The Intruder," 73.
48. Borges, 74.
49. "creo que Racine ni siquiera hubiera entendido a una persona que le hubiese negado su derecho al título de poeta francés por haber buscado temas griegos y latinos. Creo que Shakespeare se habría asombrado si hubieran pretendido limitarlo a temas ingleses, y si le hubiesen dicho que, como inglés, no tenía derecho a escribir *Hamlet*, de tema escandinavo, o *MacBeth*, de tema escocés. El culto argentino del color local es un reciente culto europeo que los nacionalistas deberían rechazar por foráneo" (Borges, *Obras completas*, 270).
50. "Fue escrito por Mahoma, y Mahoma, como árabe, no tenía por qué saber que los camellos eran especialmente árabes; eran para él parte de la realidad, no tenía que distinguirlos; en cambio, un falsario, un turista, un nacionalista árabe, lo primero que hubiera hecho es prodigar camellos, caravanas de camellos en cada página" (Borges, *Obras completas*, 270).
51. Borges, 271.
52. Borges, 272.
53. Borges, 272.
54. Borges, 274.

5. REWRITING DANTE TO PARODY LUGONES: BORGES'S "THE ALEPH"

1. Jorge Luis Borges, "Roberto Godel: Nacimiento del fuego" in *Prólogo con un prólogo de prólogos* (Madrid: Alianza Editorial, 1975), 112.

2. Some studies on Dante in Borges include Humberto Nuñez-Faraco's *Borges and Dante: Echoes of a Literary Friendship* (Berlin: Peter Lang, 2006); Julio Chiappini's *Borges y Dante* (Rosario: Editorial Zeus, 1993); Maria Bonatti, "Dante en la lectura de Borges," *Revista Iberoamericana* 43, no. 100–101 (1977): 737–44; Jon Thiem, "Borges, Dante, and the Poetics of Total Vision," *Comparative Literature* 40, no. 2 (1988): 97–120.

3. Jorge Luis Borges, "The Divine Comedy," in *Seven Nights*, trans. Eliot Weinberger (New York: New Directions, 1984), 8–9.

4. Jorge Luis Borges, *Nueve ensayos dantescos*, ed. Marcos Ricardo Barnatán (Madrid: Espasa-Calpe, 1982).

5. "*La Divina Comedia* es el libro más justificable y más firme de todas las literaturas." Jorge Luis Borges, "Sobre el 'Vathek' de William Beckford," in *Obras completas* (Buenos Aires: Emecé Editores, 1974), 731.

6. Borges, "The Divine Comedy," 20.

7. Jorge Luis Borges and Roberto Alifano, *Twenty-Four Conversations with Borges Including a Selection of Poems: Interviews by Roberto Alifano, 1981–1983*, trans. Nicomedes Suárez Araúz, Willis Barnstone, and Noemí Escandell (Housatonic, MA: Lascaux, 1984), 97.

8. Jorge Luis Borges, *Selected Non-fictions*, ed. Eliot Weinberger, trans. Esther Allen, Suzanne Jill Levine, and Eliot Weinberger (New York: Viking, 1999), 267.

9. Jorge Luis Borges, "La esfera de Pascal," in *Obras completas* (Buenos Aires: Emecé Editores, 1974), 636.

10. Borges, 637.

11. "Two or three times he had reconstructed a whole day; he had never hesitated, but each reconstruction had required a whole day." Jorge Luis Borges, "Funes el memorioso," in *Obras completas* (Buenos Aires: Emecé Editores, 1974), 488.

12. Jorge Luis Borges, "The Aleph," in *The Aleph and Other Stories*, trans. Andrew Hurley (New York: Penguin Books, 2004), 126–27. Hereafter, all citations of "The Aleph" refer to Andrew Hurley's translation; all citations of "El aleph" refer to the original Spanish text in *Obras completas* (Buenos Aires: Emecé Editores, 1974), 617–28.

13. Borges, "The Aleph," 129.

14. Borges, 129.

15. The many parallels between "The Aleph" and *The Divine Comedy* have already been investigated by critics. See for example the following studies: Francisco Ayala, "Comentarios textuales a 'El Aleph' de Borges," *Explicación de textos literarios* 2 (1973): 3–5; Gene H. Bell-Villada, *Borges and His Fiction: A Guide to His Mind and Art* (Austin: University of Texas Press, 1999); Bonatti, "Dante en la lectura de Borges"; Matei Calinescu, *Rereading* (New Haven,

CT: Yale University Press, 1993), 3–17; Daniel Devoto, "Aleph et Alexis," *L'Herne* no. 4 (Paris 1964): 280–92; George R. McMurray, *Jorge Luis Borges* (New York: Frederick Ungar, 1980), 229–30; Emir Rodríguez Monegal, *Jorge Luis Borges: A Literary Biography* (New York: E. P. Dutton, 1978), 413–17; Roberto Paoli, "'El Aleph': Bifurcazioni di lettura," in *Borges: Percorsi di significato* (Florence: Università degli Studi di Firenze, 1977), 7–49; Ruggero Stefanini "Dante in Borges: L'Aleph, Beatriz, e il Sud," *Italica* 57, no. 1 (1980): 53–65; Thiem, "Borges, Dante, and the Poetics of Total Vision," 97–120.

16. See for example Patricia Novillo-Corvalán, *Borges and Joyce* (London: Legenda/MHRA and Maney, 2011), 138. This is also the opinion of Jon Thiem, "Borges, Dante, and the Poetics of Total Vision," 100. Others have read the figure of Daneri as a parody of the Chilean poet Pablo Neruda, although this would hardly make sense given Daneri's middle name "Argentino," and the fact that his poem is published in a series of "Argentine pieces." Nuñez-Faraco suggests the possibility of parallels with the Nicaraguan writer Rubén Darío, but ultimately concludes that Daneri "embodies a complex web of literary references." See *Borges and Dante*, 45.

17. Borges, "The Aleph," 131.

18. Thiem, "Borges, Dante, and the Poetics of Total Vision."

19. To my knowledge, the only other person to have identified Daneri as Lugones is Marisa Martínez Pérsico in her essay "El dilema de los críticos practicantes: Un discurso que no puede exceder sus propios márgenes; L. Lugones a través de J. L. Borges," *Cartaphilus* 2 (2007): 107–18.

20. Pérsico, 111; Lugones was born on June 13, 1874. The Sociedad Argentina de Escritores (SADE), which he founded, designated his date of birth as the "Día del Escritor" in his honor following his tragic suicide.

21. Borges, "The Aleph," 119.

22. Pérsico, "El dilema," 110.

23. Borges, "The Aleph," 199–20.

24. Jorge Luis Borges and Betina Edelberg, *Leopoldo Lugones*, in *Obras completas en colaboración* (Buenos Aires: Emecé Editores, 1997), 457; quoted in Pérsico, "El dilema," 114.

25. Borges and Edelberg, *Leopoldo Lugones*, 508.

26. Borges, "The Aleph," 120.

27. Fort's poems appear in both vol. 1, no. 2 (February 1914) and vol. 2, no. 4 (April 1914).

28. See Emilio Carilla's article "La revista de Lugones," *Thesaurus* 39, no. 3 (1974): 501–25, 506. As Carilla points out, the journal was typical of "el enciclopedismo lugoniano" and featured articles on politics, sociology, natural science, folklore, and mathematics, in addition to literature.

29. Borges, "The Aleph," 120.

30. Borges, "The Aleph," 125.

31. Borges, "El aleph," in *Obras completas* (Buenos Aires: Emecé Editores, 1974), 619.

32. Borges, "The Aleph," 121.

33. Borges, "The Aleph," 121. The first emphasis is mine.

34. Borges and Edelberg, "Lugones y lo Helénico," in *Leopoldo Lugones*, 489–91.

35. Borges and Edelberg, 490–91.

36. Fernando Sorrentino, *Seven Conversations with Jorge Luis Borges*, trans. Clark M. Zlotchew (Philadelphia: Paul Dry Books, 2010), 23.

37. Jorge Luis Borges and Roberto Alifano, *Twenty-Four Conversations with Borges: Including a Selection of Poems: Interviews by Roberto Alifano, 1981–1983*, trans. Nicomedes Suárez Araúz, Willis Barnstone, and Noemí Escandell (Housatonic, MA: Lascaux, 1984), 112–13.

38. Sorrentino, *Seven Conversations with Jorge Luis Borges*, 21.

39. Borges and Edelberg, *Leopoldo Lugones*, 473.

40. Borges and Edelberg, 473.

41. Borges and Edelberg, 474.

42. Borges, "The Aleph," 121–22.

43. Borges, 122–23.

44. Borges, 124.

45. Borges and Edelberg, *Leopoldo Lugones*, 507; quoted in Pérsico, 110. The elipses are Pérsico's.

46. Borges, "El aleph," 620.

47. Borges, "The Aleph," 123.

48. Borges, 123.

49. Jorge Luis Borges and Osvaldo Ferrari, *Conversations*, vol. 1, trans. Jason Wilson (London: Seagull Books, 2014), 4.

50. César Fernández Moreno, "Weary of Labyrinths: An Interview with Jorge Luis Borges," *Encounter* 32 (April 1969): 10–11; quoted in Monegal, *Jorge Luis Borges: A Literary Biography*, 197.

51. Borges, "El aleph," 622.

52. Jorge Luis Borges, "Leopoldo Lugones: Romancero," trans. Alfred Mac Adam in *On Argentina*, ed. Alfred Mac Adam and Suzanne Jill Levine (New York: Penguin Books, 2010), 57–58. Emphasis in the final paragraph is mine.

53. Fernando Sorrentino, "Borges y Lugones: Entusiastas ataques y reticentes disculpas" *Espéculo* 18 (2001): "a pesar de alguna ambivalencia y de cierta actitud de arrepentimiento (puramente exterior), Borges conservó hasta el fin de su vida una opinión en general adversa o desdeñosa sobre la literatura de Leopoldo Lugones."

54. Borges and Alifano, *Twenty-Four Conversations with Borges*, 96.

55. Borges and Alifano, 111–16.
56. Borges and Alifano, 113.
57. Borges and Alifano, 113.
58. Borges and Alifano, 111.
59. Borges and Alifano, 38.
60. Borges and Alifano, 93.
61. Borges and Alifano, 97.
62. Borges and Alifano, 96.
63. Borges and Alifano, 96.
64. Borges and Edelberg, *Leopoldo Lugones*, 457.
65. Harold Bloom, *The Anxiety of Influence: A Theory of Poetry* (New York: Oxford University Press, 1973).
66. Borges, "The Aleph," 124.
67. Borges, 125.
68. Borges, 125.
69. Borges, 125.
70. Estela Canto, *Borges a contraluz* (Madrid: Espasa-Calpe, 1989), 275–76; quoted in Pérsico, "El dilema," 114–15.
71. Borges, "The Aleph," 132.
72. Borges, 132.
73. Jorge Luis Borges, "La luna," in *Obras completas* (Buenos Aires: Emecé Editores, 1974), 818.
74. Borges, "La luna," 819.
75. Borges, 820.
76. Jorge Luis Borges, 1969 prologue to *Fervor de Buenos Aires*, in *Obras completas* (Buenos Aires: Emecé Editores, 1974), 13.
77. Jorge Luis Borges, second prologue to *El otro, el mismo*, in *Obras completas* (Buenos Aires: Emecé Editores, 1974), 858.
78. "Arid camel" also brings to mind Borges's ridiculing of Gibbon's remark that there are no camels in the Koran (see "El escritor argentino y la tradicion"). Borges's argument is that there is no need for an Arab to put camels on every page in order to be Arabian. He likely perceived a similar futility in combining the adjective "arid" with "camel."
79. Specifically, Borges criticizes the line "El hombre numeroso de penas y de días." Borges and Alifano, *Twenty-Four Conversations with Borges*, 112–13.
80. Jorge Luis Borges, "A Leopoldo Lugones," in *Obras completas* (Buenos Aires: Emecé Editores, 1974), 779.
81. Jorge Luis Borges, "Foreword to *The Maker*," trans. Andrew Hurley, in *The Aleph and Other Stories*, 139.
82. Borges, "Foreword to *The Maker*," 139.
83. Borges, 139.

84. Jorge Luis Borges, "Kafka y sus precursores," in *Obras completas* (Buenos Aires: Emecé Editores, 1974), 711–12.

85. For more on the relationship between Dante and Cavalcanti and for a nuanced discussion of the semantics of friendship in Dante, see Teodolinda Barolini, "*Amicus eius*: Dante and the Semantics of Friendship," in *Dante's Multitudes: History, Philosophy, Method* (Notre Dame, IN: University of Notre Dame Press, 2022), 99–120. Barolini argues that in Dante's early poetic exchanges, "in the context of young males seeking to take their places in the poetic agora," the word *amico* as a direct address "is a word that signals posturing and rivalry masking as friendship" (102).

6. LEOPOLDO MARECHAL ON IMMIGRATION AND ARGENTINE IDENTITY

1. Federica Bertagna, "Techint e gli altri: Penetrazione industriale ed emigrazione italiana nell'Argentina peronista (1946–55)," *Studi storici* 55, no. 3 (July–September 2014): 618.

2. Federica Bertagna and Marina Maccari-Clayton, "Italy: Migration 1815 to present." In *The Encyclopedia of Global Human Migration*, ed. Immanuel Ness (Chichester, UK: Blackwell, 2013), 5–6.

3. Bertagna and Maccari-Clayton, 7.

4. See Federica Bertagna, *La patria di riserva: L'emigrazione fascista in Argentina* (Rome: Donzelli, 2006) and David Aliano, *Mussolini's National Project in Argentina* (Lanham, MD: Fairleigh Dickinson University Press, 2012).

5. See Bertagna, "Techint e gli altri."

6. Bertagna, "Techint e gli altri."

7. Lucia Capuzzi, *La frontiera immaginata: Profilo politico e sociale dell'emigrazione italiana in Argentina nel secondo dopoguerra* (Milan: Franco Angeli, 2006).

8. Capuzzi.

9. "Cronología de Leopoldo Marechal," in *Antígona Vélez* (Buenos Aires: Ediciones Colihue, 1997), 9.

10. María de los Ángeles Marechal, "Bio-cronología Leopoldo Marechal," in *Adán Buenosayres*, ed. Javier de Navascués (Buenos Aires: Corregidor, 2013), 78–80.

11. M. Marechal, "Bio-cronología Leopoldo Marechal," 80.

12. M. Marechal, 81.

13. M. Marechal, 84.

14. Juan Domingo Perón, *Perón en doctrina*, comp. Juan Carlos Rousselot (Buenos Aires: Siglo Veintiuno Editores Argentina, 2008), 63; quoted in Elena P. Picech, "Leopoldo Marechal and *Adán Buenosayres* in State of Exile," *Hispanófila* 167 (January 2007): 81.

15. Federico Finchelstein, *The Ideological Origins of the Dirty War* (Oxford: Oxford University Press, 2014), 65–92.

16. Leopoldo Marechal, "Descubrimiento de la patria," in *Obras completas*, vol. 1, *La poesia*, comp. Pedro Luis Barcia, ed. María de los Ángeles Marechal (Buenos Aires: Libros Perfil S.A., 1998), 303. In the prologue to *Adán Buenosayres* he refers to Buenos Aires as "Ciudad de la Yegua Tobiana" or City of the Pinto Mare.

17. Fernanda Elisa Bravo Herrera, "Lo épico en 'La Patriótica' de Leopoldo Marechal," in *Perspectivas de la ficcionalidad: Actas del II Simposio Internacional de Narratología*, ed. Daniel Altamiranda and Esther Smith, vol. 1 (Buenos Aires: Editorial Docencia, 2005), 269–77.

18. Leopoldo Marechal, "De la patria joven," in *Obras completas*, vol. 1, *La poesia*, comp. Pedro Luis Barcia, ed. María de los Ángeles Marechal (Buenos Aires: Libros Perfil S.A., 1998), 151–52.

19. Marechal, "De la patria joven," 151.

20. Marechal, 152.

21. Marechal, "Descubrimiento de la patria," 303.

22. Marechal, 303. In part 2 of book 1 of *Adán Buenosayres*, the protagonists Adán and Tesler are distinguished from the migrant workers who are oblivious to their poetic and philosophical concerns. The Italian construction workers munching raw onions across from Tesler's apartment stare at him as he stands in the window and laugh at his elaborately decorated kimono, the description of which is a parody of Homer's description of Achilles's shield (43). This associates Adán and Tesler wih epic and high culture, but makes them a silly spin-off thereof.

23. Marechal, "Descubrimiento de la patria," 303.

24. Marechal, 304.

25. Marechal, 304.

26. Marechal, 305–6.

27. Marechal, 305–6.

28. Leopoldo Marechal, *Adam Buenosayres*, trans. and ed. Norman Cheadle (Montreal: McGill-Queen's University Press, 2014), 405. All English translations of quotations from *Adán Buenosayres* are from that edition.

29. Leopoldo Marechal, "Proyecciones culturales del momento argentino," in *Obras completas*, vol. 5, *Cuentos y otros escritos*, comp. Pedro Luis Barcia, ed. María de los Ángeles Marechal (Buenos Aires: Libros Perfil S.A., 1998), 132.

30. Marechal, "Descubrimiento de la patria," 306–7.

31. Bravo Herrera, "Lo épico en 'La Patriótica,'" 270.

32. Marechal, "Descubrimiento de la patria," 307.

33. Leopoldo Marechal, "Carta a Eduardo Mallea," in *Obras completas*, vol. 5, *Cuentos y otros escritos*, comp. Pedro Luis Barcia, ed. María de los Ángeles

Marechal (Buenos Aires: Libros Perfil S.A., 1998), 289. First printed in *Sol y luna* (Buenos Aires), no. 1 (1938): 180–82.

34. Marechal, "Carta a Eduardo Mallea," 290.

35. Marechal, 291.

36. Leopoldo Marechal, "Fundación espiritual de Buenos Aires," in *Obras completas*, vol. 5, *Cuentos y otros escritos*, comp. Pedro Luis Barcia, ed. María de los Ángeles Marechal (Buenos Aires: Libros Perfil S.A., 1998), 105.

37. Marechal, "Fundación," 106. My emphasis.

38. Marechal, 106.

39. Marechal, 106

40. Marechal, 107.

41. Marechal, 110.

42. Leopoldo Marechal, "Didáctica de la patria," in *Obras completas*, vol. 1, *La poesía*, comp. Pedro Luis Barcia, ed. María de los Ángeles Marechal (Buenos Aires: Libros Perfil S.A., 1998), 309.

43. Marechal, "Didáctica," 309.

44. Marechal, 310.

45. Marechal, 311.

46. Marechal, 311.

47. Marechal, 312.

48. Marechal, 313.

49. Marechal, 312–13.

50. Marechal, 317.

51. Marechal, 318.

52. Leopoldo Marechal, lecture given in 1936 for the fourth centenary of the founding of Buenos Aires. Published in *Homenaje a Buenos Aires en el cuarto aniversario de su fundación*, Conferencias (Buenos Aires: Municipalidad de la Ciudad de Buenos Aires, 1936), 479–92. Also published as "La nueva generación literaria," in *Obras completas*, vol. 5, *Cuentos y otros escritos*, comp. Pedro Luis Barcia, ed. María de los Ángeles Marechal (Buenos Aires: Libros Perfil S.A., 1998), 215.

53. Leopoldo Marechal, "Carta al Dr. Atilio Dell'Oro Maini," en *Obras completas*, vol. 5, *Cuentos y otros escritos*, comp. Pedro Luis Barcia, ed. María de los Ángeles Marechal (Buenos Aires: Libros Perfil S.A., 1998), 322–23.

54. Leopoldo Marechal, "Sobre la inteligenica argentina," in *Nueva Política*, September 4, 1941; reprinted in *Obras completas*, vol. 5, *Cuentos y otros escritos*, comp. Pedro Luis Barcia, ed. María de los Ángeles Marechal (Buenos Aires: Libros Perfil S.A., 1998), 313–19.

55. Marechal, "Sobre la inteligenica argentina," 314.

56. Marechal, 317.

57. See Jorge Luis Borges, "El escritor argentino y la tradición," in *Obras completas* (Buenos Aires: Emecé Editores, 1974), 267–74.

58. Leopoldo Marechal, "La poesía lírica: Lo autóctono y lo foráneo en su contenido esencial," in *Obras completas*, vol. 5, *Los cuentos y otros escritos*, comp. Pedro Luis Barcia, ed. María de los Ángeles Marechal (Buenos Aires: Libros Perfil S.A., 1998), 144. A conference talk given on June 23, 1949, the eighth of a series organized by the Subsecretaría de Cultura de la Nación. In *Primer ciclo cultural de conferencias organizadas por la Subsecretaría de Cultura de la Nación* (Buenos Aires: Talleres Gráficos del Ministerio de Educación, 1950), vol. 1, series 3, no. 4, 181–92.

59. Marechal, "La poesía lírica," 146.

60. Marechal, 147.

61. Leopoldo Marechal, "El gaucho y la nueva literatura rioplantense," in *Obras completas*, vol. 5, *Los cuentos y otros escritos*, comp. Pedro Luis Barcia, ed. María de los Ángeles Marechal (Buenos Aires: Libros Perfil S.A., 1998), 235. First published in *Martín Fierro* (Buenos Aires), no. 34, October 5, 1926.

62. Marechal, "El gaucho," 236.

63. Leopoldo Marechal, *Adán Buenosayres*, ed. Javier de Navascués (Buenos Aires: Corregidor, 2013), 327.

64. Marechal, *Adam Buenosayres*, 132.

65. Marechal, 132.

66. The text was originally read as "La conferencia de Hoy" for LRA, Radio del Estado, Buenos Aires, Talleres Gráficos de Correos y Telecomunicaciones, 1955, 15 pp. It was also printed in *La Opinión*, Buenos Aires, Suplemento cultural, June 25, 1972, 1–2, entitled: "Un texto desconocido de Leopoldo Marechal: '*Martín Fierro* o el arte de ser argentinos y americanos'"; and as "Simbolismos del *Martín Fierro*," in *Obras completas*, vol. 5, *Los cuentos y otros escritos*, comp. Pedro Luis Barcia, ed. María de los Ángeles Marechal (Buenos Aires: Libros Perfil S.A., 1998), 157–71.

67. Marechal, "Simbolismos del *Martín Fierro*," 157.

68. Leopoldo Lugones, *El payador* (Buenos Aires: Editorial Huemel S.A., 1972), 27.

69. Marechal, "Simbolismos del *Martín Fierro*," 157.

70. Marechal, 158.

71. Marechal, 158.

72. Marechal, 158.

73. Jorge Luis Borges, "La poesía gauchesca," in *Obras completas* (Buenos Aires: Emecé Editores, 1974), 180.

74. Borges, 194.

75. Marechal, "Simbolismos del *Martín Fierro*," 160.

76. Marechal, 160.

77. Marechal, 160.

78. Marechal, 161.

79. Marechal, 161.

80. Marechal, 162.
81. Marechal, 166.
82. Marechal, 166.
83. Marechal, 168.
84. Nicolas Shumway, *The Invention of Argentina* (Los Angeles: University of California Press, 1991), 277.
85. Raúl Scalabrini Ortiz, *Yrigoyen y Perón* (Buenos Aires: Plus Ultra, 1973), 14–15; quoted by Shumway in *Invention of Argentina*, 277.
86. Marechal, "Simbolismos del *Martín Fierro*," 163.
87. All English translations of quotes from *Adán Buenosayres* are from the following edition: Leopoldo Marechal, *Adam Buenosayres*, trans. and ed. Norman Cheadle (Montreal: McGill-Queen's University Press, 2014), 62.
88. Marechal, *Adam Buenosayres*, 94. My emphasis.
89. Marechal, 155.
90. Marechal, 135.
91. For the relationship between *Adán Buenosayres* and Ortiz's essay see Norman Cheadle, "Twentieth-Century *homo bonarense:* The Buenos Aires 'Man-in-the-Street' in Raúl Scalabrini Ortiz and Leopoldo Marechal," in *Relocating Identities in Latin American Cultures*, ed. Elizabeth Montes Garcés (Calgary: University of Calgary Press, 2007).
92. Marechal, *Adam Buenosayres*, 135.
93. Leopoldo Marechal, "Las claves de *Adán Buenosayres*," in Marechal et al., *Interpretaciones y claves de "Adán Buenosayres"* (Montevideo: Acali Editorial, 1977), 13–14.

7. DANTE'S *VITA NUOVA* AND BOOK 6 OF *ADÁN BUENOSAYRES*: SOLVEIG AS BEATRICE, SOLVEIG AS ARGENTINA

1. See Washington Benavídez, "Índice episódico y temático de 'Adán Buenosayres' de Leopoldo Marechal," in Leopoldo Marechal et al., *Interpretaciones y claves de Adán Buenosayres* (Montevideo: Acali Editorial, 1977), 85–159; Donald L. Shaw, *Nueva narrativa hispanoamericana*, 3rd ed. (Madrid: Cátedra, 1985), 41; Fernanda Elisa Bravo Herrera, "Dante, Valli y Marechal: *Fedeli d'Amore* en diálogo," in *Dante en América Latina: Actas Primer Congreso Internacional sobre Dante Alighieri en Latinoamérica* (Salta, October 4–8, 2004), vol. 1, ed. Nicola Bottiglieri and Teresa Colque (Ercolano: Università degli Studi di Cassino, 2007), 285–97; José Ignacio Gallardo Ballestero, "El cuaderno de las tapas azules, «Vita Nuova» de Leopoldo Marechal," *Philologia hispalensis* 5, no. 1 (January 1990): 295–316.

2. Leopoldo Marechal, *Adam Buenosayres*, trans. and ed. Norman Cheadle (Montreal: McGill-Queen's University Press, 2014), 13. All English translations of quotations from *Adán Buenosayres* are from that edition.

3. Marechal, *Adam Buenosayres*, 14.

4. Marechal, 53.

5. Marechal, 54.

6. Marechal, 49.

7. Leopoldo Marechal, "Las Claves de *Adán Buenosayres*," in Marechal et al., *Interpretaciones y claves de Adán Buenosayres* (Montevideo: Acali Editorial, 1977), 11: "el influjo es tan grande come 'definitorio'; y mi terrible maestro lo ejerce, no como autor de la Commedia, sino como integrante y jefe de los 'Fedeli d'Amore.'"

8. Marechal, "Claves," 11.

9. The Luigi Valli books owned by Marechal are *Ritmi* (Rome: Optima, 1929); *Il linguaggio segreto di Dante e dei "Fedeli d'Amore"* (Rome: Biblioteca di Filosofia e Scienza, 1928); *Il linguaggio segreto di Dante e dei "Fedeli d'Amore,"* vol. 2 (Rome: Biblioteca di Filosofia e Scienza, 1930); *La struttura morale dell'Universo Dantesco* (Rome: Tipografica Sallustiana, 1935); *Il secreto della Croce e dell'Aquila nella Divina Commedia* (Bologna: Nicola Zanichelli, 1922).

10. Leopoldo Marechal, "Autobiografía de un novelista," *Revista Proa*, no. 49 (September–October 2000): 67.

11. For more on esoteric interpretations of the *Divine Comedy* by Valli and others, see Massimo Ciavolella, "Esoteric Interpretations of the *Divine Comedy*," in *Dantean Dialogues: Engaging with the Legacy of Amilcare Iannucci*, ed. Maggie Kilgour and Elena Lombardi (Toronto: University of Toronto Press, 2013), 215–30; and Stefano Salzani, *Luigi Valli e l'esoterismo di Dante* (San Marino: Il Cerchio, 2014).

12. Pedro Luis Barcia, notes to his edition of Leopoldo Marechal, *Adán Buenosayres* (Madrid: Clásicos Castalia, 1994), 293n.

13. Leopoldo Marechal, "De la patria joven" in *Obras completas*, vol. 1, *La poesía*, comp. Pedro Luis Barcia, ed.María de los Ángeles Marechal (Buenos Aires: Libros Perfil S.A., 1998), 151.

14. Marechal, *Adam Buenosayres*, 105.

15. Marechal, 63.

16. Marechal, 14.

17. Dante Alighieri, *La vita nuova*, ed. Kenneth McKenzie (New York: D. C. Heath, 1922), 1.

18. Dante Alighieri, *La vita nuova*, *'The New Life' of Dante Alighieri*, trans. A. S. Kline, 4, https://www.poetryintranslation.com/klineasthenewlife.php.

19. Marechal, *Adam Buenosayres*, 359.

20. Marechal, 359.

21. Marechal, 360.
22. Marechal, 360.
23. Marechal, 361.
24. Marechal, 362.
25. Marechal, 362.
26. Marechal, 363.
27. Marechal, 364.
28. Marechal, 364.
29. Marechal, 365.
30. Marechal, 365.
31. Marechal, 135.
32. Marechal, 366.
33. Marechal, 145.
34. Marechal, 366.
35. Marechal, 368.
36. Marechal, 369.
37. Marechal, 370.
38. Marechal, 371.
39. Dante, *Paradiso*, 1.55–60.
40. Marechal, *Adam Buenosayres*, 372.
41. Marechal, 373.
42. Marechal, 373.
43. "I've already said that springtime in Buenos Aires and the woman of my sleepless nights had manifested themselves at the same time," Marechal, 377.
44. Marechal, 377.
45. *Vita nuova* 14.19.
46. *'The New Life' of Dante Alighieri*, trans. A. S. Kline, 19.
47. Marechal, *Adam Buenosayres*, 384.
48. Marechal, 374.
49. Marechal, 374.
50. Marechal, 261.
51. Leopoldo Marechal, "De la adolescente," in *Obras completas*, vol. 1, *La poesía*, comp. Pedro Luis Barcia, ed. María de los Ángeles Marechal (Buenos Aires: Libros Perfil S.A., 1998), 142.
52. Marechal, *Adam Buenosayres*, 375.
53. Dante, *Vita nuova*, 3; Gallardo Ballestero, "El cuaderno de las tapas azules," 308.
54. Marechal, *Adam Buenosayres*, 375.
55. Quoted by Barcia in the notes of *Adán Buenosayres* (Madrid: Editorial Castalia, S.A., 1994), 648n, and by Norman Cheadle, in his notes to Leopoldo

Marechal, *Adam Buenosayres*, trans. and ed. Norman Cheadle (Montreal: McGill-Queens' University Press, 2014), 670n7.

56. Marechal, *Adam Buenosayres*, 375.
57. Marechal, 377.
58. Marechal, 377.
59. Marechal, 378.
60. Dante, *Vita nuova*, 19.27.
61. Marechal, *Adam Buenosayres*, 379.
62. Marechal, 380.
63. Marechal, 381.
64. Marechal, 382.
65. Marechal, 384.
66. Marechal, 385.
67. Marechal, 385.
68. Marechal, 385.
69. Fernanda Elisa Bravo Herrera, "Reescrituras de textos italianos en la producción de Leopoldo Marechal: sublimación y censura de lo erótico," in *Erotismo: clase y sectores sociales en la lengua y la literatura italianas*, vol. 1, ed. Fulvia Gabriela Lisi (Salta: Universidad Nacional de Salta, 1999), 155.
70. Marechal, *Adam Buenosayres*, 386–87.
71. Dante, *Vita nuova*, 42.70–71.
72. Marechal, *Adam Buenosayres*, 388.
73. Marechal, 388.
74. Marechal, 389.
75. Marechal, 391.
76. Marechal, 391–92.
77. Marechal, 392.
78. Dante, *Vita nuova*, 42.71.
79. *'The New Life' of Dante Alighieri*, 64.

8. THE JOURNEY TO CACODELPHIA: A PARODY OF *INFERNO* AND MODERN-DAY ARGENTINA

1. Leopoldo Marechal, *Adam Buenosayres*, trans. and ed. Norman Cheadle (Montreal: McGill-Queen's University Press, 2014), 403. All English translations of quotations from *Adán Buenosayres* are from this edition. Cheadle's translation retains the original spellings of characters' names with the exception of "Adam" for "Adán" and "Schultz" for "Schultze" (Cheadle, introduction to *Adam Buenosayres*, xviii–xix).
2. Marechal, *Adam Buenosayres*, 397.

3. Norman Cheadle, in his notes to Leopoldo Marechal, *Adam Buenosayres*, trans. and ed. Norman Cheadle, 671n3.

4. Marechal, *Adam Buenosayres*, 398.

5. Marechal, 395.

6. Santos Vega was an Argentine gaucho who was eventually defeated by the Devil, disguised as the *payador* Juan sin Ropa. Bartolomé Mitre wrote a poem about the legend.

> Tu alma puebla los desiertos,
> y del Sud en la campaña
> al lado de una cabaña
> se eleva fúnebre cruz;
> esa cruz, bajo de un tala
> solitario, abandonado,
> es un símbolo venerado
> en los campos del Tuyú.
>
> (Your soul populates the deserts,
> and the South in the countryside
> next to a cabin
> a funeral cross is raised;
> that cross, down from a felling
> lonely, abandoned,
> is a revered symbol
> in the fields of Tuyú.)
>
> (Bartolomé Mitre, "Á Santos Vega, payador argentino," lines 81–88)

Thereafter Hilario Ascasubi, who used the pen name Santo Vega, composed the long poem "Santos Vega o Los mellizos de La Flor," and Eduardo Gutiérrez wrote "Story of Santos Vega and his friend Carmona prosecuted by justice." The most famous work about the legend is Rafael Obligado's 1885 *Santos Vega*, considered along with *Martín Fierro* to be one of the most important works of Argentine literature.

7. Marechal, *Adam Buenosayres*, 403.

8. Marechal, 403.

9. Book 7, "Journey to the Dark City of Cacodelphia," is 223 pages long in Cheadle's translation.

10. Marechal, *Adam Buenosayres*, 599.

11. Marechal, 600.

12. Marechal, 601.

13. Marechal, 609–10.

14. Leopoldo Marechal, "Sobre la inteligencia argentina," in *Obras completas*, vol. 5, *Los cuentos y otros escritos*, comp. Pedro Luis Barcia, ed. María de los Ángeles Marechal (Buenos Aires: Libros Peril S.A., 1998), 315.

15. This is consistent with books 1–5, which I have not been able to discuss here. The problem with Argentine identity, according to Adán/Marechal, is that there is no communal or spiritual direction uniting the population. The immigrants coming to Argentina had somehow been stripped of their community. Many of the character sketches in book 2 serve to support the idea of Argentines as uprooted immigrants, adrift in a chaotic and materialistic world with nothing to anchor them.

16. Marechal, *Adam Buenosayres*, 618.

17. Marechal, 404.

18. Marechal, 404.

19. Marechal, 405.

20. The character of Schultz is based on Xul Solar, who, in addition to being a painter and sculptor, invented two imaginary languages: "Neo Criollo," a local blend of Portuguese and Spanish, and "Pan Lingua," a complex form of communication inspired by mathematics, visual arts, music, and astrology.

21. Marechal, *Adam Buenosayres*, 406.

22. Marechal, 407–8.

23. Marechal, 410.

24. Marechal, 411.

25. Marechal, 404.

26. Marechal, 414.

27. Marechal, 417.

28. Marechal, 417.

29. Marechal, 417.

30. Marechal, 418.

31. Marechal, 418.

32. Marechal, 419.

33. Marechal, 421.

34. Marechal, 421.

35. Marechal, 421–22.

36. An allusion to Hermann von Keyserling's *South American Meditations* (*Südamerikanische Meditationen*, 1932). Cheadle, notes to *Adam Buenosayres*, 640n23, 674n35.

37. Marechal, *Adam Buenosayres*, 424.

38. Marechal, 425–26.

39. Mark Musa, commentary notes in *The Divine Comedy*, vol. 1, *Inferno* (Penguin Classics, 1984), 37–38.

40. Marechal, *Adam Buenosayres*, 472.
41. Marechal, 430–31.
42. Marechal, 434.
43. Marechal, 434.
44. Marechal, 434–35.
45. Marechal, 438–39.
46. Leopoldo Marechal, *Adán Buenosayres*, ed. Javier de Navascués, Ediciones Académicas de Literatura Argentina Siglos XIX y XX (Buenos Aires: Corregidor, 2013), 560.
47. Marechal, *Adam Buenosayres*, 446–47.
48. "Tirifilo" is a derogatory *lunfardo* term meaning a person who puts on airs. It is synonymous with "petimetre," which derives from the French "petit-maître."
49. Marechal, *Adán Buenosayres*, 569.
50. Marechal, *Adam Buenosayres*, 449.
51. Marechal, 450.
52. Marechal, 455.
53. Marechal, 456.
54. *Abel Sanchez* (1917) is a novel by Miguel de Unamuno treating the Cain and Abel theme.
55. Leopoldo Marechal, "Las claves de *Adán Buenosayres*," in Marechal et al., *Interpretaciones y claves de Adán Buenosayres* (Montevideo: Acali Editorial, 1977), 16.
56. Patricia Waugh, *Metafiction: The Theory and Practice of Self-Conscious Fiction* (London: Methuen, 1984), 2.
57. Waugh, 2.
58. Waugh, 3.
59. Marechal, *Adam Buenosayres*, 403.
60. Marechal, 473–74.
61. Marechal, 474.
62. Marechal, 475.
63. Marechal, 476.
64. Marechal, *Adán Buenosayres*, 596.
65. Marechal, *Adam Buenosayres*, 476.
66. Marechal, 476.
67. This metaphysician is René Guénon, whose 1921 *Introduction générale à l'étude des doctrines hindous* is the basis of Schultz's discourse. Cheadle, in notes to *Adam Buenosayres*, 626n20, 628n6, and 637n7.
68. Marechal, *Adam Buenosayres*, 477.
69. Marechal, *Adán Buenosayres*, 564–65.
70. Marechal, *Adam Buenosayres*, 443–44.

71. Marechal, 444.
72. Marechal, 481.
73. Marechal, 455.
74. Cheadle, in notes to *Adam Buenosayres*, 677n59.
75. The dragon is Schultz's totemic animal. As Cheadle points out, Xul Solar painted several watercolors with the motif of the dragon: "Dos Dragos" (1920), "Dama, pájaro, drago" (1922), "Hombre y dragón" (1922), "Drago y dama fluctúo" (1923), "Drago San Jorge" (1923), and "Drago" (1927).
76. Marechal, *Adam Buenosayres*, 482.
77. Marechal, 482.
78. Marechal, 483.
79. Marechal, 555.
80. Marechal, 556. This idiom means to feel guilty or at fault.
81. Marechal, 555.
82. Marechal, 555.
83. Marechal, 555.
84. Marechal, 556.
85. Marechal, 557.
86. Beatriz Sarlo, *Borges: Un escritor en las orillas* (Madrid: Siglo, 2007).
87. Marechal, *Adam Buenosayres*, 557.
88. Marechal, 557.
89. As Cheadle notes in *Adam Buenosayres*, 684n134, the pink general store on the corner is one of Borges's famous symbols of Buenos Aires that appears in his early poetry: in "Calle con almacén rosado" in *Luna de enfrente* (1925) and in Borges, *Obras completas*, 57; and in "Fundación mítica de Buenos Aires," in Borges, *Obras completas*, 81.
90. Marechal, *Adam Buenosayres*, 557.
91. Marechal, 557.
92. Cheadle, in notes to *Adam Buenosayres*, 685n137.
93. Marechal, *Adam Buenosayres*, 558.
94. Marechal, 558.
95. Marechal, 558.
96. Marechal, 559.
97. Leopoldo Marechal, *Obras completas*, vol. 1, *La poesía*, comp. Pedro Luis Barcia, ed. María de los Ángeles Marechal (Buenos Aires: Libros Perfil S.A., 1998), 93–94 and 476.
98. Marechal, "Las claves de *Adán Buenosayres*," 17.
99. Marechal, *Adam Buenosayres*, 470.
100. Marechal, 487.
101. Marechal, 488.
102. Marechal, 490.

103. Marechal, 490.
104. Marechal, 490–91.
105. Marechal, 491.
106. Marechal, 491.
107. Marechal, 492.
108. Marechal, 493.
109. Marechal, 494.
110. Cheadle claims that Germán may be a homage to Ricardo Güiraldes, who wrote *Cuentos de muerte y de sangre* (Stories of death and of blood). Cheadle, in notes to *Adam Buenosayres*, 679n86.
111. Marechal, *Adam Buenosayres*, 500.
112. Marechal, 506.
113. Marechal, 488–89.
114. Marechal, 489.
115. Marechal, 489.
116. Marechal, 508.
117. Marechal, 409.
118. Marechal, 527.
119. Marechal, 481.
120. Albert de la Fuente, "La estructura interna de *Adán Buenosayres* de Leopoldo Marechal," *Hispania* 58, no. 2 (May 1975): 261.
121. Marechal, *Adam Buenosayres*, 135.
122. Marechal, 135.
123. Marechal, 430.
124. Marechal, 430.
125. Marechal, 431–32.
126. Marechal, 432.
127. Leopoldo Marechal, "Proyecciones culturales del momento argentino," in Marechal, *Obras completas*, vol. 5, *Los cuentos y otros escritos*, comp. Pedro Luis Barcia, ed. María de los Ángeles Marechal (Buenos Aires: Libros Perfil S.A., 1998), 136.
128. First published in French: Victoria Ocampo, *De Francesca à Béatrice: À travers la Divine comédie* (Paris: Editions Bossard, 1926).
129. Victoria Ocampo, *De Francesca a Beatrice: A través de la Divina Comedia* (Madrid: Rivista de Occidente, 1924), 10.
130. Ocampo, *De Francesca a Beatrice*, 11.
131. Marechal, *Adam Buenosayres*, 432.
132. Ocampo, *De Francesca a Beatrice*, 27.
133. Ocampo, 7.
134. Javier de Navascués's notes to his edition of *Adán Buenosayres*, 549n.

135. Eduardo González Lanuza, "Leopoldo Marechal: Adán Buenosayres." Leopoldo Marechal, *Adán Buenosayres*, ed. Jorge Raúl Lafforgue and Héctor Fernando Colla (Madrid: Allca XX, 1997), 877; quoted in Elena P. Picech, "Leopoldo Marechal and *Adán Buenosayres* in State of Exile," *Hispanófila* 167 (January 2013): 89. Not all reviews were negative, however. Julio Cortázar did recognize the novel's importance in a review published in *Realidad* in 1949.

136. Picech, 80.

CONCLUSION. ARGENTINA'S FAILURE TO PRODUCE A *DIVINE COMEDY*

1. Nicolas Shumway, *The Invention of Argentina* (Los Angeles: University of California Press, 1991), x.

2. Pertaining to the port city of Buenos Aires.

BIBLIOGRAPHY

Albarracin, Julia. "Selecting Immigration in Modern Argentina: Economic, Cultural, International and Institutional Factors." PhD diss., University of Florida, 2004. https://ufdcimages.uflib.ufl.edu/UF/E0/00/83/85/00001/UFE0008385.pdf.

Alberdi, Juan Bautista. *Bases y puntos de partida para la organización política de la República Argentina.* In *Obras completas de Juan Bautista Alberdi*, vol. 3. Buenos Aires: La Tribuna Nacional, 1886–87. English translation by Ian Barnett as "Bases and Starting Points for the Political Organization of the Argentine Republic (1852) (Excerpts)," in *Liberal Thought in Argentina, 1837–1940*, ed. Natalio R. Botana and Ezequiel Gallo, 115–76. Indianapolis: Liberty Fund, 2013.

Alcántara, José Godoy. *Ensayo histórico etimológico filológico sobre los apellidos castellanos desde el siglo X hasta nuestra edad.* Madrid: Rivadeneyra, M., 1871.

Aliano, David. *Mussolini's National Project in Argentina.* Lanham, MD: Fairleigh Dickinson University Press, 2012.

Alighieri, Dante. *Dantis Alagherii Epistolae: The Letters of Dante.* Emended text with introduction, translation, and notes by Paget Toynbee. Oxford: Clarendon, 1966.

———. *De vulgari eloquentia.* Edited and translated by Stephen Botterill. Cambridge: Cambridge University Press, 1996.

———. *La divina commedia.* Edited by Carlo Grabher. Florence: La Nuova Italia, 1934–36.

———. *La divina commedia.* Translated by Bartolomé Mitre. Buenos Aires: Jacobo Peuser, 1894.

———. *La vita nuova.* Edited by Kenneth McKenzie. New York: D. C. Heath, 1922.

———. *La Vita Nuova: 'The New Life' of Dante Alighieri.* Translated by A. S. Kline, 2001. https://www.poetryintranslation.com/klineasthenewlife.php.

———. *The Inferno.* Translated by Robert Hollander and Jean Hollander. New York: Anchor Books, 2002.

———. *Paradiso.* Translated by Robert Hollander and Jean Hollander. New York: Anchor Books, 2002.

———. *Purgatorio.* Translated by Robert Hollander and Jean Hollander. New York: Anchor Books, 2002.

Altamirano, Carlos, and Beatriz Sarlo. *Ensayos argentinos: De Sarmiento a la vanguardia.* Buenos Aires: Centro Editor de América Latina, 1983.

Anderson, Benedict. *Imagined Communities: Reflections on the Origin and Spread of Nationalism.* London: Verso, 1991.

Andrés, Alfredo. *Palabras con Leopoldo Marechal: Reportaje y antología.* Buenos Aires: Carlos Pérez, 1968.

Ascoli, Albert Russell, and Krystyna von Henneberg, eds. *Making and Remaking Italy: The Cultivation of National Identity around the Risorgimento.* Oxford: Berg, 2001.

Ayala, Francisco. "Comentarios textuales a 'El Aleph' de Borges." *Explicación de textos literarios* 2 (1973): 3–5.

Baily, Samuel L. "The Adjustment of Italian Immigrants in Buenos Aires and New York, 1870–1914." *American Historical Review* 88, no. 2 (April 1983): 281–305.

Balán, Jorge, John D. Gould, and Tulio Halperin Donghi. "[The Integration of Italian into the United States and Argentina: A Comparative Analysis]: Comments." *American Historical Review* 88, no. 2 (April 1983): 330–42.

Balbo, Cesare. *Delle speranze d'Italia.* Edited by Achille Corbelli. Turin: Unione Tipografico, 1925.

Barański, Zygmunt G. "Inferno XVIII." In *Lectura Dantis Bononiensis*, vol. 3, edited by Emilio Pasquini and Carlo Galli, 81–110. Bologna: Bononia University Press, 2014.

Barolini, Teodolinda. "Dante and Francesca da Rimini: Realpolitik, Romance, Gender." *Speculum* 75, no. 1 (January 2000): 1–28.

———. *Dante's Multitudes: History, Philosophy, Method.* Notre Dame, IN: University of Notre Dame Press, 2022.

———. "Inferno 18: Fraud and Sex in a Post-Geryon World." *Commento Baroliniano, Digital Dante.* New York: Columbia University Libraries, 2018. https://digitaldante.columbia.edu/dante/ divine-comedy/inferno / inferno-18/.

Battistessa, Ángel J. "Dante y las generaciones argentinas." *Boletin de la Academia Argentina de Letras* 30, no. 115–16 (June 1965): 7–27.

Bayer, Osvaldo. "The Influence of Italian Immigration on the Argentine Anarchist Movement." Posted on libcom.org by Quinlan Vos, January 24, 2010, https://libcom.org/library/

influence-italian-immigration-argentine-anarchist-movement-osvaldo-bayer. First published as "L'influenza dell'immigrazione italiana nel movimento anarchico argentino," in *Gli italiani fuori d'Italia*, edited by Bruno Bezza, 145–62. Milan: Franco Angelo, 1983.

Becco, Horacio J., Félix Weinberg, Rodolfo A. Borello, and Adolfo Prieto. *Trayectoria de la poesía gauchesca*. Buenos Aires: Plus Ultra, 1977.

Bell-Villada, Gene H. *Borges and His Fiction: A Guide to His Mind and Art*. Austin: University of Texas Press, 1999.

Benavídez, Washington. "Índice episódico y temático de 'Adán Buenosayres' de Leopoldo Marechal." In *Interpretaciones y claves de Adán Buenosayres*, 85–159. Montevideo: Acali Editorial, 1977.

Bertagna, Federica. *La patria di riserva: L'emigrazione fascista in Argentina*. Rome: Donzelli, 2006.

———. "Techint e gli altri: Penetrazione industriale ed emigrazione italiana nell'Argentina peronista (1946–55)." *Studi storici* 55, no. 3 (July–September 2014): 615–44.

Bertagna, Federica, and Marina Maccari-Clayton. "Italy: Migration 1815 to Present." In *The Encyclopedia of Global Human Migration*, edited by Immanuel Ness. Chichester, UK: Blackwell, 2013.

Bloom, Harold. *The Anxiety of Influence: A Theory of Poetry*. New York: Oxford University Press, 1973.

Bollati, Giulio. *L'italiano: Il carattere nazionale come storia e come invenzione*, 2nd ed. Torino: Einaudi, 1983.

Bonatti, Maria. "Dante en la lectura de Borges." *Revista Iberoamericana* 43, no. 100–101 (1977): 737–44.

Borello, Rodolfo. *Hernández: Poesía y política*. Buenos Aires: Plus Ultra, 1973.

Borges, Jorge Luis. "A Leopoldo Lugones." Prologue to *El hacedor*. In *Obras completas*, 779. Buenos Aires: Emecé Editores, 1974.

———."The Aleph." In *The Aleph and Other Stories*, translated by Andrew Hurley, 118–33. New York: Penguin Books, 2004.

———. *The Aleph and Other Stories, 1933–1969: Together with Commentaries and an Autobiographical Essay*. Edited and translated by Norman Thomas di Giovanni in collaboration with the author. New York: E. P. Dutton, 1978.

———. "Commentaries." In *The Aleph and Other Stories, 1933–1969: Together with Commentaries and an Autobiographical Essay*, edited and translated by Norman Thomas di Giovanni in collaboration with the author. New York: E. P. Dutton, 1978.

———. "The Divine Comedy." In *Seven Nights*, translated by Eliot Weinberger, 6–25. New York: New Directions, 1984.

———. "El aleph." In *Obras completas*, 617–28. Buenos Aires: Emecé Editores, 1974.

———. "El escritor argentino y la tradición." In *Obras completas*, 267–74. Buenos Aires: Emecé Editores, 1974.
———. *El "Martín Fierro."* Buenos Aires: Editorial Columba, 1953.
———. "El tamaño de mi esperanza." In *El tamaño de mi esperanza*, 11–14. Buenos Aires: Espasa Calpe/Seix Barral, 1993.
———. "Fundación mítica de Buenos Aires." In *Obras completas*, 81. Buenos Aires: Emecé Editores, 1974.
———."Funes el memorioso." In *Obras completas*, 485–90. Buenos Aires: Emecé Editores, 1974.
———. "Infierno, V, 129." In *Poesía completa*, 559–60. New York: Vintage Español, 2012.
———. "The Intruder." In *Doctor Brodie's Report*, translated by Norman Thomas di Giovanni, 67–74. New York: E. P. Dutton, 1972.
———. "Kafka y sus precursores." In *Obras completas*, 710–12. Buenos Aires: Emecé Editores, 1974.
———. "La esfera de Pascal." In *Obras completas*, 636–38. Buenos Aires: Emecé Editores, 1974.
———. "La intrusa." In *Obras completas*, 1025–28. Buenos Aires: Emecé Editores, 1974.
———."La poesía gauchesca." In *Obras completas*, 179–97. Buenos Aires: Emecé Editores, 1974.
———. "Leopoldo Lugones: Romancero." Translated by Alfred Mac Adam. In *On Argentina*, edited by Suzanne Jill Levine and Alfred Mac Adam, 57–59. New York: Penguin Books, 2010.
———. "The Mythical Founding of Buenos Aires." Translated by Alastair Reid. In *On Argentina*, edited by Suzanne Jill Levine and Alfred Mac Adam, 16–17. New York: Penguin Books, 2010.
———. *Nueve ensayos dantescos*. Edited by Marcos Ricardo Barnatán. Madrid: Espasa-Calpe, 1982.
———. *Obras completas*. Buenos Aires: Emecé Editores, 1974.
———. *Poesía completa*. New York: Vintage Español, 2012.
———. Prologue to *El otro, el mismo*. In *Obras completas*, 857–58. Buenos Aires: Emecé Editores, 1974.
———. Prologue to *Fervor de Buenos Aires* (1969). In *Obras completas*, 13. Buenos Aires: Emecé Editores, 1974.
———. Prologue to Leopoldo Lugones, *La estatua de sal*, 9–14. La Biblioteca de Babel 19. Madrid: Siruela, 1985.
———. "Roberto Godel: Nacimiento del fuego." In *Prólogo con un prólogo de prólogos*. Madrid: Alianza Editorial, 1975.
———. *Selected Non-fictions*. Edited by Eliot Weinberger. Translated by Esther Allen, Suzanne Jill Levine, and Eliot Weinberger. New York: Viking, 1999.

———."Sobre el 'Vathek' de William Beckford." In *Obras completas*, 729–32. Buenos Aires: Emecé Editores, 1974.

Borges, Jorge Luis, and Roberto Alifano. *Twenty-Four Conversations with Borges Including a Selection of Poems: Interviews by Roberto Alifano, 1981–1983*. Translated by Nicomedes Suárez Araúz, Willis Barnstone, and Noemí Escandell. Housatonic, MA: Lascaux, 1984.

Borges, Jorge Luis, and Betina Edelberg. *Leopoldo Lugones*. In *Obras completas en colaboración*, 453–508. Buenos Aires: Emecé Editores, 1997.

Borges, Jorge Luis, and Osvaldo Ferrari. *Conversations*. Vol. 1. Translated by Jason Wilson. London: Seagull Books, 2014.

Botana, Natalio R., and Ezequel Gallo, eds. *Liberal Thought in Argentina, 1837–1940*. Translated by Ian Barnett. Indianapolis: Liberty Fund, 2013.

Bourdieu, Pierre. "À propos de la famille comme catégorie réalisée." *Actes de la recherche en science sociales* 100 (1993): 32–36.

Bravo Herrera, Fernanda Elisa. "Dante, Valli y Marechal: *Fedeli d'Amore* en diálogo." In *Dante en América Latina: Actas Primer Congreso Internacional sobre Dante Alighieri en Latinoamérica* (Salta, October 4–8, 2004), vol. 1, edited by Nicola Bottiglieri and Teresa Colque, 285–97. Ercolano: Università degli Studi di Cassino, 2007.

———. "Lo épico en 'La Patriótica' de Leopoldo Marechal." In *Perspectivas de la ficcionalidad: Actas del II Simposio Internacional de Narratología*, edited by Daniel Altamiranda and Esther Smith, vol. 1, 269–77. Buenos Aires: Editorial Docencia, 2005.

———. "Reescrituras de textos italianos en la producción de Leopoldo Marechal: sublimación y censura de lo erótico." In *Erotismo: Clase y sectores sociales en la lengua y la literatura italianas*, vol. 1, edited by Fulvia Gabriela Lisi, 149–59. Salta: Universidad Nacional de Salta, 1999.

Calinescu, Matei. *Rereading*. New Haven, CT: Yale University Press, 1993.

Canto, Estela. *Borges a contraluz*. Madrid: Espasa-Calpe, 1989.

Capuzzi, Lucia. *La frontiera immaginata: Profilo politico e sociale dell'emigrazione italiana in Argentina nel secondo dopoguerra*. Milan: Franco Angeli, 2006.

Carilla, Emilio. "La revista de Lugones." *Thesaurus* 39, no. 3 (1974): 501–25.

Cheadle, Norman. "Introduction to *Adam Buenosayres*." In *Adam Buenosayres*, translated by Norman Cheadle, xi–xxx. London: McGill-Queen's University Press, 2014.

———. "Twentieth-Century *homo bonarense:* The Buenos Aires 'Man-in-the-Street' in Raúl Scalabrini Ortiz and Leopoldo Marechal." In *Relocating Identities in Latin American Cultures*, edited by Elizabeth Montes Garcés, 13–34. Calgary: University of Calgary Press, 2007.

Chiappini, Julio. *Borges y Dante*. Rosario: Editorial Zeus, 1993.

Ciavolella, Massimo. "Esoteric Interpretations of the *Divine Comedy*." In *Dantean Dialogues: Engaging with the Legacy of Amilcare Iannucci*, edited by Maggie Kilgour and Elena Lombardi, 215–30. Toronto: University of Toronto Press, 2013.

Ciccarelli, Andrea. "Dante and Italian Culture from the Risorgimento to World War I." *Dante Studies, with the Annual Report of the Dante Society*, no. 119 (2001): 125–54.

Concise Encyclopedia of Latin American Literature. Edited by Verity Smith. New York: Routledge, 2013.

Coulson, Graciela. "Leopoldo Marechal: La aventura metafísica." *Hispamérica* 3, no. 7 (July 1974): 29–39.

Davidson, Sylvie. "Borges and Italian Literature." *Italian Quarterly* 27, no. 105 (Summer 1986): 43–49.

de la Fuente, Albert. "La estructura interna de *Adán Buenosayres* de Leopoldo Marechal." *Hispania* 58, no. 2 (May 1975): 260–66.

Delaney, Jeane. "Making Sense of Modernity: Changing Attitudes toward the Immigrant and the Gaucho in Turn-of-the-Century Argentina." *Comparative Studies in Society and History* 38, no. 3 (July 1996): 434–59.

De Seta, Cesare. *L'Italia nello specchio del Grand Tour*. Milan: Rizzoli, 2014.

Devoto, Daniel. "Aleph et Alexis." *L'Herne* no. 4 (1964): 280–92.

di Núbila, Domingo. *La época de oro: Historia del cine argentino*. Buenos Aires: Ediciones del Jilguero, 1998.

Echeverría, Esteban. *El Dogma Socialista a la juventud argentina (1837)*. Biblioteca Virtual Universal, 2003.

Encyclopedia of Latin American and Caribbean Literature, 1900–2003. Edited by Daniel Balderston and Mike Gonzalez. New York: Routledge, 2004.

España, Claudio. "El cine sonoro y su expansión." In *Historia del cine argentino*, edited by Jorge Miguel Couselo. Buenos Aires: Centro Editor de América Latina, 1984.

Even-Zohar, Itamar. *Polysystem Studies*. [= *Poetics Today* 11, no. 1.] Durham, NC: Duke University Press. A special issue of *Poetics Today*.

———. "The Position of Translated Literature within the Literary Polysystem." In *Papers on Poetics and Semiotics 8: Papers in Historical Poetics*, edited by B. Hrushovki and Itamar Even-Zohar, 21–26. Tel Aviv University: Porter Institute of Poetics and Semiotics, 1978.

Finchelstein, Federico. *The Ideological Origins of the Dirty War*. Oxford: Oxford University Press, 2014.

Gallardo Ballestero, José Ignacio. "El cuaderno de las tapas azules, «Vita Nuova» de Leopoldo Marechal." *Philologia hispalensis* 5, no. 1 (January 1990): 295–316.

Gálvez, Manuel. "¿Cuál es el valor del *Martín Fierro*?" *Nosotros*, no. 50 (June 1913).

Gioberti, Vincenzo. *Del primato morale e civile degli italiani*. Edited by Gustavo Balsamo-Crivelli. 3 vols. Turin: Unione tip.-editrice torinese, 1920.

Guglielminetti, Marziano. "'Decadenza' e 'progresso' dell'Italia nel dibattito fra classicisti e romantici." In *La restaurazione in Italia: Strutture e ideologie, Atti del XLVII Congresso di storia del Risorgimento italiano* (1974). Rome: Istituto per la storia del Risorgimento italiano, 1976.

Halperín Donghi, Tulio. *José Hernández y sus mundos*. Buenos Aires: Editorial Sudamericana, Instituto Torcuato di Tella, 1985.

———. "Para que la inmigración? Ideología y política inmigratoria y aceleración del proceso modernizador: El caso argentino." *Jahrbuch für Geschichte von Staat, Wirtschaft und Gesellschaft Lateinamerikas* (JBLA) 13. Cologne: Bohlau Verlag, 1976.

Hernaiz, Sebastián. "*Adán Buenosayres:* La armonización tutelada." In *El peronismo clásico (1945–1955): Descamisados, gorilas y contreras*, vol. 4 of *Literatura argentina del siglo XX*, edited by David Viñas. Buenos Aires: Paradiso, 2007.

Hernández, José. *La vuelta de Martín Fierro*. Buenos Aires: Imprenta de Pablo E. Coni, 1879.

———. *Martín Fierro*. Bilingual edition. Translated by Emily Stewart. Buenos Aires: Ediciones Lea S.A., 2016.

Hobsbawm, Eric, and Terence Ranger, eds. *The Invention of Tradition*. Cambridge: Cambridge University Press, 1983.

Klein, Herbert S. "The Integration of Italian Immigrants into the United States and Argentina: A Comparative Analysis." *American Historical Review* 88, no. 2 (April 1983): 306–29.

Longhi de Bracaglia, Leopoldo. *Mitre traductor de Dante*. Edited by Nicolás Besjo Moreno. Buenos Aires: Centro Cultural "Latium," 1922.

Lugones, Leopoldo. *El payador*. Buenos Aires: Editorial Huemul S.A., 1972.

———. "Francesca." In *Lunario sentimental*, 343–54. Buenos Aires: M. Gleizer, 1926.

———. *Lunario sentimental*. Buenos Aires: M. Gleizer, 1926.

———. *Obras poéticas completas*. Edited by Pedro Miguel Obligado. Madrid: Aguilar, 1959.

———. *Odas seculares*. In *Obras poéticas completas*, edited by Pedro Miguel Obligado. Madrid: Aguilar, 1959.

———. "On Immigration." In *Leopoldo Lugones: Selected Writings*, translated by Sergio Waisman. Oxford: Oxford University Press, 2008.

———. Prologue to *Lunario sentimental*. In *Leopoldo Lugones: Selected Writings*, translated by Sergio Waisman. Oxford: Oxford University Press, 2008.

Marechal, Leopoldo. *Adam Buenosayres*. Translated and edited by Norman Cheadle. Montreal: McGill-Queen's University Press, 2014.

———. *Adán Buenosayres*. Edición crítica, introducción y notas de Javier de Navascués. Ediciones Académicas de Literatura Argentina Siglos XIX y XX. Buenos Aires: Corregidor, 2013.

———. *Adán Buenosayres*. Edited by Pedro Luis Barcia. Madrid: Clásicos Castalia, 1994.

———. *Antígona Vélez*. Buenos Aires: Ediciones Colihue, 1997.

———. "Autobiografía de un novelista." In *Revista Proa*, no. 49 (September–October 2000): 61–71.

———. "Carta a Eduardo Mallea." In *Obras completas*, vol. 5, *Los cuentos y otros escritos*, compilación y prólogo de Pedro Luis Navascués, edición coordinada por María de los Ángeles Marechal, 289–91. Buenos Aires: Libros Perfil S.A., 1998. (Hereafter cited as *Obras completas*, 5.)

———. "Carta al Dr. Atilio Dell'Oro Maini." In *Obras completas*, 5:322–23.

———. "De la adolescente." In *Obras completas*, vol. 1, *La poesía*, compilación y prólogo de Pedro Luis Barcia, edición coordinada por María de los Ángeles Marechal, 142–43. Buenos Aires: Libros Perfil S.A., 1998. (Hereafter cited as *Obras completas*, 1.)

———. "De la patria joven." In *Obras completas*, 1:151–52.

———. "Descubrimiento de la patria." In *Obras completas*, 1:303–8.

———. "Didáctica de la patria." In *Obras completas*, 1:309–18.

———. "El gaucho y la nueva literatura rioplantense." In *Obras completas*, 5:235–36.

———. "Fundación espiritual de Buenos Aires." In *Obras completas*, 5:105–16.

———. "La nueva generación literaria." In *Obras completas*, 5:215–16.

———. "La poesía lírica: Lo autóctono y lo foráneo en su contenido esencial." In *Obras completas*, 5:143–56.

———. "Las claves de *Adán Buenosayres*." In Leopoldo Marechal, Julio Cortázar, Adolfo Prieto, Graciela de Sola, and Washington Benavídes, *Interpretaciones y claves de Adán Buenosayres*. Montevideo: Acali Editorial, 1977.

———. "Mano a mano con un creador." Interview by Mario Mactas. *Gente y la actualidad* 5, no. 241 (1970): 60.

———. *Obras completas*. Vol. 1, *La poesía*, compilación y prólogo de Pedro Luis Barcia, edición coordinada por María de los Ángeles Marechal. Buenos Aires: Libros Perfil S.A., 1998.

———. *Obras completas*. Vol. 5, *Los cuentos y otros escritos*, compilación y prólogo de Pedro Luis Barcia, edición coordinada por María de los Ángeles Marechal. Buenos Aires: Libros Perfil S.A., 1998.

———. "Proyecciones culturales del momento argentino." In *Obras completas*, 5:322–23.

———. "Simbolismos del *Martín Fierro*." In *Obras completas*, 5:157–71.

———. "Sobre la inteligencia argentina." In *Obras completas*, 5:313–19.

Marechal, Leopoldo, Julio Cortázar, Adolfo Prieto, Graciela de Sola, and Washington Benavídes. *Interpretaciones y claves de Adán Buenosayres*. Montevideo: Acali Editorial, 1977.

Marechal, María de los Ángeles. "Bio-cronología Leopoldo Marechal." In *Adán Buenosayres*. Edición crítica, introducción y notas de Javier de Navascués. Ediciones Académicas de Literatura Argentina Siglos XIX y XX, 77–86. Buenos Aires: Corregidor, 2013.

Mazzini, Giuseppe. "Dante." In *La commedia*. Milan: Istituto Editoriale Italiano, 1914.

McMurray, George R. *Jorge Luis Borges*. New York: Frederick Ungar, 1980.

Mitre, Adolfo. *Italia en el sentir y pensar de Mitre*. Cuadernos de la "Dante" 15. Buenos Aires: Asociación Dante Alighieri, 1960.

Mitre, Bartolomé. *Archivo del General Mitre*. Edited by Jorge Adolfo Mitre. Buenos Aires: Biblioteca de "La Nación," 1911–14.

———. *Correspondencia literaria, histórica y política del general Bartolomé Mitre*. Museo Mitre. 3 vols. Buenos Aires: Imprenta de Coni Hermanos, 1912.

———. "Discurso en el Senado de la Nación (septiembre de 1870)." In *Arengas de Bartolomé Mitre: Colección de discursos parlamentarios, políticos, económicos y literarios, oraciones fúnebres, alocuciones conmemorativas, proclamas y alegatos in voce pronunciados desde 1848 hasta 1902*, vol. 2. Buenos Aires: Biblioteca de la Nación, 1902.

———. "Teoría del traductor: Introducción a la *Divina Comedia*." Buenos Aires: Peuser, 1897.

Monegal, Emir Rodríguez. *Jorge Luis Borges: A Literary Biography*. New York: E. P. Dutton, 1978.

Moreiro Prieto, Julián, and Ricardo Sánchez. *Escritores a la greña: Envidias, enemistades y trifulcas literarias*. Madrid: Edaf, 2014.

Moreno, César Fernández. "Weary of Labyrinths: An Interview with Jorge Luis Borges." *Encounter* 32 (April 1969): 6–12.

Morgan, Edmund S. *Inventing the People: The Rise of Popular Sovereignty in England and America*. New York: Norton, 1988.

Musa, Mark. Commentary notes in *The Divine Comedy*. Vol. 1, *Inferno*. New York: Penguin Books, 1984.

Novillo-Corvalán, Patricia. *Borges and Joyce*. London: Legenda/MHRA and Maney, 2011.

Nuñez-Faraco, Humberto. *Borges and Dante: Echoes of a Literary Friendship*. Berlin: Peter Lang, 2006.

Ocampo, Victoria. *De Francesca a Beatrice: A través de la Divina Comedia*. Madrid: Revista de Occidente, 1924.

Olea Franco, Rafael. "Lugones y el mito gauchesco: Un capítulo de historia cultural argentina." *Nueva revista de filología hispánica* 38, no. 1 (1990): 307–31.
Onega, Gladys. *La inmigración en la literatura argentina (1880–1910).* Rosario: Facultad de Filosofia y Letras, Universidad Nacional del Litoral, Cuadernos del Instituto de Letras, 1965.
Paoli, Roberto. "'El Aleph': Biforcazioni di lettura." In *Borges: Percorsi di significato*, 7–49. Florence: Università degli Studi di Firenze, 1977.
Patriarca, Silvana. "Indolence and Regeneration: Tropes and Tensions of Risorgimento Patriotism." *American Historical Review* 110, no. 2 (April 2005): 380–408.
Paz, Martin. "El Infierno de los traductores: El noveno círculo." *Página 12, Radar Libros*, June 15, 2003. http://www.pagina12.com.ar/diario /suplementos/libros/10-615-2003-06-15.html.
Perón, Juan Domingo. *Perón en doctrina.* Compiled by Juan Carlos Rousselot. Buenos Aires: Siglo Veintiuno Editores Argentina, 2008.
Pérsico, Marisa Martínez. "El dilema de los críticos practicantes: Un discurso que no puede exceder sus propios márgenes; L. Lugones a través de J. L. Borges." *Cartaphilus* 2 (2007): 107–18.
Picech, Elena P. "Leopoldo Marechal and *Adán Buenosayres* in State of Exile." *Hispanófila* 167 (January 2007): 79–94.
Quevedo, Francisco de. *Sueños y discursos.* Madrid: Clásicos Castalia, 1972.
Rama, Ángel. "El sistema literario de la poesía gauchesca." Prologue to *Poesía gauchesca*, ix–xlvii. Caracas: Biblioteca Ayacucho, 1977.
———. *Los gauchipolíticos rioplatenses.* Buenos Aires: Centro Editor de América Latina, 1982.
República Argentina. *Censo general de la Ciudad de Buenos Aires, 1887*, 2. Buenos Aires, 1889.
República Argentina, Dirección de Inmigración. *Resumen estadística del movimiento migratorio en la República Argentina, 1857–1924*. Buenos Aires, 1925.
Rock, David. *Argentina, 1516–1982*. Los Angeles: University of California Press, 1985.
———. *State Building and Political Movements in Argentina, 1860–1916.* Stanford, CA: Stanford University Press, 2002.
Romero, José Luis. *Breve historia de la Argentina.* Buenos Aires: Eudeba, 1967.
———. *El desarrollo de las ideas en la sociedad argentina del siglo XX.* México/ Buenos Aires: Fondo de Cultura Económica, 1965.
Salzani, Stefano. *Luigi Valli e l'esoterismo di Dante.* San Marino: Il Cerchio, 2014.
Sarlo, Beatriz. *Borges: Un escritor en las orillas.* Madrid: Siglo, 2007.
———. *Jorge Luis Borges: A Writer on the Edge.* New York: Verso, 1993.

Sarmiento, Domingo Faustino. *Facundo.* Madrid: Editorial América, 1922.

———. *Facundo.* Buenos Aires: Editorial Losada, 1981.

———. *Facundo: Civilization and Barbarism.* Translated by Kathleen Ross. Berkeley: University of California Press, 2003.

———. *Viajes por Europa, África y América: 1845–1847.* In *Obras completas de Domingo Faustino Sarmiento*, vol. 5. Buenos Aires: Luz del Día, 1949.

Sava, Walter. "Literary Criticism of *Martín Fierro* from 1873 to 1915." *Hispanófila* 75 (May 1982): 51–68.

Scalabrini Ortiz, Raúl. *Yrigoyen y Perón.* Buenos Aires: Plus Ultra, 1973.

Scobie, James R. *Buenos Aires: Del centro a los barrios, 1870–1910.* Buenos Aires: Solar/Hachette, 1977.

Shaw, Donald L. *Nueva narrativa hispanoamericana.* 3rd ed. Madrid: Cátedra, 1985.

Shumway, Nicolas. *The Invention of Argentina.* Los Angeles: University of California Press, 1991.

Solari, Juan Antonio. *A un siglo del "Dogma Socialista."* Buenos Aires, 1937.

Solberg, Carl. *Immigration and Nationalism: Argentina and Chile, 1890–1914.* Austin: University of Texas Press, 1970.

Sorrentino, Fernando. "Borges y Lugones: Entusiastas ataques y reticentes disculpas." *Espéculo* 18 (2001).

———. "Dante's Afterlife in Argentina." *California Italian Studies* 9 (2019): 1–22. https://escholarship.org/uc/item/2qq1510s.

———. *Seven Conversations with Jorge Luis Borges.* Translated by Clark M. Zlotchew. Philadelphia: Paul Dry Books, 2010.

Speier, Claudia Fernández. "Las traducciones argentinas de la Divina Commedia." PhD diss., Universidad de Buenos Aires, 2013.

Stahringer Ofelia I. *La política migratoria argentina.* Buenos Aires: Depalma, 1975.

Stefanini, Ruggero. "Dante in Borges: L'Aleph, Beatriz, e il Sud." *Italica* 57, no. 1 (1980): 53–65.

Subieta, Pablo. "Martín Fierro: Quarto artículo." Accessed December 1, 2015. http://www.biblioteca.org.ar/libros/157849.pdf.

Thiem, Jon. "Borges, Dante, and the Poetics of Total Vision." *Comparative Literature* 40, no. 2 (1988): 97–121.

U.S. Bureau of the Census. *Historical Statistics of the United States, Colonial Times to 1972.* Washington, DC, 1975.

Waisman, Sergio. "Foundational Scenes of Translation." *Estudios interdisciplinarios de America Latina y el Caribe* 21, no. 1 (2010): 53–75.

Waugh, Patricia. *Metafiction: The Theory and Practice of Self-Conscious Fiction.* London: Methuen, 1984.

White, John W. *Argentina: The Life Story of a Nation.* New York: Viking, 1942.

INDEX

HEATHER RENEE SOTTONG is an Assistant Professor of Literary and Cultural Studies at FLAME University in Pune, India. Her research focuses on the Italian diaspora in Argentina and the literary appropriation of Dante in the Americas.

Critical Studies in Italian Migrations

Nancy C. Carnevale and Laura E. Ruberto, *series editors*

Heather Renee Sottong, *Transnational Dante: Inventing Argentine Cultural Identity*

www.ingramcontent.com/pod-product-compliance
Lightning Source LLC
Chambersburg PA
CBHW020414110726
47899CB00006B/1980
* 9 7 8 1 5 3 1 5 1 0 4 4 2 *